God
in
Popular Culture

God
in
Popular
Culture

Andrew Greeley

THE THOMAS MORE PRESS
Chicago, Illinois

ISBN 0-88347-234-1

The author and publisher wish to make grateful acknowledgment to the following for permission to include copyrighted material in this book:

Quotations from *A Morbid Taste for Bones, Monk's Hood, The Virgin in the Ice, The Sanctuary Sparrow,* and *The Devil's Novice* by Ellis Peters. Copyright © by Ellis Peters. Reprinted by permission of the publisher, William Morrow & Company, Inc. New York, NY.

Quotations from *For Better or for Worse* by Lynn Johnston, *Cathy* by Cathy Guisewitte, *Doonesbury* by Garry B. Trudeau, and *The Far Side* by Garry Larson. By permission of Universal Press Syndicate, Kansas City, MO.

Quotation from a journal by Mario Cuomo used by permission of the author.

Quotations from *Bloom County* by Berke Breathed used by permission of Washington Post Writers' Group, Washington, DC.

Quotation from the script of *Hannah and Her Sisters* by Woody Allen. Copyright © by Woody Allen. Used by permission of the author and Untitled Productions, Inc. New York, NY.

Quotations from the "Madonna" interview in *Rolling Stone Magazine,* Issue # 508, by Mikal Gilmore. Copyright ©1987 by Straight Arrow Publishers. All rights reserved. Reprinted by permission

Excerpts from *Past Master* by R.A.Lafferty. Copyright © 1968 by R.A. Lafferty. And excerpts from *Apocalypses* by R.A. Lafferty. Copyright ©1977 by R.A. Lafferty. Reprinted by permission Virginia Kidd Literary Agency.

For Jacob Neusner

Table of Contents

1

Introduction

I propose in this book to develop a theology of popular culture.

My thesis is simple enough: Popular culture is a "locus theologicus," a theological place—the locale in which one may encounter God. Popular culture provides an opportunity to experience God and to tell stories of God or, to put the matter more abstractly, to learn about God and to teach about God.

I am not able to develop my theory unless I discuss first of all a theology of the religious imagination. That, in turn, requires some statement of the sociology of the religious imagination. All culture is imaginative, popular culture no more so and no less so than high culture. One cannot reflect religiously on the meaning of any sort of culture unless one understands that religion is imaginative activity before it becomes cognitive activity.

So first of all, I will lay out a theory of the religious imagination. Then I will attempt a constructive statement about the theological implications of popular culture. And finally, I will discuss certain manifestations of popular culture, because of my training manifestations that are more likely to be literary and verbal than pictorial or musical.

In these introductory remarks, I must now define and to some extent defend popular culture. Popular culture is produced by those arts and crafts which people enjoy as opposed to those arts and crafts which the "self defined" elites enjoy. Krystoff Penderecki is high culture. Bruce Springsteen is pop culture. David Mamet is high culture. Bill Cosby is pop culture. John Barth is high culture. John P. MacDonald is pop culture. Jean Luc Godard is high culture. John Hughes (of *Some Kind of Wonderful*) is pop culture.

The distinction between that which the elites like and that which the folks like has always been implicit. The Mozart concerti were played in palaces, not in plazas. The antics of Pierrot, Columbine, and Harlequin in the Italian Commedia dell'Arte A La Improviso rarely made it into the palaces. Some works seemed to have appealed to both groups. The plays of Shakespeare, for example, did not fail to amuse the "groundlings," and some novels by distinguished "serious" novelists make the national best-seller lists—works by Saul Bellow, Walker Percy, Louise Erdrich, Umberto Eco, and D.M. Thomas, for example.

However, the distinction between that which the elites like and that which the rest of folk like only became a pejorative distinction in the present century, with the rise of the university whose professors need tenure and universal higher education in which the elites have watched with dismay as the folk invade their bastions of literacy. Only in relatively recent decades have the intellectual elites (herein defined as those who've attended graduate school in the arts and sciences) come to the conclusion that if a work is popular it cannot be any good. And indeed, if ordinary people like something, it must of course be trash.

In much of what passes for literary criticism today, there is both snobbery and envy of the artists and writers whose works attract large audiences. There is a temptation, therefore, for the theologian, even for the Catholic theologian, to accept the judgment of his fellow elitists: if people like it, it must be trash!

Sometimes the would-be critics, with a self-conscious air of sophisticated bravado, will take up a popular writer of science fiction, perhaps, or mystery—such as John P. MacDonald, Elmore "Dutch" Leonard, Robert Heinlein, or Stanislaw Lem. They even manage occasionally not to sound patronizing when they review such popular works. However, as a columnist in the *Chicago Tribune* nervously assured his readers one Sunday morning, while Dutch Leonard's works are topflight in their own genre, the genre itself is inferior. Why one must compare different literary genres is not immediately evident. Why indeed they are not permitted to exist in their diversity is also not immediately evident. But those are not the kind of questions one addresses to a literary critic who has a compulsive need to assure himself and others of his own importance.

Some scholars (among others, John Cawelti and Bruno Bettelheim) have examined the "function" of popular culture in society and have argued that popular fiction or fairy stories, for example, reassure their readers that there is meaning and purpose in life. They conclude that these literary genres are, finally, deceptive because there is in fact no meaning or purpose in life. "Serious" literature realizes that life is pointless and absurd and acknowledges that fact. Popular literature does not.

Popular literature is guilty of what the literary critic, Frank Kermode, calls the "fallacy of the end," that is to say, it wraps up the tangled webs of plot in the final chapter and provides order, symmetry, solution, conclusion. In fact, life does not do this at all, and life indeed ends on a note of enormous ambiguity. Cynthia Ozick, a gifted storyteller herself, worries that stories may be idolatry, that they may become more than just paradigms for life and actually, to the storyteller and the listener (or reader), turn into substitutes for life.

Popular culture, in brief, is no good because it tends to provide happy endings to its stories. High culture is not trash because it does not fall victim to the temptation of happy endings.

A favorite scenario of book reviewers, literary critics, book review editors, college professors of criticism, and teachers of "creative" writing is the story of the hardworking and gifted novelist who is not appreciated by the people of his own day who devote their attention to trash instead of to "quality" writing.

Then, after the writer is dead, he is enthusiastically hailed by subsequent generations. Thus, many young writers will confide that their only intention is to write something that "will last." They don't care whether they're read now, so long as they're read someday, that someday in the future when the contemporary writers of trash are not read.

There is much envy in such a scenario; most of those young writers who posture about their delight that people don't read their books would enthusiastically accept a large advance for paperback rights of one of their books if people suddenly did begin to read them. More to the point, however, the scenario doesn't measure up to reality. Most writers who are unread in their own day are also unread in the future. The writers from the past who we read now are the writers that were read by their own contemporaries. Dickens, Scott, Dostoyevsky, and Proust were all serialized in the popular newspapers of their day. Similarly, the most important American writers—Faulkner, Fitzgerald, Hemingway—had good-sized audiences in their own time and, in the case of Fitzgerald and Faulkner, might have lived to have much larger audiences if their self-destructiveness had not been so powerful.

I shall return later to the question of happy or, as I prefer, hopeful endings. But two observations seem in order:

1) While it is certainly true that under the influence of "modernity" most works of high culture end absurdly (rather than tragically), for most of human history, high culture has not been absurd and has not always even been tragic.

2) Works of pop culture tend to have endings and, often implicitly, tend to provide paradigms of meaning. This would only make them "trash," however, if the assumption of the critics and the professors that life is absurd were certainly valid. But it is not certainly valid. The use of it as a criterion by professors and critics inappropriately transfers a theological assumption from their own world to literary criticism. Indeed, in its simple form, criticism of the "fallacy of the end" is in fact a fallacy of begging

the question: it assumes that which remains to be proven, namely that life is absurd.

I will concede to the critics and the professors, however, that pop culture in its various forms does tend, implicitly or explicitly, to offer paradigms of meaning. It is precisely this phenomenon—pop culture as a search for meaning—which makes it an appropriate area for theological concern.

My contention in this introduction is modest: I do not insist that all popular culture is good, much less theological. I merely insist that some popular culture is excellent and, therefore, given pop culture's propensity to search for meaning, possibly theological.

(I will also assert, for the record, that some high culture is theological: the work of Flannery O'Connor, Cynthia Ozick, Walker Percy, and Graham Greene, for example. But I will quickly add that some high culture is most certainly trash, even if it gets published in the literary magazines or performed at summer music festivals.)

I prefer a distinction among literary genres instead of the distinction between high culture and popular culture (and parallel distinctions among musical and artistic genres). The important question from a genre perspective is not whether a work is "serious" or "trash" (writers like Stephen King and Robert Parker—the author of the Spenser series—quite properly insist that their works are "serious") but whether a work is comedy or tragedy or romance. A story or a work of art must be judged, as I will suggest at greater length later on, in terms of the genre in which the artist or writer decides to work and not in terms of the genre that a critic or a reviewer or a professor or a theologian wishes to impose upon the artist or the writer.

If, for the purposes of this book, I accept the distinction between high culture and popular culture, between "serious" work and work that is labeled "not serious," the reason is that the distinction is so common that to fight it throughout this series of notes would be counterproductive.

Nonetheless, the Catholic analogical imagination, precisely because it says "both/and"—as opposed to the dialectical imagination which says "either/or"—must keep an open mind on the subject of popular culture and must be very uneasy about what seems to be an exercise of the dialectical imagination in the paradigm "serious/trash." The very comprehensiveness and catholicity of the Catholic imagination ought to find that distinction abhorrent.

My colleague and friend, Professor Michael Marsden of the Popular Culture Department at Bowling Green State University, has suggested to me that the rise of popular culture as a serious interdisciplinary field (with three thousand members in the Popular Culture Association) may well be the result of migration into the Academy of the children and the grandchildren of Catholic ethnics. Marsden suggests that the members of the Popular Culture Association may well be disproportionately Catholic precisely because the Catholic sensibility does not and perhaps cannot abhor that which appeals to people.

Catholicism at its best moments, I would submit, embraces an empirical sensibility. In its early days, it appropriated to Catholic worship and practice everything that was good, true, and beautiful in the pagan world around it: the Brigid Cross (sun symbol), the Celtic Cross (intercourse symbol), Brigid the Goddess (of spring, poetry, and new life), the angels and the saints, the rhythms and cycles of nature in the liturgical year, the art and music and literary forms of the pagan world, and even the titles and customs of spring festivals. (Easter is the name of a festival in honor of the Anglo-Saxon goddess of the dawn and of spring, a goddess whose symbols are eggs and lilies and rabbits. She is a first cousin, doubtless, of the Irish spring goddess Brigid.) The fire and water rite of the Easter vigil was lifted intact from pagan Roman fertility rituals. Let us find what is good, true, and beautiful, the early Christians said, and then define it as "naturally Christian."

For most of Christian history, religious leaders were

selected in popular election, bishops by the vote of priests and people, even the Bishop of Rome. The cardinals, the parish priests of Rome, would gather in Saint Peter's and select a nominee to be the new Bishop of Rome. They would then present the nominee on the balcony of Saint Peter's. If the people cheered, then he was considered to be duly elected Bishop of Rome, and if they booed, the cardinals went back and chose another candidate. This bit of Catholic history is cheerfully ignored today by those who will try to persuade you that Catholicism is not a democracy. In fact, for most of its history, it was so democratic that several popes said that it was a grave sin to choose a bishop by any method other than the free election of priests and people (and it probably still is a grave sin). The argument supporting this democratic process was simple: the Holy Spirit is most likely to work through the local clergy and laity who know the religious needs of a bishopric far better than anyone else. God's will, you see, was to be determined empirically and not deductively.

Moreover, for the first thousand years of Catholic history, the "consent" or "assent" of the faithful was considered to be necessary to confirm and validate official teaching. Most definitive documents always included a statement something like "with the assent of the whole Christian people." It was assumed as a matter of course, not subject to question or debate, that the Holy Spirit worked through the people of the church as well as through the leaders of the ecclesiastical institution and that their consent was absolutely essential to confirm the validity of the teaching. Theologians at the service of the Roman curia today will argue that the consent of the faithful or the "sense of the faithful" is to be found only among those lay people who already accept the official teaching. This position effectively safeguards the power of the curia, but it rejects the obvious intent of the first thousand years of Catholic history.

Finally, the natural law theory in its original form held that third-level principles of the natural law are to be discovered empirically. First-level principles, do good and avoid evil, and second level-principles, thou shalt not kill, are deductive; but when the issue is determining the third level of principles (what is lying, what is theft, what is adultery), Saint Thomas Aquinas and the other great natural law thinkers argued that it was necessary to go to the *gentes*, the people, and determine what the ordinary definition of these sins were among various communities of humankind. The common practice of church leaders and teachers today of deriving third-level principles deductively would horrify the great teachers of the natural law tradition, and in fact, what passes for natural law in the Church today is usually a perversion of natural law which stands traditional natural law theory on its head.

All of these "popular" practices in the Catholic tradition are based on the same theological assumption: God speaks through the people to the institutional church just as He/She speaks to the people through the leaders of the institutional church. Both the learning church and the teaching church represent the voices of God. Presumably, no bishop or no theologian would deny that premise today, but often, indeed normally in ecclesiastical practice, the assumption seems to be that bishops and/or theologians have a monopoly on religious truth and that the ordinary laity must be hassled, persuaded, converted, or denounced so that they will accept the answers that bishops and/or theologians know to be true—usually without the bishops or theologians even having to bother to listen to the questions.

This traditional Catholic empiricism (reinforced but certainly not created by Saint Thomas' Aristotelian philosophy) has battled down through the centuries with another tradition, a prioristic, deductive, and Platonic (and perhaps best represented in Catholic history by Saint Augustine). While theologians argued for centuries—almost entirely for deductive reasons—that sex was almost evil and that marital intercourse for pleasure was wrong, the ordinary practice of priest and people in the parishes of Christianity, particularly in the marriage rituals, continued to celebrate sexual love as a revelation and a sacrament of God's love. The theologians and teachers and leaders were wrong. The a prioristic, Platonic tradition was wrong, and the priests and people and the empirical tradition were correct. At its best moments, Catholicism has always gone with its gut instinct, and at its worst moments, it has relied on the dangerous propensity to provide deductive answers to questions that have not been asked.

The failure to listen to the voice of the Spirit speaking through the people is by no means limited to the Catholic right wing. Those enthusiasts within contemporary American Catholicism for "the people" or, more recently, for "the poor" rarely, if ever, spend much time listening to what "the people" or "the poor" actually want. Rather, they impose on the people their own vision of what the people *should* want. Liberation theology, for example, that illegitimate offspring of Marxism and Christianity, when constrained to produce evidence that the people want what liberation theology says they want, will not fall back on empirical studies of people but rather on quotes from Marx.

In both the Catholic right and the Catholic left there is very little willingness to listen to the people because there is little respect for the people; little confidence in their insights; and precious little belief that God may, in fact, actually speak through them.

On the other hand, if one believes, as Catholics must believe, that people are sacraments of God, that God discloses Himself/Herself to us through the objects, events, and persons of life, then one must concede the possibility that in the sacramentality of ordinary folk, their hopes, their fears, their loves, their aspirations represent a legitimate experience of God, legitimate symbols of God, and legitimate stories of God. Therefore, the Catholic sensibility requires that we keep an open mind about the possibility that experiences, images, and stories of God are to be found in popular culture and indeed that these experiences, images, and stories provide a wealth of material of immediate practical use in catechetics and homiletics.

Later I will return to the subject of the "empirical" nature of the Catholic religious sensibility. I will be content at the beginning of this book if my readers are willing to suspend judgment on this subject and keep an open mind on the possibility that God may indeed be encountered in works of the fine and lively arts which ordinary people enjoy.

I ask the reader to entertain the possibility that the spirit may still blow whither She will—in the Vatican Palace, in the diocesan curias, in the theological faculties, indeed, but also in the neighborhoods, the communities, the families, the friendships, and the loves of the faithful and in the experiences, images, and stories where the faithful find articulation and representation of their own experiences of God.

2

The Creative Imagination

At the heart of my theory of the religious imagination and my corollary theory of popular culture is a model of the creative imagination, derived from social science and from philosophy. Culture of whatever sort is the result of creative imagination leaping to creative imagination—from the writer to the reader, the artist to the viewer, the musician to the listener.

Moreover, religion, I will argue subsequently, begins in this same dimension of the personality, the result, as St. Paul would have said, of the Spirit talking to our spirit—to the most open and sensitive aspect of the self.

Everyone, therefore, has a creative imagination, the creator as well as the consumer of culture. In fact, what occurs when we are in contact with a work of art is that we re-create the work that the creator has already done.

A conclusion of this assumption is that culture and religion are always intimately linked because both take their origins in the creative self. Animals don't have religion because they cannot reflect on their imagery. Angels don't have religion because they don't have imagery.

Unless, in the case of angels, St. Bernard and St. Augustine are correct when they say angels have spiritual bodies.

In this chapter, while I am developing my theory of the creative imagination, I will suggest that it is a dimension of the self which must be treated with reverence and respect. It is a full-fledged partner, a lover who is also a mate, to the rational self.

In the film *8 1/2*, Federico Fellini shares with us the confusion of a film-maker who has lost his muse. It's a film about making a film when you have no idea what the film is about. The white-clad muse, portrayed by the wondrous Claudia Cardinale, slips by him occasionally with a magic smile and then vanishes. Once, she appears in his bedroom at night, straightens it out, makes modest romantic advances to him, and promises to remain and bring order and love to his life.

Then the phone rings and the muse disappears once again. She returns at the last moment to lead Anselmi (the film-maker) and his cast of characters in search of a plot in a madcap parade down the beach, a parade which, astonishingly, crystalizes the disorder in the film-maker's imagination into a work of art.

During the film, the muse occasionally seems to blend with an actress (also played by Ms. Cardinale and called, appropriately, Claudia) and Anselmi's wife, played by the enchanting Anouk Aimee. Somehow, the muse is related to real-life women, reflects and is reflected by them, and eludes the film-maker just as they do.

Inspiration, Fellini seems to be saying, is rather like a lover, a notion that he shares with the Greeks; but she is also rather like a wife—a partner who maintains cleanliness and order and serenity in the imagination and who whispers, in moments of ingenious passion, the creative themes with which the artist will work.

Such is the nature of the relationship between discursive mind (*ratio* to scholastic philosophers) and creative mind (*fantasia* to the schoolmen), between rationality and imagination, between, if you will, left brain and right brain, between full consciousness and the preconscious daydream world that lurks on the threshold of the unconscious. There are times when the voice we hear in this daydream world is the adoring whisper of a tender lover. There are other times when she is imperious and demanding, like a full partner in a complex relationship. And yet other times when she's not there at all.

Should we, Fellini asks, treat her as a partner or a hand-maid, a spouse or a slave?

His answer seems to be both, depending on her mood—a thoroughly Mediterranean answer, it might be noted. A Celt, wiser perhaps in this matter than his southern cousins, already knows that the only possible response to a woman, si-multaneously lovely and demanding, is to straighten up, get one's act together, act right, and do what one is told.

Would a woman artist, it should be asked in passing, imagine creativity as a man? It has been suggested to me that instead of a sexual lover, a woman might picture the muse as a close woman friend. I note this response in passing and leave it to others for discussion. For the purposes of this book, it is enough to say that anyone who has chased creativity around the park and has been chased by her knows that she is both an erratic, if tender, lover and a loyal, if often absent, friend. And one who can be exorcised, as in 8 1/2, by the ring of the telephone.

The point in this theory is that however the creative dimension of the personality is to be pictured, she/he/it must be treated with respect, a partner in the human enterprise and not a slave to be summoned when we are in need of the slave's services.

What do I mean by creative imagination? Leonard Kubie called it the preconscious, the scholastics called it the agent intellect, Mihaly Cizsintmihaly calls it "flow"; Michael Polanyi called it "personal knowledge"; Bernard Lonergan called it in-sight; others call it the creative intuition, nondiscursive knowledge, an altered state of consciousness, the process by which you know the answer to a problem even before you have defined the terms of the investigation, the dimension of the self which knows the end of a journey before it even begins, the skill by which researchers pursue the truth long before they get around to describing their theories in the first few paragraphs of a scholarly article.

In the Aristotelian framework, *fantasia* is more important because it is charged with "reproduction" both to the intellect and to the outside world through art. Dante, perhaps the greatest of the Aristotelians, was convinced that *fantasia* could do what *ratio* could not — describe the world which is to come.

Let me note in passing that I think the *fantasia/ratio* model is far too simple, a product of the Platonic thought which has dominated the Western World for far too long. Moreover the subordinate place of *fantasia* in the platonic model (which has so influenced Christian spirituality down through the ages) does violence to human nature.

The "altered states of consciousness" model allows for many different kinds of consciousness, scores, perhaps hundreds, functioning in hierarchies, rhythms and periodicities that we have only begun to understand.

To use a computer metaphor, many if not all of the various "states of consciousness" (ways of knowing) can be oprating in "background mode" while others are operating in "foreground mode."

I am not altogether easy with the word "altered" which seems to imply that "ordinary" or "waking" consciousness is the norm and that all the other states, if not deviant are at least unusual.

Perhaps a jazz orchestra metaphor is better. The ways of knowing are like the instruments of the combo which work simultaneously, serially, sequentially, dialectically in loose but harmonious (sometimes) relationships with one another as they work through various melodies.

Creativity. then, is that experience when something inside

the self takes over and tells you, often quite imperiously, what comes next. Did I say something? But those who know the experience realize that I understate what happens. Someone tells us what comes next. If we are forced to imagine what that someone is like, there is no reason to deny the power of Fellini's picture of the white-clad Ms. Cardinale—a gentle and demanding lover, a handmaid and a spouse.

Let us be candid: we hear the answers, often with the grateful humility of an amanuensis who knows that he does not deserve credit for what he is writing down.

A software programmer on a roll, a poet racing through a sonnet, a storyteller watching the actions and listening to the words of his characters as they take over the story and write it themselves, a data analyst constructing ingenious models out of the blue (or so it seems), a quarterback observing a pass pattern open up and the other team responding to it, a surgeon during a long and complex operation reacting to a crisis with quick and sure instinct—all of us know that someone else takes over. Demon, god, muse, call it what we will, we are in the grip of a force that seems outside of ourself, at least outside the normal, rational self of everyday life.

We know a great deal about the creative imagination, although the definitive research and syntheses on the subject still needs to be done. There is a dimension of the self, resident to some extent though not exclusively in the right hemisphere, which—like a radar scanner or a computer compiler—seems to continuously scan the image traces of our memory in a mostly silent, lunatic game of bricolage. It playfully juxtaposes and separates, combines and readjusts, changes and undoes, assembles and tears down and then reconstructs again complex, intricate, brilliant, and absurd imaginative structures—and then patiently waits till we fall asleep so that it will really have some fun.

Creativity seems to be nothing more than the accessibility of this scanning, compiling dimension of the self, an ability to slip through the boundaries of discursive reasoning and join the fun and games going on in the preconscious. Crossing such barriers requires patience, respect, craftspersonship, and determination—like all love affairs. There are no shortcuts, no wonder drugs, no weekend seminars which will make us creative. But there are skills and disciplines which facilitate access to our creative intuition and enhance our ability to express what we find there when we return from the journey.

I often think that the difference between God and us is that, in the former, rationality and imagination are combined. Creating a whole poem in a marvelous burst of energy in which rationality and creativity combine to produce the total work is rather like creating a cosmos of your own, a god-like experience. Characters in stories are not the result of carefully engineered construction work in which bits and pieces of people we already know are carefully assembled in conformity with a detailed plan. Rather, Venus-like, the character bursts forth, a creature of passion with which to contend as well as love. Is that not what God experienced when She made us?

Recognizing the double helix or the weak force or the right model or the fitting equation—do these experiences not make us want to laugh and celebrate because now we, too, understand how the machine works and, in some sense, are the creators of it? The way She felt when she jumped over Planck's wall in the first fraction of a second of the Big Bang?

It follows, then, that the distinction between art and science, however useful it may be, is ultimately invalid. Science is certainly artistic in its procedures. Now theoretical physicists, if not yet sociologists, admit that they seek elegance, beauty, symmetry. Stephen Hawking tells us that the very name "black hole"—mysterious, threatening, fascinating—has facilitated research on this important area of theoretical physics. Perhaps only the social scientists, still pathetically eager for acceptance in the world of "hard" science, are reluctant to admit the artistic aspects of their craft. But even we, as we become addicted to model fitting, are charmed by the elegance of the real and are willing to readmit creativity into our lexicon.

Whether art is also science might be another matter, one perhaps to be hotly disputed by the humanists—many of whom are simultaneously envious and contemptuous of the respectability of the world of "hard" science as they see it—the kind of humanists who see the typewriter as the last bastion of defense against the mechanization of the word processor (though they are not willing, as logic demands, to retreat to the quill or, perhaps more appropriately, to the chisel).

Perhaps it is enough to say that both are committed to the pursuit of truth with no holds barred and the expression of that truth, once discovered, in the most charming and attractive models. Both the humanist and the scientist, the writer and the teacher seek the charms of the real in order to charm others with what they have discovered. The tools may be different, but the core of both discovery and method are the same.

Peace will no more be declared in this battle between science and humanism than it will be in the conflict between science and religion or in the lanes and fields of Ulster. Perhaps in the next century, however, some of us will come to realize that we have a common interest in and dependency on the creative imagination which necessitate at least an armed truce. In the absence of the muse, you see, science becomes pedestrian and art becomes dull. Both artist and scientist need her—and one adds, both had better accept her as a full partner to discursive reason. For it is in the combination of rationality and imagination, in the fertile and passionate union of the two, that the work, whatever it might be—Rasch model in sociology, unified field theory in physics, sonnet, story, painting of a beach in summertime—is born.

Hopefully, I have made it clear that I am not advocating the abandonment of reason, of rational and discursive knowledge. I am not supporting the surrender of intellect to the wilder and more demonic dimensions of the self. The image of the muse as lover should make it clear that the appropriate goal is union, not disjunction; comprehension, not isolation; "both/and," not "either/or." Because "creativity" has often been a password for those wishing to depart on a far-out trip to the never-never lands of substance-induced dreaming or on a mystical voyage to what the Celts called the multicolored lands, it does not follow that we should consign the muse to the bleary-eyed concern of psychedelic pilgrims. She is too wonderful, too lovely, and too important to be left in their dubious care.

What difference is there between the religious imagination of the artist and the consumer of art—between Mozart and those who listen to him, for example?

The difference, even in the case of Mozart, is, I suspect, a difference of degree, partly based in nature (genetic endowment), partly based in nurture (life experiences, particularly in the family while growing up), and partly based in the self-discipline by which the artist acquires the skills of the craft necessary to bring his vision to life. We all are storytellers, but not everyone has the genetic endowment or the life experience which enables her/him to tell stories that others will want to hear or read. And even the endowment of nature and nurture (which I suspect consists in substantial part of an ability to access easily the workings of the creative imagination) is not enough if the person is unwilling to work at the acquisition of the craft skills required to express his/her vision. Unless you want to communicate with no one (and some of the poems and stories in literary magazines suggest that such is the goal of the writer), you must learn how to communicate.

In my role as a writer of tales, I am often asked to read novels written by unpublished novelists. Not one in a hundred merits publication, many because there is little storytelling vision revealed in the work, but many more because the writer has not bothered to learn how to tell stories, not even to the extent of studying the techniques of those who are successful storytellers. So consumed are they with the fiction of "self-expression" that they think having a story to tell and telling it well are the same thing and that no one has the right to impose on them rules for storytelling.

To be a creative consumer of works of culture also requires some discipline. To read a story requires first of all that you are able to read (and some college graduates are not able to read). It also requires that you are in sufficient control of your life to have time to read. Finally, it requires that you permit the writer to tell his/her story and not the story you want him/her to tell.

Without the creative imagination, then, there is no culture either created or consumed. And without skills and discipline imposed on the frantic energies of the creative imagination, there is no communication.

Cultural communication is the sharing of experiences; the artist attempts to activate in the imaginative memory of the consumer experiences that parallel the artist's own so that the consumer can say (implicitly in ordinary circumstances), "Oh, I know what that's about. Something like that once happened to me."

Culture and religion are linked because religion too is about experiences. It takes its origins and its raw power from experiences that suggest that there are grounds for hope. Since the creative imagination as such is utterly agnostic about the separation between various kinds of experiences, it automatically scans "sacred" images and "secular" images and pieces them together in its rambling game of bricolage. No matter how hard the creator and consumer of culture may try, s/he cannot exclude religious experiences from the other experiences of life. Long before questions of meaning arise in the discursive self, the creative self is already playing its riotous game with images of the kinds of experiences that fill it with hope—even before the discursive self has time to put the label "hope" on the experiences.

The creativity in each of us—radar scanner, compiler, manic bricolage game—is, in the final analysis, Herself (to use a

Celtic expression), a beauty ever ancient, ever new, charming, attracting, drawing us on, seducing us along the beach of life with a promise of yet more beauty to be found further down the beach.

And whether you spell her name with a capital "H" or a small "h" doesn't matter, not so long as you know that once she's captivated you, She'll never let you go.

3

The Religious Imagination in Nature Religions

In the next three chapters, I intend to summarize the history of the Catholic religious imagination. Thus I hope to provide raw material out of our historic experience of religion for the sociological and theological conclusions to be derived in subsequent chapters.

In the process, I will be sustaining my argument that Catholicism does not shun the ordinary religious experiences of people. Like Judaism, but with much more self-confidence, it absorbs any and all religious experiences which seem to disclose the presence of grace.

Even if one does not accept the Catholic conclusion about the religious nature of secular experience, one is forced to admit that most of the religions the world has known (excepting, each in their own way, Protestantism, Judaism, and Islam) sensed that the sacred was not "totally" other but lurked in the midst of the secular, the "every day."

One can, I presume, develop a theology of the religious imagination and popular culture on other than Catholic premises. Even if one holds that God is almost totally absent and that the only sacrament of God is Jesus and him crucified, one may still be able to find hints of sacramentality in creation and in culture.

But it's a lot harder.

Under the influence of David Tracy, some Protestant theologians have discovered the importance of religious metaphor. They try, however, to accept metaphor and still reject the Catholic principle of analogy. They are driven to this odd behavior because if you accept analogy, God is less the Totally Other than S/He is the Always Present. In fact, metaphors for God are meaningless or at best extrinsic predicates of God unless analogy is true. Father Tracy, despite his wonderful ecumenical style, has put these Protestant theologians in a bind.

Catholicism is a religious heritage in which the world is seen as a metaphor for God. Catholicism in its essence is distinct from all the other great world religions—Protestantism, Islam, Judaism, the Zoroastrian religion in Persia, Buddhism, and Hinduism—in that it looks on creation as a metaphor for God. God is like the world. Where all the other religions would be hesitant about saying that, Catholicism says it bluntly and confidently, and takes the risks involved.

Now to make this case that Catholicism stands on the notion that the world is a metaphor for God, I'm going back deep into history to see how the ceremonies and symbols of our religion emerged and what their roots are in our pagan past. In a decisive move somewhere between the return of Jesus to the Heavenly Father and the year 500 A.D., Catholicism took the great gamble of trying to assimilate all that it could out of paganism.

There are three feasts, three sets of symbols in particular, which I want to emphasize as quintessentially displaying what Catholicism is all about: Easter and Christmas and the feasts of Mary, the Mother of Jesus. And also, by way of conclusion, I'll say something about St. Valentine and suggest that we have let the good saint of romantic love slip out of our grip. We have let him become a nice, pagan, secular saint; forgotten that he's ours;

and forgotten the enormous Catholic possibilities that are to be found in his mid-winter romantic festival.

Let us go back five thousand years. We are in a time when most of the human race can't read or write because they haven't developed an alphabet. We are in pre-history, only the people who lived then didn't know it was pre-history because they didn't know anything about history. There was no history because records weren't being kept. But still, we can piece together from archaeology and anthropology and other disciplines something about what life was like then. So let us to try to imagine the world about 2800 B.C., somewhere in Northern Europe. A group that has split off from their tribe or their clan is moving northward through the forests to begin a settlement of their own.

These people are Indo-Europeans, only they didn't know they were Indo-Europeans. They also could be called Aryans but they certainly didn't know they were Aryans. We have only the faintest idea of who they thought they were. Their original tribe lived in Southern Poland, but these people didn't think of themselves as Polish because Poland wasn't there either. They were probably tall for their time, with light blonde hair; vigorous, athletic, brave fighters; and heavy drinkers. The Indo-European peoples, as we call them now, were the ancestors of all of us—from Norway to North Africa, from Ireland to India.

Today, most of us in these areas are descendants of that relatively small tribe because our ancestors had a big advantage over everybody else: they were the first ones to figure out that a human being could get on top of a horse and ride it.

At the time we are following the breakaway group, they were, for the most part, herdsmen. They may have had little farms of their own, but they supported themselves by raising animals. Because they were good on horses, they were good at raising animals, and they made themselves, for that period, a lot of wealth in animal raising. That meant that they had more children and more of their children survived to adulthood and the land on which they lived grew, by their standards, very profitable. So it was necessary, periodically, for offshoots to leave the main tribal lands and go off into the wilderness, go north to what would become Ireland, go west to what would become Spain, south towards what would become Italy and Greece, or east towards India.

We know what these people were like mostly by selecting cultural artifacts from the farthest movements of their culture, from Ireland and India. Whatever traits the Irish and the Indians have in common in their laws and their culture and their religions and their symbols probably go back to that little tribe in Southern Poland which learned how to ride horses.

So now we are with this group made up of fifteen or twenty families maybe, thirty or forty at the most, who left behind the old village, the old neighborhood if you will; got on their horses and rode out into the sunset. They were mostly very young people. They were probably the second or third children in the family who were not going to inherit the family fields and flocks. They were, in a certain sense, like their descendants who came to this country in the immigrant years. Since there wasn't any chance for them in the old neighborhood, they gathered their young wives and their baby children and climbed on their horses and rode out. There was nothing else for them to do. They rode over the hills and maybe over the mountains and into the deep, thick forests that covered Europe five thousand years ago, after the last of the glaciers had slipped back to the north. And they rode and they rode and they rode until they were able to find a spot that looked like it would be a good place for a settlement.

We can imagine it to be a clearing or a meadow in the middle of a forest, with a stream flowing through it and possibly a lake that they could use as a partial defense. But certainly a stream, so there would be running water and quick and easy sanitation. We can picture these ancestors of ours riding into the meadow, late into the day, unloading their horses, putting up little shelters, perhaps made of skins, the mothers nursing and feeding the babies, the men outlining where their village would be with a series of stones, quite possibly stones they had brought with them in their saddlebags, sacred stones that represented the boundaries of the world.

This little village that they were forming late at night (let's think of it as an evening in spring) represented their world, order and system imposed on a reluctant and resistant chaos. When they outlined the village with stones and put up their tents and perhaps piled another set of stones somewhere near the bank of the stream and built their fires, they were continuing the work of creation. They were participating in the God-like activity of replacing chaos with cosmos, disordered creation with ordered creation.

They had brought fire with them, of course, in their saddlebags, protected, because without fire they were at a loss. They couldn't cook their food, they couldn't keep themselves warm at night. Fires were easily extinguished by rain. So you protected your fires and you always made sure that there were several of them around so that if the rain came, you would still have a little bit of a fire left. Picture then, if you will, the setting: a dense forest, a meadow in the middle of it, an outline of stones, another pile of stones, fire by the stream, and the little camp settling in at night, with some of the young men taking turns patrolling the perimeter. It was probably a night, you may im- agine, with the full moon high in the sky. The men (kids, really, in their late teens, early twenties) would be very restless and nervous as they patrolled the rim of stones which represented their little world because they knew how many other such offshoots of the tribe had died, attacked by the savages that lurked out in the woods, destroyed by evil spirits, carried off by plagues.

The forest was filled with enemies, human enemies and supernatural enemies. There were demons and goblins and ghosts and haunts out there, and every sound through the night must have brought a touch of terror into those young men's hearts as they patrolled the borders of their world.

Outside there was evil and chaos. Inside, around the camp fires and around the sacred stones, there was a little bit of order because there was a little and very new community—their new tribe and their new world.

In the stories these young men and women had heard about how the world was put together, the act of creation by the gods was an imposition of order on chaos. The world was chaotic, confused, ugly, messy, and the gods came along and did something; they cut it in half and they walked on it, and a little bit of order came together. Every time a new village was started, every time new flocks were organized, every time new plants were put in the fields, the work of creation continued. Darkness was pushed back a little more. Light was given a chance to shine. Chaos and confusion were pushed to the edge of the meadow, and order and reason began to prevail. The new tribe was not only finding land on which they could support themselves and their wives and their children, they were creating a little bit of order. They were continuing the gods' work of creation.

As the days went on, in all likelihood the sacred stones at the rim of the camp were not supplanted but assisted by the erection of a stockade. The stones represented the contact with the gods whose work the tribe was continuing. While you trusted in the gods, you also realized you had to do your part, so you put up a wooden wall. And the pillar of stones around the fire by the riverside maybe became one giant stone that they had found somewhere out in the forest and rolled to erect there. That stone was the center of their kingdom, of their community, of their little universe, but it also reached to heaven where it linked itself and their work with the work of the gods. The stone was the male organ rising to the female organ of the sky to bring down water and sun, to bless the fields, and to grant fertility and increase to the flocks. When it came time to raise animals and plant fields, everyone knew what to do, not because they had Ph.D.'s in animal husbandry or agricultural economics to advise them but because the religious rituals of the tribe told them how to plant the fields and how to raise the animals.

They were involved in a spiritual work. With the help of the gods, they were spreading the work of the gods, pushing back ugliness and evil and confusion; when therefore, they learned how to plant, how to continue the work of the gods, they encoded their knowledge and skills in religious rituals. Bit by bit the forests were cleared, more fields were planted, more animals were collected and domesticated. The village community began to flourish and the world expanded. In the struggle between cosmos and chaos, cosmos was winning.

They were troubled by sickness, undoubtedly. They were perhaps attacked by barbarian savages who didn't have horses and who painted their faces yellow (while our folks, being civilized, painted their faces blue), and maybe they had internal conflicts. By following the rituals that they had brought with them, by honoring the work of the gods to whom they were united by the fire and water and stones, they knew that they could conquer their problems. Also, they had the best horses. Never leave out the horses because they were terribly important.

It's hard for us to imagine a world like that, where the good spirits and evil spirits were so deeply integrated in human existence; where your emotions in your planting and in your harvesting and in your cultivating and in your presiding over your flocks were so intimately linked with religious ritual; where the major actions in life—love making, rearing children, making food—were all somehow, through the stones and through the water and through the fire, linked to the gods; and where your daily work was considered sacred because it was continuing the work of creation.

The gods were out there someplace, but more important, the gods were down here; they were in the fields and in the animals. They were in the rain and in the sun and in the streams and in the sacred stone and, especially, in the community that had brought the stones and the fire and tamed the water.

Moreover, the evil spirits were out there, too. They, too, were in the stones and in the trees and in the storms and in the plagues. Every event that threatened the community, every scary place out beyond the boundaries of the village and beyond the boundaries of the community was under the domination of evil spirits, the forces of chaos resisting cosmos, disordered creation trying to snuff out ordered creation.

Our ancestors, forty-eight hundred years ago, lived in a world permeated by gods and demons in which the divine forces of good and evil were all around them. You had to placate the evil forces so they wouldn't attack you and you had to appeal to the good forces so they would remember their promises to you. All of this was not something you did merely when you had your festivities in the center of the village. You did this all the time. Your life was not sharply distinct from the conflict between the good spirits and the evil spirits. Quite the contrary. You worked out your existence in the context of the forces of good and evil fighting one another.

The sacred and the secular were inextricably mixed for these ancestors of ours, and both were this-worldly. The rituals were a joining together of the gods and humans in their joint activity of fighting off chaos and confusion. Human religion was not distinct from the rest of life; rather, it was that part of life in which humans and the gods together contended against evil.

It is not clear that humankind can do without some element of that cosmic fight of life against death in its religion. In later years, we would try to divorce religion from the forces of nature, with mixed success at best.

The religion of these "Proto Celts" was not greatly different from that in every other part of the world since the beginning of human self-awareness, and not greatly different from many of the nature religions which remain today, often in coexistence (as in Brazil) with more advanced religious forms.

The change to horses would not have affected human religion as much as it did if it were not joined by another authentically religious transformation. At about the same time as the Proto-Celts were riding through Europe, human self-reflection in other countries had produced a breakthrough inside: If we can reflect about ourselves, maybe we are capable of transcending ourselves.

To some religious leaders, this meant that the nature religions ought to be abandoned because they were related to the body and not to the spirit.

Catholic Christianity alone thought you could combine a religion of body and a religion of spirit, a religion of fertility ritual and of self-transcendence.

4

Imagination in the World Religions

While our Indo-European friends were building their community in the forests of Western Europe, some other members of the human race were engaging in the most dangerous activity in which the species can engage. In the great cities of the Middle East, they were thinking.

In the cities, humankind had yet to learn to ride horses, but some humans were very wealthy because they were such successful producers of agriculture. In the great farming cities like Nineveh, Babylon, Memphis and Thebes, humankind began to think abstractly. As the centuries turned into millennia about the time our friends settled in their meadow in Northern Europe (a place that, to tell you the truth, was in West Cork), an idea began to emerge almost simultaneously (at least within a thousand-year range) in China, in India, in Iran or Persia, in Egypt, among the Hebrews, and in Greece. This idea was that there were such things as ideas; that thought was somehow independent of body; that there was mind and body; and while they worked together in the known world, there might very well be mind somewhere else that was pure mind. Everything in the known world might be merely a reflection of that pure mind.

During this critical turning point in history, what happened in each of these places (and perhaps it was going on in the civilizations of the Western Hemisphere, too) was that people began to imagine or, perhaps better we should say, to conceive that there was a god beyond the gods; that the ultimate power of the universe was independent of matter; and indeed that everything we did was a pale, pale reflection of this enormous supermind that existed above all creation.

Human beings, sometime between 1500 B.C. and 500 B.C., began to explicitly conceptualize transcendence, a God that existed beyond the world and independent of the world.

Out of this notion of a transcendent god, a god independent of matter, all the great religions of the world came to be: Prophetic Judaism, Christianity, Islam, the higher forms of Hinduism, Confucianism in China, the worship of the solar disk in Egypt, Platonism in Greece, and Zoroastrianism in Iran. All these religions thought of god as spirit and religion, therefore, as something that ought to be independent of the forces of nature. Because it was a religion of idea and not of flesh, this religion of the mind was also universal, something that embraced all humankind.

This emergence of what Karl Jaspers called the Axial Age was happening at about the same time as the Indo-Europeans were sweeping across Europe with their horses, some of them becoming what we call Proto-Celts.

Thus, almost simultaneously, two breakthroughs, one intellectual and other technological, were creating the matrix for the modern world and for the religious heritages of which we are a part.

Let's go back to our friends in the village, which we decided has to be in West Cork. They didn't read because they couldn't. And they didn't know any philosophers. So these ideas of the transcendence of God didn't get to them. They continued to have their own celebrations. Their religious rituals dealt almost entirely with fertility because, while the sun was powerful and the moon was powerful and the thunder was powerful and the forest was powerful and the ocean was powerful, that which was really critical in their lives was fertility. Would the fields reproduce and provide harvest? Would the males and the females of the flocks come together, goats and horses and sheep, and reproduce? Would there be young lambs and young horses and young goats, which meant the tribe could continue to live? Would the members of the tribe themselves conceive and produce children? Would the children live or would they die?

The reproduction of the plants and the animals and the members of the tribe was a very chancy and uncertain thing. Sometimes there would be fertility and the tribe would flourish, and sometimes, perhaps even during the same year, the crops would die and the animals would die and the children would die and many of the mothers would die in childbirth. Then the people would be gripped by the terrible fear that maybe the tribe was coming to an end. Perhaps the gods were displeased with them because they had failed in their mission of spreading the world of the gods against the world of demons, of overcoming chaos with cosmos.

So their ritual celebrations were a worship of fertility, a plea for successful fertility, a horror of failed fertility. Each spring, when the first animals were reproduced and stood up off the ground as healthy lambs and healthy colts, they would heave a huge sigh of relief. The gods were still pleased with them. Fertility was still on their side. So they would assemble around the central shrine, which now might be more elaborate, and they would kill one of the first fruits of the flocks, a lamb or a goat, and they would roast its meat. Then the community would eat the roasted meat of the sacrificial victim, and they would celebrate in that little springtime meal the continuation of their work.

The spring festival would celebrate their unity with God or the gods and their community with one another. Farming people who were more settled than our friends in West Cork, would, when their wheat was harvested and their bread made, throw out the old yeast that they had used for their bread, and while the new yeast was fermenting would eat bread without yeast.

There were two very ancient fertility rituals, meals both of them, a meal in which a sacrificial victim was eaten, a meal when new bread was eaten; meals that brought people together, celebrated the continuation of their work, celebrated the unity of the tribe, and celebrated their unity with God or the gods. This was the annual spring fertility festival that, in one form or another, can be found in most of the primitive peoples of the world. It was a celebration of rebirth and spring. Naturally, celebrations often got out of hand, and not only in Ireland, people drank too much and they loved too much; but winter was over and it was spring and it was time to celebrate.

There was another festival that was important as well—a mid-winter, hope-against-hope, fingers-crossed anticipation of the coming spring. These mid-winter festivals also existed almost everywhere in the world. But they would be particularly important in those parts of the world, such as northern Europe, where the winters were severe.

Four or five thousand years ago, winters perhaps weren't quite as severe as they are now. The climate might have been a little warmer. But it was still cold. And the sun, which was a pretty important thing in life, started to go away. Our friends in the little village knew that the sun returned every year. In fact they probably had pretty good records of exactly when it was going to happen, so they weren't all that surprised. Indeed it may have been that the stones that they put around their village were ways of measuring where the sun was going and when it would come back. But for all their abilities that seemed to predict the return of the sun, it was still scary to see it keep getting lower and lower and lower in the sky.

In Northern Europe, the sun gets pretty far away in

November and December, barely peeking above the southern horizon, sometimes only four or five hours of decent daylight and the rest darkness. You say to yourself, What if it doesn't come back? It's come back every year, but what if it doesn't come back this year?

The wise men and the priests and the monsignors and the bishops (though they didn't use those names then) of the tribes would go out and watch when the sun would come up every morning, and they'd measure it against the stone and they'd say, Well it's right on schedule. This is what it's done every year. It gets lower and lower and then it will get as low as possible where it's marked by this stone way out here and then, you watch, it will come up a little higher the next morning and then the day will be a little longer and we'll know for sure that the sun is returning.

The skeptics of the tribe said, Oh yeah, that's the way it's always happened before but how do we know it's gonna keep on happening? Finally, when the turning point day came and the day was a little longer as the bishops had predicted, there were big celebrations. Spring was closer than it had been, and they could be reasonably sure that spring would come again. Thus it was proper and indeed essential to have a mid-winter festival. Again it was a fertility festival, a prayer for the return of life to the fields and to the animals and to their own relationships.

They drank and they loved and they celebrated and in the center of the celebration was a sacred evergreen tree, which perhaps they had now moved into the camp and put next to the sacred stone. The tree and the stone were the same thing. They were earth reaching to heaven. Why an evergreen tree? Because, you see, an evergreen tree was always green. It didn't lose its leaves. It remained green and fertile through the winter. And so, it was the world and god's promise. The evergreen tree was a promise that spring would come. They put lights around the tree because they said the lights represented the light that's coming back into the world. They hung fruits on the tree because fruits are the result of the fertility that marked the passionate union of the sky (female) and the earth (male) through the tree by which the earth had penetrated the sky.

Thus the two major festivals of nature religions were both fertility festivals, a celebration of fertility achieved and an anticipation of fertility still to come.

The religious thinkers and philosophers dismissed these festivals as ignorant, stupid, and physical; the last adjective was the strongest: humans are spirit. The physical body constrains the spirit and therefore is evil. Bodily religion degrades human spirit.

They also pointed out that, in addition to being fundamentally corrupt because of its physical nature, popular religion became even more corrupt because it was so easily turned into magic and superstition and frequently became an excuse for degrading roistering and wenching. In most lands, however, the philosophers were willing to permit the ordinary people their depraved religious forms because such folk were not capable of anything else. Some of the wise men even participated in the harmless pagan rites on the grounds that they were necessary to bind together the civic community.

The first attempt to provide a transcendent religion for ordinary people took place among the Hebrews. This ragtag collection of desert tribes—some already living in Canaan, some refugees from Egypt, some wandering desert nomads—possessed a traditional memory of a powerful experience of God uniting them as one people and, indeed, His People. Moreover, their God, who had been originally a desert god of battle, came to be experienced as a transcendent God, one who was utterly superior to the nature deities of the other Semitic and Canaanite peoples.

The development of Yahweh into a transcendent God probably took many years, although it is not unreasonable to assume there were hints of such transcendence in the primal experience at Sinai. As the religious leaders of the people became gradually aware of the fact that Yahweh was not a god like other gods but was utterly different from and far superior to them, they did a very wise thing. They appropriated (perhaps only gradually) two of the pagan fertility festivals—the festival of the unleavened bread and the festival of the spring lamb—and they made them their own. They said, We are no longer honoring the gods of fertility who inhabit our fields and our animals and our own bodies. We are now honoring the transcendent Yahweh for whom all fertility and all sexuality is an obedient servant. So we eat the unleavened bread and we offer the Pascal lamb and, in the process of doing this, we celebrate our unity with Yahweh and our unity with one another and remember that great time at the foot of Mt. Sinai when all the tribes came together and were seized by this enormous experience of Yahweh making them a people.

This decision was a decisive turning point in the history of humankind. It produced the first world religion designed for all the people and not only for the wise folks in the elite. This world religion—the religion of a transcendent God—converted as best it could two of the pagan festivals and put them to the use of a transcendent religion.

From the prophets' denunciations, we know that this transcendent religion had a hard time of it. The Hebrew people did not want to give up completely the pagan, fertility elements that had been eliminated from their religion. No one ought to be surprised at that fact. On the contrary, what is surprising is that the extraordinary innovation of the Hebrew "transcendence for everyone" worked at all.

The festivals were no longer fertility rituals. They had been "cleaned up" so that the forces of nature were no longer worshiped, but only the God who dominated completely the forces of nature. Eventually, by the time of the Second Temple era, the pagan cults were eliminated in most of Palestine, though, according to recent archaeological discoveries, they survived elsewhere. (In a temple in Alexandria, for example, Yahweh still had a wife, a consort who in prophetic Judaism has been reduced to the shekinah, the "spirit" of Yahweh.)

The achievement of the Hebrew religion, however, was enormous. In other lands, the "axial" thinkers were philosophers and poets, men who had little interest in ordinary people. Among the Hebrews, the transcendental religion emerged out of the religion of the people under the direction of men who had little interest in philosophy and much interest in ordinary people.

One suspects that some of the prophets were uneasy with the temple cult precisely because they didn't even like the sanitized Passover liturgy. They had a point: how could one engage in fertility rites and at the same time honor a transcendent Yahweh? If you permitted any nature religion (of the Canaanite variety in the trees and in the "high places") would not the worship of creation taint the worship of the Creator? And would not all the excesses of fertility worship return again?

Thus by the beginning of the Common Era, there were three different religious imaginations in the world, each with its own experience of God and its own imagery to convey that experience. Paganism, sophisticated and decadent, still reigned in the Roman Empire and in much of the rest of the world. Transcendental religion preoccupied the philosophers and many of the elite of society in the various gnostic cults and in similar groups beyond the empire. Prophetic Judaism had produced transcendence for everyone, a God who—like the old desert warrior from whom he emerged—was in a love relationship with his people but who now was also a transcendent deity who entered into intimate personal relationships with not only the people but with people, with each individual person, and, by so doing, made holy not only spirit but also flesh.

Some Jewish thinkers, most notably Jacob Neusner, contend that in the stories of the relationship between God and people, there was already a demand for incarnation. Perhaps by expropriating the two fertility festivals, the leaders of the Hebrew people also built into their religion, if not an incarnation, at least an incarnational element.

Certainly the Hebrew religion did not have to assert the evil of the human body in order to defend the transcendence of God.

But despite the compromise of the transformed Passover festival, Judaism was (and still is) horrified of idolatry, of the possibility that human rituals will taint with idolatry the worship of the transcendent Other.

Catholic Christianity later decided that you could have both, that the power of God manifested in the risen Jesus was so great that the worship of the God of Jesus could absorb all that was good, true, and beautiful in the cults of the groves and the high places. And every other pagan cult, too.

It was a brave, if risky, decision.

Whether it was also a wise decision is a question on which all the evidence is not in.

5

The Catholic Imagination

With Catholic Christianity there appeared one of the most interesting phenomena in the history of the religious imagination. Somewhere between Ignatius of Antioch and Gregory I, what Hebrew prophets did with the pagan Passover customs, early Catholic Christians did with everything in sight. They took over paganism.

It's hard for us to imagine what a sacred world our very sophisticated ancestors from Greece and Rome lived in. Every field had a shrine. Every cave had an oracle. Every scary place in the forest had a god. Every neighborhood in the city had its own little temple. Every house had its own gods by the fireplace. There were feasts every day in honor of the gods of the farmers and the gods of the hunters and the gods and goddesses of love and the god of war and the goddess of the tin merchants and the iron merchants and the copper merchants.

Everybody had their own god and their own oracle and their own ceremonies and their own cults. How seriously did folks take this omnipresent religion? Perhaps about as seriously as we take religion. Some of them were very serious. Some weren't serious at all. Some were skeptical. Some were deeply religious. Some of the ceremonies were civic rituals of no more importance than Presidents' Day is. And others were of as much importance as Valentine's Day is, which is pretty important to people if not to the Church.

At the time that Constantine decided that he was going to become Christian, only five percent of the people in the Roman Empire (according to the best information we have) were Christian. It took another one hundred years before the majority of people in the empire were Christian. So the Church was faced with a very challenging situation: it was officially the religion of the empire. Paganism was in retreat and the pagan gods had not been able to protect it. Christianity was going to win. But what do you do with all these shrines and ceremonies and patron gods and goddesses around? At that point, Catholic Christianity made the fateful decision.

In the tremendous optimism of their experience of the risen Jesus, Catholic Christians had already decided that everything that was good, true, and beautiful was "naturally" Christian. In the years after Constantine, Catholic Christianity generalized from the tentative compromise that the Hebrew prophets had made with pagan rituals: if everything good and true and beautiful was Christian, they would baptize and make Christian anything in pagan ceremony and in custom which looked like it was good and true and beautiful.

Islam revolted against this decision, and later, Protestantism revolted against it. Most of the great spiritual religions of the world still look in horror on this fateful compromise attempted by Catholic Christianity.

It must not be forgotten that the compromise was attempted because early Catholicism was permeated with optimism generated by its faith in the Incarnation and Resurrection of Jesus. If Jesus became man, if Jesus took on human flesh, if Jesus was part of the material things of this world, then everything is sanctified, everything is Christian, everything's a sacrament, everything will tell us something about God.

In Ireland Brigid, the goddess of spring and poetry and

new life, was converted to become the patron saint of these things, and her shrine at Kildare became the shrine of St. Brigid of Kildare and her sacred fire became the sacred fire of Brigid of Kildare. The phallic stones were said to represent the tree of the cross; the fertility symbol of the male and the female—the Celtic Cross—was said to represent Jesus and its circle to represent Mary.

All through the Roman Empire the same thing happened. The old festivals were taken over. The old shrines and the old rites were not sprinkled with holy water. Rather, they were eliminated and quickly replaced. The explanations for the changes given were good explanations. The Irish, for example, said, Well now, Brigid isn't a goddess. She's not a goddess at all. No, she's just a plain, old saint. She's a human being like us. But because she did such good work when she was alive here in the world, God is especially likely to hear her, and so she's been given charge of certain responsibilities in this world. And we talk to her so she can talk to God. She's got clout. Of course God hears us. He doesn't need Brigid. But sure, we need her because she represents somebody that we know that knows God well.

It was a marvelously human explanation. It was also thoroughly Christian because now divine power wasn't in the sacred rivers and the sacred forests and the sacred stones. Divine power was in God. The gods and goddesses who had previously presided over creation with power of their own now became saints, humans like us, with special access to God because they were God's friends.

It didn't always work out that neatly. Since the pagan religion of Ireland believed in reincarnation, when the Irish said that Brigid was the Mary of the Gaels, they meant it quite literally: Brigid was the Blessed Mother reincarnate.

Many, many times down through history, this calculated risk, this gamble of Catholic Christianity to take over all the rites and the ceremonies and the objects and the events of the world of human life and make them sacred, has led to superstition and folk religion. Protestantism and Islam don't have that problem because they feel the world is essentially bad and bleak and human nature is related directly to God without any of these intermediaries. Superstition, magic, folk religion are much less likely to happen. Since their people are humans too, they have their superstitions, but not the kind of superstitions which can readily be integrated into their religion. The Catholic compromise, the Catholic appropriation of the material world, leaves us open to superstition. The Protestant, Jewish, and Islamic suspicion of the material world leaves the world in which we live a bleak place.

Both sides need each other to correct them. One is not better than the other. They need to listen to us about the presence of God in the world in which we live. We need to listen to them to realize that God and the world are identified too much when we slipped back into the world.

The early Christians celebrated a Passover just like the Jews. It was held at the same time as the Jewish Passover. They ate the Pascal meal with one another every Sunday. Especially at Passover time, the Eucharist commemorated the resurrection of Jesus. Just as at Sinai the Hebrews had been brought together and constituted a people, so in the upper room at the Last Supper, the Christian community had been constituted the new people of God. Just as Moses had led the Israelites out of slavery into a new life of freedom, the land flowing with milk and honey, so Jesus led us out of the slavery of sin and death into a new life in his death and resurrection.

First of all, there were the original two pagan festivals. Then there was an overlay of the Jewish religious experience and another overlay of the Christian experience of the death and resurrection of Jesus. The old festival was not thrown away as new overlays were put on it.

Then an interesting development occurred between Ignatius of Antioch in 150 A.D. and Gregory the Great in about 600 A.D. A ceremony taken over completely from Roman paganism was inserted in the Christian Passover celebration: the Roman pagan spring fertility rite of fire and water was baptized and became part of baptism.

There was some justification for this appropriation: in the Jewish Passover tradition, the water of the Red Sea and the pillar of cloud by day and the pillar of fire by night gave a hint of fire and water symbolism. Although those two symbols never became important in the Jewish Passover, they provided justification for the baptism of the fire and water symbolism in the Christian Passover.

In most fertility rituals in the world, the lighted candle represents the male and water represents the female. When you plunge the candle into the water, you are virtually re-enacting intercourse. The Romans did this as part of their spring fertility festival because it was spring, a time when plants, animals, and humans blossomed with new life. The Roman Christians said, We will take this ceremony and make it our own. We'll say that when Jesus rose from the dead, he consummated his nuptials with his bride, the Church. We who are baptized in the sanctified waters of Easter are the first fruits of this passionate union between Jesus and his Church. It was an explicitly erotic ceremony. The old Latin words said, "May this candle fructify these waters; may this candle impregnate these waters; give life"—an explicitly nuptial and sexual interpretation and symbolism attached to the Passover Feast. Yet another layer was thus added to the paganism of the Semite tribes and the Jewish reinterpretation and the Christian reinterpretation: the overlay of the fire and water ritual.

The final overlay was Anglo-Saxon. In most of the nations of the world, the names for the Christian spring festival and the Jewish one are the same. The Passover is the Passover. The Jews have their Passover. We have ours. They are linked, and theoretically, they should even occur at the same time—the first Sunday after the first full moon in the beginning of spring.

But in English we call it Easter. How come?

Easterne, or Eastern, was a pagan, Anglo-Saxon goddess,

the goddess who appeared in the eastern sky, the goddess of the dawn, like the Latin Aurora. Like her cousin, the Celtic Brigid, Easterne was the goddess of spring. The Christian Passover in the Anglo-Saxon countries came at the same time as the festival of the pagan goddess Easterne. The pagan festival was replaced by the Christian Passover, but the name of pagan festival was retained.

Moreover, and this is the final overlay of meaning, as the goddess of dawn and the goddess of spring, the pagan Easterne had three symbols, three familiars that traveled with her: lilies, rabbits, and eggs, all symbolisms of the implacable power of life. At "Easter" we celebrate the Resurrection of Jesus, the triumph of life over death *par excellence*, the most brilliant of all the victories of fertility over decay. So pagan fertility symbols—bunnies, eggs, and lilies—are baptized and converted to Christian use.

The same process of piling on layers of meaning has constituted our Christmas. The northern European Tannenbaum, the mid-winter solstice tree reaching between earth and heaven, the evergreen impregnating the sky to bring down spring rain and spring warmth, becomes our Christmas tree. The tree, we say, represents the cross, the cross on which hung the light of the world, the cross that reunited earth and heaven. The ornaments on the cross are the fruits. They represent us humans, who are the offspring of the passionate new union between earth and sky, between human nature and God.

When we celebrate Christmas and when we celebrate Easter, we return five or six thousand years at least. And we plunge down deeply into the swirling mass of images in the borderland between our preconscious and are our unconscious. We continue ceremonies that our pre-Christian ancestors performed. We continue them with the same meaning that they had but with new overlays of meaning of our own. We continue them in one way or another as part of that compromise which said, in effect, you can respect and reverence the transcendent deity without denying the goodness and the truth and the beauty of the things of this world.

We also continue our pagan ancestors' reverence for the maternity of nature when we honor Mary the Mother of Jesus. It often seemed to our ancestors that God was cruel. He killed our animals, destroyed our fields with storms, let our wives and husbands and children die. He has doomed us to die too. What kind of a God is that?

But at other times God seemed very gentle, very tender, very affectionate, and very loving. This is how the idea that God is a Mother as well as a Father began to develop in humankind. It was females, animals and humans, who were especially responsible for the new life that began in springtime. Perhaps, then, God loves us as the mother hen loves the chick, as the mare loves her newborn colt, as particularly as a human mother cuddles her newborn child. Israel tried everything it could to extirpate all traces of a womanly deity from Galilee, though Lady Wisdom in the Jewish Scriptures is a reflection of the womanliness of God and Yahweh displays many womanly traits.

Catholic Christianity reversed the process completely. It purified the notion of a womanly God and brought her back in as Mary, the Madonna, the Mother of Jesus, representing the mother love of God. It was probably the most brilliant ploy in the whole history of religion. The ploy, like all human efforts, has not always worked perfectly because, often, Mary has not been understood properly. She's been made into a negative goddess of sex, a goddess of virginity. She's been covered with saccharin. Sometimes her role has detracted from the worship of God. But still, Mary represents in Catholic Christianity an enormously important insight that goes way, way back to our ancestors in that little wooded village on the shores of County Cork: God loves us like a Mother as well as like a Father.

So three of our symbols — Mary, the Christmas Tree, and Easter—are rooted deep, deep in the past and deep, deep in the human unconscious. They are still alive with us and they will always be alive in some fashion as long as we are enfleshed creatures—creatures with a soul that yearns for the transcendence of God, creatures with a body that is very much part of the ordinary physical world. And creatures whose soul and body are going to stay together in whatever resurrection the Lord God and Lady Wisdom prepare for us.

The Catholic Christian experiment has often not been successful. But it represents a recognition of our curious blend of body and spirit, of a spirit that soars to the heavens and a body that is very much a part of and rather enjoys the material world. The fact that Jesus took on human flesh is the theological justification for the Catholic experiment. In the light of the Incarnation, validated by the Resurrection, all that is good, true, and beautiful is Christian. Grace is everywhere and everything.

Contemporary Catholicism is often embarrassed by this tradition, especially as it applies to the Mother of Jesus. We are afraid to stage big May crowning processions because Protestants might say that Catholics worship Mary. If the Catholic compromise means anything, it means that we have to rearticulate our insights, not abandon our ceremonies and rituals. Mary represents the womanliness of God—God's tender, affectionate, merciful love.

It's not all that difficult to rearticulate. But somehow or the other, in the turbulent transition after the Vatican Council, we would sooner repudiate our angels and our saints and our Blessed Mother and our ceremonies and our rituals than try to explain them.

This brief and schematized history of the Catholic imagination is essential for the development of a Catholic theology of popular culture. Even though we may be ashamed of them now, the devotions of the Catholic tradition were taken from the popular customs and ceremonies of ordinary people in years past. In former times, the Church was not ashamed of what its people liked. The triumph of propositional theology over imaginative liturgy is the result of universal literacy and the development of theological requirements for being Catholic. The Vatican Council was a propositional Council, uninterested in imagination. The liturgical "reform" of the Council was interested only in theology, not in art or culture or the popular imagination.

The Council fathers could not have cared less about the imagination of the people. The Catholic tradition was theology, of course; what else could it be?

I emphasize again that propositional religion is essential because humans are reflective creatures as well as experiencing creatures. But a full comprehension of the Catholic tradition requires respect not only for its proposition dimension but also for its imaginative dimension, especially since religion seems to originate in and draw its raw power from the imagination—as we shall see in the next three chapters.

The Vatican Council was a left-brain Council. It acted as if the right brain did not exist. Much of the post-conciliar troubles can be traced to that failure.

6

A Sociological Theory of the Religious Imagination

In this chapter, I will present a sociological theory of the religious imagination, a final preliminary to stating my theological theories of the religious imagination and of popular culture.

My thesis in this chapter is that a religious imagination is the source of the power and energy of faith. I will use sociological theory and research evidence to sustain this thesis, though I will note that it is congruent with both Bernard Lonergan's notion of "perception" and Alfred North Whitehead's conception of "prehension." Both philosophers, as I understand them, hold that "out of the corner of our eye," so to speak, in the act of knowing, we perceive purpose, design, even love binding together the cosmos. I contend that the "out of the corner of the eye" aspect of knowing is precisely where religion finds its origin and power and that, therefore, religion is primarily an activity of the creative imagination.

As I have indicated before, there are a number of different

names for that dimension of the human personality which I will call in this paper the creative imagination—a word I have taken from the psychoanalyst, Leonard Kubie, who also calls it the preconscious—an aspect of the self somewhere between the unperceived unconscious and the fully perceived conscious.

Jacques Maritain, in words similar to Kubie's, calls it the "creative intuition" and compares it to Thomas Aquinas' agent intellect (*intellectus agens*, if you prefer the mother tongue.) Others would call it the poetic intuition or the poetic faculty. St. Paul seems to refer to the same dimensions of the person when he says that the spirit speaks to our spirit, to, it would seem from the context, the spontaneous, creative, fine edge of the soul.

By whatever name, this dimension of the personality may be conceived (or perhaps imagined)—as I have suggested in an earlier chapter—as a radar screen on which are scanned in endlessly shifting arrangements the images that have been drawn by the senses out of the world of experience. In this scanning process, images are juxtaposed in constantly changing constellations that are inchoate poems and stories, metaphors and narratives which combine various elements in our experience, past and present. The creative imagination edits and compares, connects and separates, simplifies and distorts, convolutes and modifies; it performs these activities sometimes "mindlessly" in the strict sense that the mind is not attending and, at other times, with deliberate purpose in that the mind is carefully listening, searching for insight and understanding.

It seems not unreasonable to link the creative imagination with the right lobe of the brain and to define the times when it is given the full freedom to operate in an altered state of consciousness. At such times (which can, of course, be deliberately induced by one means or another), one can literally hear the stories and poems which are being created, so much so that the Greek myth of the Muse, the outside, inspiring agent, takes on a certain amount of plausibility. It is worth noting, by the way, that in certain kinds of scientific analysis (including sociological work with a conversational computer system), this "preconscious" dimension also operates.

I contend that it is precisely in this creative imagination where religion has its origin and power and that, therefore, the priest with a poorly developed creative imagination will be so devoid of religious sensibility as to be ineffective as a priest.

It is necessary here to make two precisions so that my argument will not be misunderstood.

1) I am not excluding from religion the importance of discursive intellect or rational reflection. On the contrary, because we are reflecting creatures, we must be able to go beyond story and poem, beyond picture and song, to philosophize about religion. Creeds, catechisms, and *Summae* are utterly essential to the human condition. Because religion begins in the imagination, that does not mean that it should end there but merely that we ought not to forget the fact that it does, indeed, begin there. Among certain right-wing Catholics now there is a contempt for "religious experience" as though it was utterly irrelevant to the human condition and to human faith. Perhaps there is some merit in their contempt because today much of what passes for religious experience in the Church is both shallow and unreflective. It is not of such experiences that I am speaking.

2) Nor is either religious experience or the religious imagination, in which the stories and pictures of the experience resonate and remain, pure "emotion." Quite the contrary, the religious imagination is an aspect of the personality of an intellectual creature and is both affected by that creature's intellectual development and operated as a dimension of intellect. It is precisely because it is "preconscious" that it is still intellect. The conscious mind is not absent from the creative imagination, not ever; and it is especially present when it pauses to listen during the creative process. Indeed, the term "preconscious intellect" is in my judgment the perfect description of the dimension I am describing—so too, is Thomas' "agent," or if you will, "active intellect."

I will not enter into a dispute as to whether the development of conscious intellect or the development of the creative imagination is important for the work of the priest, though it is my impression that neither is taken very seriously these days. Both are important, indeed. Both are indispensable, and that seems to be enough.

However, one must say that if sermons are terrible—and the judgments of the laity are that they, indeed, are terrible—the problem may be more in the lack of creative imagination in the priest than in the lack of cognitive knowledge.

I now turn to the sociological theory that supports my thesis. I will describe this theory under nine headings.

1) Human nature has a built-in propensity to hope. Whether that hope is genetically programmed, as Lionel Tiger has argued, or merely a powerful psychological need is not pertinent for my theory. It is sufficient to say that in William McCready's research, more than four fifths of the American people gave hopeful or optimistic responses to potentially tragic situations. Death research, resuscitation research, and dream analysis all demonstrate this powerful and persistent tendency of humans to hope even when the situation seems hopeless, even when they can find no specific content to their hope.

2) Humans also have the capacity for experiences that renew their hope. These experiences may for some people be the spectacular experience of which William James wrote in his *Varieties of Religious Experience*. These experiences may also be much less spectacular—a desert sunset, the touch of a friendly hand, a reconciliation after a quarrel, the grin on the face of a toddler, solving an ethical or mathematical problem, even a good night's sleep. Experiences like these, as David Tracy points out in his book, *A Blessed Rage for Order*, are experiences of "gratuity," nice things that didn't have to happen but did. We encounter with them the limitations of our existence (Tracy calls them "limit" or "horizon-experiences"), which also confirm that

despite these limitations, our existence is "gifted," something that didn't have to happen, didn't have to be, yet is. Such experiences occur with varying degrees of intensity in virtually everyone's life, providing hints of purpose, "rumors of angels," intimations of. . . something, encounters with "otherness."

Creatures born with the propensity to hope, we are confirmed in that propensity by certain "encounters" in our lives. Most often, that which is "encountered" is experienced simply as "otherness"; but on occasion, or frequently for some people, it can be a powerful, demanding, passionately loving "otherness." Hence, on reflection, we speak of the "otherness" as "The Other." Both historically and psychologically, we believe this to be the origin of first the image and then the concept of "God."

Philosophically, an examination of religion may well begin with the question of whether God exists (a question that has been brilliantly addressed recently by Professor Hans Kung). But, humanly, the experience of gratuity and the encounter with The Other precedes the question of whether God exists (though most of us, of course, come to our limit-experience with an existing notion of God, a notion that may or may not fit that which we experience). However, both the God concept and the God issues are derivative. The more fundamental and primordial question is whether reality is such as to guarantee the propensity to hope. Perhaps even more basic, is reality truly that which we experience in our interludes of hopefulness? John Macquarrie, an English theologian, put the question nicely when he said that the primary question is whether reality (or Reality) is gracious (or Gracious). From the point of view of the social scientist approaching religion, the basic questions are "What are the stories that reveal reality as gracious?" "What impact do such stories have on a person's life?"

3) While any reality may trigger a "grace" experience (and, hence, everything is sacramental in the sense that everything has the potentiality of revealing the source of our hopefulness), there are certain realities that because of their power, their importance,

or their prevalence, are especially likely to trigger such experiences (hence, are sacraments par excellence): fire, the sun, water, the moon, oil, love, sex, marriage, birth, death, community. For reasons of biology, psychology, or culture, these realities seem especially likely to trigger grace experiences for many human beings.

In previous chapters, I have discussed the Christmas tree as a link between heaven and earth, an application of the traditional symbolism of tree. Let us consider here three different but not totally unrelated experiences of tree.

The first is from Jean Paul Sartre:

> The roots of the chestnut tree were sunk in the ground just under my bench. I couldn't remember it was a root anymore. I was sitting, stooping forward, head bowed, alone in front of this black, knotty mass, entirely beastly, which frightened me. The chestnut tree pressed itself against my eyes. Green rust covered it halfway up; the bark, black and swollen, looked like boiled leather. Knotty, inert, nameless, it fascinated me, filled my eyes, brought me back unceasingly to its own existence. The whole stump gave me the impression of unwillingness, denying its existence to lose itself in a frenzied excess. I scraped my heel against this black root: I wanted to peel off some bark. For no reason at all, out of defiance, to make the bare pink appear absurd on the tanned leather: to play with the absurdity of the world. Suddenly I knew that every existing thing is born without reason, prolongs itself out of weakness and dies by chance.

The second is from Avery Dulles' account of his conversion:

> As I wandered aimlessly something impelled me to look contemplatively at a young tree. On its frail, supple branches were young buds attending eagerly the spring which was at hand. While my eyes rested on them the thought came to me suddenly with all the strength and novelty of a revelation, that these little buds with their innocence and meekness followed a rule, a law of which I as yet knew nothing. How could it be, I asked, that this delicate tree sprang up and developed and that all the enormous complexity of its cellular operations combined together to make it grow erectly and bring forth leaves and blossoms? The answer, the trite answer of the schools, was new to me: that its actions were ordered to an end by the only power capable of adapting means to ends—intelligence—and that the very fact that this intelligence worked toward an end implied purposiveness—in other words, a will. As I turned home that evening, the darkness closing round, I was

conscious that I had discovered something which would introduce me to a new life. Never, since the eventful day which I have just described, have I doubted the existence of an all-good and omnipotent God.

And the third, my favorite of all them because it is so very, very Catholic, is from Mario Cuomo:

Friday, October 22, 1982
4:30 A.M.
Tired, very tired, feeling the many months of struggle, last night I went up to the den to make some notes. I was looking for a pencil, rummaging through some papers in the back of my desk drawer, where things accumulate for years, when I turned up one of Poppa's old business cards, the ones we made up for him, that he was so proud of: "Andrea Cuomo, Italian-American Groceries—Fine Imported Products." Poppa never had any occasion to give anyone a calling card, but he loved having them. He put one in a little gold frame on a red-velvet background on the nightstand near his bed. Momma has one of them now, framed like Poppa's, on display in a prominent place in her china closet.

I couldn't help wondering what Poppa would have said if I had told him I was tired or—God forbid—that I was discouraged. Then I thought for a few minutes about how he dealt with hard circumstances. A thousand different pictures flashed through my mind—he was so used to dealing with hard circumstances. Almost everything was hard.

But one scene in particular came sharply into view.

We had just moved into Holliswood from behind the store. We had our own house for the first time; it even had some land around it, even trees—one, in particular, was a great blue spruce that must have been 40 ft. high.

Holliswood was hilly. Our house sat 10 or 15 ft. above the road itself, and the blue spruce stood majestically like a sentinel at the corner of our property, where the street made a turn, bending around our property line.

Less than a week after we moved in there was a terrible storm. We came home from the store that night to find the great blue spruce pulled almost totally out of the ground and flung forward, its mighty nose bent in the asphalt of the street. Frankie and I knew nothing about trees. We could climb poles all day; we were great at fire escapes; we could scale fences with barbed wire at the top—but we knew nothing about trees. When we saw our spruce, defeated, its cheek on the canvas, our hearts sank. But not Poppa's.

Maybe he was 5 ft. 6 if his heels were not worn. Maybe he weighed 155 lbs. if he had a good meal. Maybe he could see a block away if his glasses were clean. But he was stronger than Frankie and I and Marie and Momma all together.

We stood in the street looking down at the tree. The rain was falling. We waited a couple of minutes figuring things out and then he announced, "O.K., we gonna push 'im up!" "What are you talking about Poppa? The roots are out of the ground!" "Shut up, we gonna push 'im up, he's gonna grow again."

We didn't know what to say to him, you couldn't say no to him; not just because you were his son, but because he was so sure.

So we followed him into the house and we got what rope there was and we tied the rope around the tip of the tree that lay in the asphalt, and he stood up by the house, with me pulling on the rope and Frankie in the street in the rain, helping to push up the great blue spruce. In no time at all we had it standing up straight again!

With the rain still falling, Poppa dug away at the place where the roots were, making a muddy hole wider and wider as the tree sank lower and lower toward security. Then we shoveled mud over the roots and moved boulders to the base of the tree to keep it in place. Poppa drove stakes in the ground, tied rope from the trunk to the stakes, and maybe two hours later looked at the spruce, the crippled spruce made straight by ropes, and said, "Don't worry, he's gonna grow again."

I looked at the card and wanted to cry. If you were to drive past the house today you would see the great, straight blue spruce, maybe 65 ft. tall, pointing straight up to the heavens, pretending it never had its nose in the asphalt.

I put Poppa's card back in the drawer, closed it with a vengeance. I couldn't wait to get back into the campaign.

4) The experience is recorded, first of all, in that aspect of the personality we normally call "the imagination." The experience of grace, first of all, is an impact on the senses, and then it is filtered through the imagination where it has an enormous and sometimes overwhelming effect. Even long after the experience is over, the residue remain in the imagination, capable of recollection and of exciting once again resonances of the experience. The interaction between experience and imagination is complex and intricate. For the repertory of images and pictures available to any given person's or community's imagination, the individual or community will respond to the experience and shape both the perception and the recollection of the experience, if not the experience itself. Thus the apostles' Easter experience of Jesus not dead but alive was encoded in the imagery of contemporary Judaism. Jesus as Moses, Jesus as Adam, Jesus as prophet, as messiah, even as "resurrected" in accordance with the "story" common in Pharisaic Judaism, all these are images or "stories" which were part of the imaginative repertory available to the followers of Jesus. Their experience of

Jesus perceived as alive triggered such images and pictures. The images and pictures shaped the experience or, at least, their resonance to it. In the process, the images, pictures, and stories were themselves transformed so that they meant something rather different to the apostles afterwards, when they tried to describe the experience. Jesus was "like" a new Adam, and yet there was more to be said because the Adam "story" had been changed as a result of the Easter experience.

I cite this classic, tradition-shaped, grace experience because it provides such a clear example of the subtle interaction between imagination and experience. Presumably, interactions of this sort occur in many, if not all, experiences of grace, although until we have much more research on the psychology of the experience itself, no one will be able to chart the precise process with any degree of confidence.

5) The purpose of religious discourse, at least of the most elementary variety, is not to communicate doctrinal propositions but to stir up in the other person resonances of experiences similar to those which the religious storyteller himself or herself has had. Thus the telling each year in Holy Week of the story of the death and resurrection of Jesus, complete with all the profoundly resonating liturgical imagery, is not designed primarily to communicate doctrinal propositions but to rekindle memories of death-rebirth experiences that have marked the lives of the hearers and to link those resonances to the historic experience of Christians through the ages, leading back to the founding experience itself. The Easter story is designed primarily to rekindle memories of grace experiences and link them with overarching memories in the historical tradition. Religion as story leaps from imagination to imagination and only then, if at all, from intellect to intellect.

6) Religion becomes a communal event when a person is able to link his own grace experience with the overarching experience of this religious tradition (or a religious tradition), when he perceives a link between his experience of grace and

the tradition's experience of grace, when he becomes aware that there is a correspondence or a correlation between the resonating picture or story in his imagination and the story passed on by his religious heritage. At that point, the experience of grace is a private event or at least one that is not perceived as linked to anything formally known as religion. (In our subsequent discussion of the film *All That Jazz*, we will illustrate how a profound grace experience need not be perceived at all as formally religious.) However, it is worth noting that most of us are products of religious heritages, and there is a powerful tendency in most of our personalities to resonate our experiences in and through the images that we inherited from our tradition. Our own experiences of grace give an inchoate meaning to the stories of our lives. They hint at purposes which exist beyond ourselves. They suggest that the story of our life, which has a beginning, a middle, and a trajectory toward conclusion, may well have a gracious purpose. Articulated with and resonating together with stories of religious heritage, these religious stories constitute a fundamental theme, a basic leitmotif that underpins and validates our own existence. They have now become a set of "unique" symbols which Geertz refers to in his definition of religion.

We are all storytellers, playing the leading role in the story that is our own life. Even if some philosophers insist that our life is a series of random events, we perceive life events linked through a number of basic themes within the context of beginning, middle, and thrust toward conclusion. One of the basic themes is religious or ultimate; it is the theme or, if you will, the subplot of the play of our lives which gives life final meaning by linking our own experiences of grace to the overarching story themes of our religious heritage.

7) Just as much of the story of anyone's life is a story of relationships, so each person's religious story is a story of relationships. (We walked the hills of Galilee and Jerusalem with him and knew he was special but did not know just how special he was.) The principal sacraments in our lives are other human

beings or, more precisely, our relationships with other human beings. While non-human objects, such as fire, water, sunset, or mountain, may stir up experiences of grace, loving goodness is perceived mostly through relationships with other humans. We are, in other words, the principal sacrament, the principal sign, the principal symbol through which other persons encounter grace and experience hope validated, just as they are the principal sacraments, the confirming grace and validating hope for us. Ultimate loving goodness, if it does indeed reveal itself, seems to reveal itself mostly through loving goodness.

8) Thus, while religious teaching must certainly deal with ideas and in cognitive propositions, it must also stir up imaginative resonances and use stories and images. The teacher must be a storyteller and a poet so that he can describe the experiences of loving goodness which are part of his life and religious heritage in such a way that resonances of parallel experiences in the lives of those who are listening to him are excited. The loving goodness in their own lives then is linked to the Loving Goodness of the heritage. These linked stories of goodness are then able to illumine the ambiguity in the lives of the listeners. The listeners are then free to permit their own narratives to be shaped by the theme of the overarching narrative. To create such an exercise requires a considerable degree of skill in the art and the craft of expressing the creative imagination.

9) Religious storytelling—the essence of this theory of religious communication—is an attempt to communicate from imagination to imagination, to leap, as it were, from two energy poles and establish a circuit of current. One attempts to set up such a current by evoking images from the surging imaginative dynamics in the preconscious of the other and restructuring to some extent the configurations of those dynamics. One evokes by discharging, as it were, the imagination configurations in one's own preconscious through the process of storytelling so that these imaginative energies of one's own may enter into an affective or quasi-affective link with those of the other. Such, of

course, is the nature of all imaginative work—storytelling, poetry, musical composition. Religious storytelling is no different. The more skillful the storyteller, that is to say, the more evocative, the more powerful will be the energy discharge and restructuring which occurs.

Note well that such evocation is not a nice adjunct to religious communication, not a cute little trick, but the essence of it—and an essence that requires a great deal of professional skill, of art and craft, of work and discipline, of patience and concentration.

Evocation is a prelude to provocation—we stir up the imaginations to move to action: "Come follow me"; "Lift up your heads and see"; "Come dance with me." Normally, I would submit, cognitive reflection comes after the evocation and the provocation have done their work. It is, I insist, absolutely indispensable. It is not, however, the starting point.

Thus, in brief summary of the theory, there are four phases in the hope experience's impact on the religious imagination— the experience itself, the image or symbol which stores the experience (normally an image of the person, object, or event which triggered the experience but which now has been imbued with paradigmatic status), the story by which we share the experience with others, and the community of those who share our imagery and stories and who provide us with an interpretive repertory for encoding the experience (and probably the predisposition to be triggered by the cause of the experience).

The remaining question for this chapter is whether such a model of religion generates hypotheses that can be tested against the data so that the theory is at least not "disconfirmed" before we go on to reflecting on it theologically. Since I am an empiricist by training, I cannot go on to reflect religiously or theologically on a theory unless it cannot be rejected by empirical data. (In the logic of our science, theories are not confirmed. Rather, the null hypotheses denying the theory are rejected.) Thus I will conclude that the data are such that the null hypothesis that says the religious imagination has no effect on social and political attitudes and behaviors must be rejected.

1) Images of God as a mother and a friend (as opposed to a father and a king) correlate at levels of statistical significance with attitudes towards the death penalty, civil liberties, feminism, and racial justice—the warmer the story of God in one's images, the more likely one is to project a warmer story on social reality. Moreover, these correlations are not eliminated by controls for age, sex, education, region, or political or religious liberalism.

2) Moreover, those with a "warmer" or more "graceful" religious imagination were at least ten percentage points more likely to vote against Ronald Reagan in the 1980 and 1984 presidential elections.

3) The relationship between religious images and voting against Reagan persisted in all political groups ("Liberal," "Moderate," and "Conservative") and in all political identifications ("Democrat," "Independent," and "Republican") except among "Conservatives." Thus the voting pattern was not merely the result of party identification or political orientation.

4) The net correlations between the religious imagination and political and social attitudes and voting behavior were such that, on the average, they were more important than age, sex, and region. It would make as much sense to exclude religious image questions from surveys as it would to exclude questions about age, sex, and region.

5) In our study of young adults carried out with the generous assistance of the Knights of Columbus, we discovered that images of God as mother and lover; Mary and Jesus as warm, patient, kind and sympathetic; and heaven as an action-filled paradise of pleasures and delights could be combined into a scale that was a far more powerful predictor of religious behavior than propositional orthodoxy. Our "grace scale" correlated positively with devotion, thoughts of a religious vocation, commitment to social and racial justice, hopeful response to tragedy, and even sexual fulfillment in marriage at a level many times more power-

ful than the doctrinal orthodoxy scale. Indeed the latter rarely produced any statistically significant relationships. Your "story of God" is a much more powerful influence on your religious behavior and your secular behavior than what you think about hell, papal authority, and papal infallibility.

6) Furthermore, the religious imagination is shaped primarily by relational experiences of loving goodness—with one's parents, with nature, directly with God, with school teachers, with friends, with parish priest and community, and with spouse. Indeed the longer the marriage and the more sexually fulfilling it is, the more powerful the mutual influences of husband and wife on each other's "story of grace." More than half of the variance in the grace scale can be accounted for by these relationships, a very powerful finding in social research.

Note that it is the quality of the relationship which matters. There is no correlation at all between years of Catholic education, years of CCD, or indeed years of education, on the one hand, and the grace scale on the other hand. However, the young person's rating of the quality of religious instruction has a very strong effect on the shaping of the religious imagination, both directly and indirectly in the enhancement of the impact of subsequent forces such as spouse and current parish community.

7) The most notable effect of the parish community on both the religious imagination and on virtually everything else in the lives of young adults is the quality of preaching in the parish. Everything else in parish life and, indeed, in church life is unimportant compared to the quality of preaching. All the "media" issues—birth control, divorce, abortion, authority, the ordination of women—account for one fourth as much of the variances in church identification as does Sunday preaching.

Moreover, the impact of preaching on identification seems to be mediated by the religious imagination. Good sermons enhance the religious imagination of young people—make their imaginations more graceful—and, thus, incline them to be more likely to identify with the church. Alas, only ten percent of the young people think that the Sunday preaching is excellent. That which is the most important thing we do, we do badly. And we seem to do it badly precisely because we cannot stir up stories of grace in the religious imagination of our congregations.

8) The Mary image is especially strong in the religious imagination of young Catholics. It encodes a benign experience of maternity in childhood and relates to a benign (sexually fulfilling) experience of potential maternity or relation to a potential mother in adult life. The Mary image survives despite the fact that May crownings and rosary devotions no longer take place, despite the fact that young people no longer can sing "Bring Flowers of the Fairest," despite the almost total absence of sermons and instructions about Mary, and precisely because young people hear stories of Mary from their mothers and at Christmas time. The Mary Myth will survive no matter how much it is smothered by one kind of propositional religion and ignored by another kind of propositional religion because, I assume, little kids will always see crib scenes and because their mothers will always tell them that the Lady in the scene is God's mommy. For the child's religious imagination it is but a short jump then to think of God as Mommy (and we can establish that correlation too). At a somewhat more sophisticated level, the possibility that God loves us with the tender care, the sensitive passion, and the fierce protectiveness of a mother with a young child has rich imaginative resonances and enormous power to rekindle hope. It is so appealing that it is unthinkable that the charm and the energy of the Mary imagery will ever be lost, no matter how desiccated formal religious instruction might become.

The persistence and the impact of the Mary image proves, I think, that despite the invention of the printing press and the spread of literacy, religious heritages are still transmitted to young people the way they have always been—through story and picture. We are fond of looking back somewhat patronizingly at those illiterate ages that did not have schools and textbooks as only semi-civilized religiously. Yet it would seem that the basic power of religious socialization is still where it always was—in the story and the picture described by the parent and the parish priest. Schools are important, of course, and do represent net gain, so long as they do not snuff out the imagination. But they are an adjunct to the traditional forms of religious socialization and not a substitute for them. More precisely, the combination of formal instruction and informal imagination ought to be the goal of all Catholic teaching so that both can reinforce one another. Again, the data sustain the importance of this combination.

No sociological theory is ever "proven." All the investigator can report is that it has not been disproven: the available data do not force us to accept the null hypothesis that the theory is wrong. My theory of the religious imagination outlined in this and the previous chapter, as a prelude to theological reflection on religious imagination and popular culture, has surely not been disproven by the data. Moreover, it explains a modest but significant amount of the variance in empirically measured behavior, all that any sociological theory can do.

I do not think it likely that anyone will produce better evidence that says the religious imagination is unimportant. I fondly hope that others will take the theory seriously enough to attempt to refine and improve it.

For the moment, all that I will contend is that it is reasonable to reflect theologically on this theory on the grounds that it is in some limited, partial, and inchoate way not completely untrue.

Not much?

OK. But a lot better empirical verification than most theological reflections enjoy—including the whole house of cards of liberation theology!

7

Empirical Liturgy: The Search for Grace

Liturgy, both as a practical craft and as a scholarly science, ought to be empirical; it ought to seek out the experiences of grace to be found in the secular world among those to whom it ministers. This assertion summarizes the argument of the first six chapters of this book and points towards the development of a Catholic theology of popular culture.

I base my assertion in the first paragraph on two assumptions:

1) The self-communication of God (experiences of hope renewal, sacraments of grace, the dance of the Spirit, whatever name one wants to use) occurs not only (I would add "and not primarily") in interludes of worship but also (and I would "and especially") in the grace-full persons, events, and objects of daily, secular life.

2) Among the purposes of Sacramental Experience in the liturgy is the "correlation" of the experiences of the self-communication of God in secular life with the overarching experiences of the religious Tradition so that each correlate may illumine the other. The goal of Sacraments is to rearticulate, refine, re-collect, and re-present secular sacraments and thus to deepen and enrich and challenge them by integrating them into the Com-

munity and the Tradition (which have already shaped the secular experience by forming the symbol repertory of the members of the Community who are heirs to the Tradition).

For those who require definitions: while a Sacrament is an outward sign instituted by Christ to confer Grace, a sacrament is any created reality that can reveal the presence of grace. For those who require a terminological link with the past: there is little difference between the traditional "discernment of spirits" and my "search for grace."

I do not believe that theologians or liturgists will disagree with my two assumptions. They may find the order and the vocabulary troubling, but on reflection, they will admit that they are unexceptionable.

Note, however, that, as stated, the assumptions—true to the analogical imagination of David Tracy—reject the usually postulated opposition of the sacred and the secular. The sacred, it is assumed, is experienced in the secular and then is correlated and re-presented through liturgy. Since there is no reason to believe that God's self-communication diminishes, the "secularization" phenomenon (for which little evidence can be found in this country) means not that grace experiences have vanished from secular life but that the correlating mechanisms have broken down—those responsible for the administration of the Sacraments have lost their ability to sense sacraments in secular life.

Theologians and liturgists like to emphasize practice (which they call praxis for reasons that escape me). I believe in narrative. Hence I propose to suspend for several paragraphs intellectual argument and narrate two practical experiences.

Following the suggestion of John Shea, I have in recent years asked parents before a baptism to tell those present what message they would like to give their child if the child were able to understand them. Invariably, they express powerful sentiments of love, joy, pride, and good wishes, often in their first explicit articulation of what the birth of the new baby means to them. All that remains for me is to resonate with their experiences of grace in the baby and respond that God and Church rejoice with them and love both the child and them. If this "correlation" is recorded on video tape (as it often is), the child will have in the years to come a powerful reminder of what her parents and her priest said about her on the day she was baptized.

(I suspect that the marriage toasts, given usually at the wedding banquet and often moving and grace-full descriptions of the love of the bride and groom for each other, could also be integrated into the wedding service itself. Thus the homily could also be a response to the grace that is already present, the self-communication of God which has already occurred between the two young lovers.)

Several years ago, with the timidity I always experience when I try to reduce theory to practice, I began a CCD class in Tucson with the request "Tell me about your experiences of God."

The teenagers, once they were convinced that I was really interested in their experiences, overwhelmed me with their stories of grace, stories that often made my own experiences seem impoverished by comparison. Once again, my task was to relate their experiences to the stories and symbols of the Community and the Tradition so that their experiences might be illumined by the Tradition and the stories of the Tradition might take on new vitality in the light of their own experiences.

Since then I have used this approach with many groups. It always works, once people understand that you are indeed interested in their experiences and do not intend to twist their stories to fit the point you had intended to make all along.

All experiences of grace must be subject to the critique of the Community and the Tradition. Only I have yet to hear, in the two contexts I have described, either error or unrestrained emotionality (a statement I could not make about some of the narrations I have heard from enthusiasts of the Charismatic Renewal). Grace experiences affect the whole personality, intellect as well as emotions; and since these experiences are shaped by the symbols and the stories of the Tradition, it requires no great effort or advanced religious education for the people describing their experiences of grace to rearticulate them in categories that are perfectly acceptable to the tradition—even if they had not thought of making the correlation until they were asked to do so.

(Should anyone be interested, the theory behind my praxis is contained in my book *Religion: A Secular Theory*.)

But is there not a responsibility to stand over against our people in prophetic judgment on their graceless attitudes and behavior towards, as is often said, disarmament, poverty, blacks, women, gays, AIDS victims?

Challenge (along with comfort) is an essential component of correlation. One must strive to call forth from the grace experiences of the people insights that they previously had perceived only dimly, to urge them to sympathy, understanding, and action in the terms of their own encounter with God's loving generosity. But for challenge to be effective, it must be offered in the categories of their own experience and not in the categories of an ideology that is alien to their experience. Moreover, challenge forbids that we who make it seem to claim a monopoly on righteousness and to be unaware of our own failings in matters of social justice—as when we urge a "fundamental option for the poor" and continue to pay our own employees poverty wages.

Denunciation of our people is simple and often enjoyable. Challenge, on the other hand, is a difficult and complex art. Challenge as I have described it, however, can often effect growth. Denunciation never does.

I contend that it is difficult to find in the liturgical theology available today (by which I include the theological statements supporting the related activities mentioned in my second paragraph) much interest in the secular grace experiences of daily life (self-communication of God, Dance of the Spirit).

I may have missed some examples, but virtually all of the concern of contemporary liturgical thinkers is focused on the self-communication of God in the Seven Sacraments as they bring Grace to the lives of the faithful. There is no discussion of how the Sacraments might correlate with the sacraments of secular life, with the grace already present in the lives of the faithful. There is, in other words, much concentration on Redemption, less on Incarnation, and hardly any on Creation.

In the writings on Baptism (excuse me, Christian Initiation, and I'll buy you a candy bar for every lay person who spontaneously uses that term), there is no allusion to the joy and pride of parents over their new baby.

Research on the sociology of mystical experiences shows that childbirth is a frequent trigger of mystical experiences, for father as well as mother. Ought not the joy of the magical event of birth, whether mystical or not, be the foundation of the Sacrament's response to the sacrament?

Moreover, one would search in vain in writings on Marriage to discover that sexual intercourse is a source of tremendous pleasure and joy to humans, a joy—sometimes verging on the ecstatic—which binds and heals and renews. Does not God communicate Herself, not infrequently with overwhelming power, to spouses through sexual love? Why, then, is physical sex not seen as a grace, often even a grace par excellence? Social science findings of which these authors are apparently unaware confirm that sex is a frequent trigger of mystical experiences and that the intensity of marital intimacy is a powerful influence on the developing personality and character of the children of such intimacy.

Sex, we are often assured, is not the only aspect of marriage. The point need not be argued. Nonetheless, without sex there would be no marriage, both because marriage has been created precisely to be a socially legitimate context for enjoying sex and because, if it were not for the power and pleasure of sex, few humans would risk the friction and frustration of sharing the same house, the same bedroom, and the same bed with another human. Indeed, marriage is difficult, for most impossible, without a satisfactory sexual adjustment; and while a satisfactory sexual adjustment does not guarantee a happy or a stable marriage, it sure helps.

Yet in this age after Freud and after Masters and Johnson, in this age when even Catholic medical schools have sexual dysfunction clinics, liturgists barely seem to be aware of its existence as a unique and compelling source of grace. (And they have permitted the sexual content to be removed from the fire and water symbolism in the Easter Vigil.)

If sex is a powerful grace, an energetic sacrament, then liturgists should not overlook its importance in the Sacrament of Matrimony. If it is not grace, then God has made a tasteless mistake in ordaining the mechanics of the procreation and nurturing of human offspring and the dynamics of binding together human parents to preside over the rearing of such offspring.

There is no doubt where Pope John Paul II stands on the issue: in his neglected Audience Talks on marriage, he discusses at considerable length the sacramentality of the nakedness of man and woman for each other—a notion, one suspects, which would scare some of our bloodless liturgists half to death.

It might also delight married couples if it could be incorporated into the liturgy of the Sacrament. However, liturgists who take the sexual symbolism out of Easter surely would not discuss the sacramentality of nakedness, not even in words written by a Pope.

Similarly, when liturgical thinkers discuss the Sacrament of Reconciliation, there seems to be little awareness that sacraments of reconciliation are the warp and the woof of all human intimacies. The parables of Jesus tell us that God's forgiveness is a constant (impeded only by our refusal to accept it). Does not the forgiving God communicate Herself in every human reconciliation? Does not God forgive us (not, I note for heresy hunters, with Sacramental absolution) when we are forgiven by our spouses, our parents, our children, our friends, our lovers? Does not the reconciling God reveal His own reconciling love in every human reconciliation? Does not the Spirit dance with joy when we celebrate the joy of beginning again, of falling in love again, with those we love?

Yet rarely if ever does one hear from liturgists about the correlation between human reconciliation and the Sacrament of Reconciliation. They do not seem to comprehend that our experience of human forgiveness (every day) helps us to understand God's forgiveness and that the story of God's forgiveness as revealed by Jesus gives strength and depth to our own experiences of forgiving and being forgiven. Can they not comprehend that the Sacrament gathers together all human reconciliations and binds them to Reconciliation?

Nor does there seem to an understanding among the liturgists of the close links between marriage and reconciliation and hence between Marriage and Reconciliation. Human sexuality is distinct from that of the other higher primates precisely in its design to link the male and the female together through the ever-present possibility of the renewal of passion. It developed in the evolutionary process (and hence is "natural law") to facilitate reconciliation. In reconciliation between sexual partners, excited by, validated in, and celebrated with erotic passion, is there not a powerful hint of Reconciliation with a passionate God, the same Reconciliation that the Community offers in God's name through its minister?

And if there is, then is it not almost blasphemy to ignore the sacramentality of sexual renewal in marriage?

(I'm told on occasion that I am obsessed with sex. To which I reply that humans are designed by God to be obsessed with sex and that if the person who is attacking me is not obsessed by it, s/he needs to see a doctor.)

Life, love, renewal—the most elementary experiences of human —are the sacramental experiences that correlate with the Sacraments. They merge in the Eucharist as a correlate of the experiences of community through which humans find their life, exercise their love, and experience their renewal. The Eucharist is not the central Sacrament because God or Church arbitrarily determined that it be so but because community is the central experience of the human condition; the common meal is the most normal and ordinary method of celebrating life and love and renewal in community.

In our day, the family meals at Christmas and Thanksgiving, interludes which purport to be and often are celebrations of life and love and renewal, are superb correlates of the heavenly banquet.

There is much talk (I almost said "babble") among liturgists about the Eucharist and community, but it usually assumes that the Eucharist "makes" or "creates" community. In fact, communities already exist. It is the function of the Eucharist to correlate communities with Community, a function that presents enormous opportunities to the one who ministers the Eucharist.

I ask myself, Why don't the liturgists see the presence of grace in the secular world?

Their cultural analysis, usually naively negative, of American society may blind them to its possibility. America is an individualist society, they often say, religiously indifferentist, consumerist, materialist, capitalist. Our society and culture are so bad, one might conclude from these jeremiads, as to be utterly grace-less. Only among the oppressed and those who protest, it would seem, is there a possibility for grace. As one famous liturgical writer notes, we have been changed from a nation of book readers to a nation of TV watchers, and rock singers like Bruce Springsteen shape American culture.

This view is one-sided and inaccurate and is not, despite the claims of some liturgical writers, supported by social science. But it does account for inattention to the possibility that God can communicate Himself wherever He wants.

Incidentally, more books are read in America today than in the past; and we should be so lucky as to have our culture shaped by Springsteen in whose most recent album there is a sacrament (and a potential homily) in every song.

Moreover, many theologians today have strong ideological commitments. Because marriage as an institution is flawed by patriarchalism, it may seem that there can be little self-communication of God in marital relationships. If woman is a sexual slave, how can sexual intimacy be grace-full?

I suspect, however, that the blind spot in the liturgists' approach to the Dance of the Spirit in the secular world is a flaw that has affected clergy (in the broad sense of that word) since the memory of humans runs not to the contrary: a priorism. Or, to give it another name, Idealism in the continental sense of the term. (In any dialogue between Empiricism and Idealism, the Empiricist always loses because he has to listen.)

There is a hint of this flaw in a quotation from a noted liturgist: The Rite of Christian Initiation for Adults is "conversion therapy."

Now, with respect, I would suggest that in addition to being arrogant and patronizing, such a notion is inaccurate. The grace of conversion, normally through another human, has already touched the person of the potential convert. Our first obligation is to listen to and to learn how the Spirit has danced with this person and to fashion our response to that self-communication of God in the experience of grace that has already happened (and from which we might possibly learn more about God).

The Idealist knows better than God, however. He has the right answers, the proper attitudes, the powerful rituals, the effective pedagogy. He will process you through his system, and then you will be like him. He will make up, in other words, for the imperfections in what God has begun. He will "convert" a person who is grace-less into one that is grace-full.

Which doesn't leave much room for the Spirit and Her dance, does it?

I am open to other explanations, but I do not understand

why the very best and the very brightest of our liturgists do not seem aware that She does dance in the world, is always blowing whither She will, and that our efforts to budget Her time and arrange Her agenda are doomed to fail. Those of us who are blessed with the analogical imagination believe that Grace is everywhere. Why don't the liturgists see that?

Let me propose an example of the Spirit at Play, of God's self-communication, which will seem both trivial and offensive to many, though I hope not the St. John's scholars: St. Valentine's Day.

It began as a pagan feast of romantic love, was transformed by popular culture into a Christian feast of romantic love, and has once again become a mostly secular feast of romantic love.

It is also the second busiest day of the year (after Mother's Day) for restaurants. Moreover, as a walk through a shopping mall the week before that day would demonstrate, it is an enormously important day for shopkeepers, especially those who sell greeting cards, candy, and women's clothes and, most especially in the latter category, for those who sell women's lingerie.

The theme of the festival is obvious, even blatant: in the middle of winter it is now time to renew romantic and erotic love.

"Commercialism," some liturgists will snap dismissively, believing that the label renders a phenomenon worthless.

Consider, however, this parable.

A certain businessman was traveling in a city distant from his home. He noted from the ads in the morning paper that the next day was Valentine's Day. Oh boy, he thought, I'd better buy a present for my wife. He went therefore to a nearby shopping mall and purchased a "romantic" card, a two-pound box of candy, and a red lace undergarment for his wife (with hearts in the appropriate places). He put them in a Federal Express package and shipped them off to her. For the rest of the day, he went about his work with a secret smile of complacency as he contemplated the warm reception his gifts would win for him when he returned home. In fact, the welcome he received was much warmer than he had expected.

Note how "commercial" this story is: the certain man read about Valentine's Day in the newspaper ads; he went to a shopping mall; he bought presents from stores in the mall; he mailed them home by Federal Express. What could be more American? And hence, for some, more grace-less? Do any of these facts affect the love his gifts demonstrated, the desire they stirred up in him and his wife, or the intensification of their love the desire occasioned?

Is the gift spoiled by the "commercial" circumstances? Do they prevent God's self-communication through the renewal of romantic love between husband and wife? Or are the commercial circumstances "neutral," open to either the grace—full or the demonic? Does the fact that it costs money to produce greeting cards and candy and lingerie make the gifts any less appealing? Is it wrong that men and women earn their living by making and selling cards, candy, and lingerie? Are there not less honorable ways of earning a living (not excluding the practice of the role of a full professor)? Is the demand for grace untainted by commerce in fact a demand for grace disincarnated from the human condition?

Theologians often devalue romantic love, as though God made a mistake in programming it into our species. Yet do not married people testify that the healing power of erotic renewal is often what seems to hold their unions together? Did not the sage of Dallas (Roger Staubach) say that he had fallen in love often during his life, just as often as Broadway Joe Namath, but always with the same woman?

Must the Spirit be excluded from such interludes? Is it forbidden to the God of love to communicate Herself in such rebirth of passion? Or is marriage not, after all, the Great Sacrament?

A "romantic" greeting card, two pounds of chocolate, a

flimsy red garment trimmed in lace—can these possibly be sacraments, occasions of God's self-communication? Or, as a writer in the Commonweal recently remarked, if such can be sacraments, then anything can be a sacrament.

Indeed yes. To respond with Nathan Scott, for some realities to be Sacraments it is necessary that all realities be capable of being sacraments.

Grace is everywhere. So the parish should have perhaps a renewal of marriage vows in a Valentine's Day service and a romantic dance afterwards. Reclaim the good saint. He was ours to begin with and we want him back.

If the reader does find this suggestion trivial or offensive, then it might be well to ask whether s/he lacks the analogical imagination and does not seriously doubt that grace is everywhere.

If the Spirit does not dance with the passion of married lovers, then where can She dance? If God does not communicate Himself in such intimacy, where can He communicate Himself?

Grace is especially to be sought in popular culture, even in unlikely places. The singer Madonna has been dismissed by a prominent woman columnist as a slut; but in her plea "like a virgin" is there not to be found the plea of every woman, indeed of every human, to be treated like someone fragile, new, and wonderful? Is this not the way God claims that She love us? Is not the song a cry of longing (not necessarily recognized as such) for Easter renewal?

It requires a special skill for a liturgist (as one who exercises the craft) to resonate to the grace experiences of secular life, to be sensitive to wonder in creation as it discloses the Wonder of Creation. One must have access to both the riches of the tradition, the depths of one's own selfhood, the riches of creation, and the sensibilities of the faithful. Such resonance is an exercise in the creative imagination (preconscious, poetic intuition, agent intellect) which, it is to be feared, is often a vestigial capability in many clergy.

The good liturgist must be a poet and a storyteller.

Because they themselves are drawn from secular life, the liturgical Sacraments are powerful symbolic narratives. They readily correlate with the secular sacraments even when their performance is inept—a fact that does not justify inept performance but merely establishes that sometimes the story is more powerful than the storyteller. (A question for theologians: might it be said that the power of the Sacrament to confer Grace is, in part at any rate, precisely its power to correlate?) Without raising the ex opere operato issue, it seems to me that the Eucharist, even when mumbled quietly in Latin or a bit more loudly in English, had and has great power over the faithful precisely because they perceive, perhaps only preconsciously, that it is a time of the coming together of the secular and the religious, of meals and The Meal, of our banquets on earth and the Banquet in the Father's kingdom.

It is necessary, I believe, to develop a spirituality of the secular. By this I do not mean the "secular asceticism" recommended in past decades which assumed that there was no more sacred in the world and that one must therefore devote oneself to the discipline of social activism. With all due respect to the need for social commitment, there also must be a spirituality that helps men and women recognize the sacred— God's self-communication as She manifests Herself in the wonders and the graces and the renewals of hope in secular life.

(Pantheism, some label-slappers may murmur. Ah, no, merely the analogy of being—Being disclosing Itself through beings.)

If liturgy is to become empirical both in craft and scholarship, it will have to wrench itself away from an a priorism which, however unintentionally, is often supercilious and sometimes arrogant.

Can one expect such a wrenching? Or should one expect that liturgists, always eager, in the current fashionable vocabulary, to engage in dialectic against others, might bitterly resent it when the dialectic is turned against them?

An empiricist must wait and see.

(An earlier version of this chapter appeared in America*.)*

8

Theology, the Religious Imagination, and Popular Culture

I now come to the central task of this exercise in religious reflection: the development of a theology of the religious imagination and of popular culture.

They are two separate tasks, and the latter does not follow necessarily from the former. If I can construct a persuasive or useful theology of the religious imagination, it does not follow that I am correct when I write about popular culture. On the other hand, I cannot even begin my task of reflecting on popular culture unless I prepare the groundwork through a theology of the religious imagination.

Imagination is the source of religion because we are experiencing, ordering, and reflective beings. Unlike angels (assuming that they do not have bodies) who intuit reality, we relate to reality through our bodily organisms and through the senses that are the reality-contacting nerve endings of the organism. We experience reality first, and only after our total personality is absorbed by the experiences do we attempt to order and organize our experiences around stories. And only after we articulate our stories to ourselves and one another are we prepared to go on to the final task of reflecting on the meaning of the stories and the experiences that are encoded in our stories.

In some primordial fashion, the meaning of the experiences is in the experiences themselves since they happen to an organism that is always sensitive to possible nuances of meaning. Storytelling and reflection do not add to experiences something new that is not in them but, rather, draw out of the experience and make explicit hints of meaning which are already there.

Therefore, religion must inevitably begin in experience (shaped of course by the images and symbols which our heritages make available to us) and be told in stories as a prelude to and the raw material of religious reflection. Just as the old scholastic adage said that nothing was in the intellect which was not at first in the senses, no religion can become rational unless it first exists as experience and narrative.

I quickly add that experience and narration must be subjected to critical reflection and that all three must in turn be critiqued by the community that is the inheritor of the religious tradition. I am not saying that religious experiences and stories are more important than reflection, that narrative is more important than theology. I am saying something much more modest: the experience and the story come first, both in the religious tradition and in our own lives. We cannot speak about the theos unless we first encounter Her/Him in experiences that impinge on our imagination.

The temptation of literate and reflective Christian elites is to short-circuit the organic development from experience to theory so that as little time as possible is spent on experience and narrative and as much as possible on reflection. Such disdain for the experiential and the narrative is what Maritain would have called "angelism"—a rejection of the bodily and sensual and imaginative aspects of human nature the way God created it.

And also a rejection of the Incarnation in which God revalidated the goodness of human nature the way He created it.

In Catholic theology, which believes that human nature is deprived but not depraved, experiences of the Holy and the hope renewing and stories out of those experiences are not evil or idolatrous but revelatory. Certainly such experiences and stories are subject to self-deception because of the limitations and frailties to which finite human nature is subject. But we minimize the potential errors into which our preconscious can lead us by examining our images and narratives against the overarching stories and reflections of our tradition.

The requirement of a community to provide a reality check is not a belief that Catholicism arbitrarily imposes. Rather, it is an inevitable requirement of our conviction that our experiences and stories of the Holy tend to be valid sacramental activities but need external guidelines so that they do not become instruments of self-deception.

Hence, Catholicism at its best and from the very beginning has embraced the works of culture not as a useful adjunct to religion but as an essential part of it.

Later I will turn to the question of how contemporary Catholicism seems to have lost its instincts about the importance of the senses and of culture that appeals to the senses. At this point, I must note that Catholicism has been, at certain times, more open to the good, the true, and the beautiful as they strive to disclose God in the world outside the Church than it has been at other times.

The missionaries to Ireland had no difficulty adapting Irish religion to the needs of Catholicism. A few centuries later, Cyril and Methodius only just succeeded in doing the same with Slavic culture. At the same time, the Synod of Whitby forced the Irish Church to pull back from its cultural experiments. Still later, the Jesuits in India and China (DeNobili and Ricci) were forced to give up similar attempts that might have won the whole of Asia to Christianity. At the time of the Vatican Council, it seemed not unreasonable to many missionaries that, as Belloc put it, "Europe is the faith and the faith is Europe." While that attitude has changed, it is not clear that we are free enough and hopeful enough—as were our early Christian predecessors — to discern and adapt in African and Brazil.

Catholic theology does not need my sociological theory to know that the imagination is critical for religion. It should know that truth from the philosophy of St. Thomas, from the traditional practice of the Church, and from its own theology of the nature of human nature and the meaning of the incarnation.

But many Catholic theologians, teachers, and administrators seem to have forgotten their traditional model of the nature of human nature and the nature of human knowledge. My sociology of religion may serve them to recall their own tradition and realize that imagination is not essential for religion only when the creatures involved do not have bodies.

Sometimes I think that some of our leaders and teachers (right wing and left wing alike) are so obsessed with ideas that they rather think God made a mistake in giving humans bodies and would rather like to be able to exclude bodies from religion save as objects of negative prohibitions.

Such might be an interesting religion. It is not, however, Catholicism.

Popular culture fits into this picture precisely because popular culture is essentially the work of storytellers, men and women who attempt to order the phenomena of experience. And sometimes the ordering of the popular culture storyteller is inept, deficient, shallow, or just plain wrong.

I do not claim anything more for popular culture than that some of its stories deserve to be considered as possible sources of the sacramental, that is of the presence of God seeking to disclose Herself in and through creation and our experiences and narratives of creation.

Essentially the imagination works at metaphor. It says

something is like something else. The religious imagination reports that God is like something else (Mother, Father, spouse, lover, friend, etc.). The imagination cannot help but make metaphors; it is a metaphor-making reality. Neither, despite the warnings of our separated brothers about dangers of anthropomorphizing God, can the religious imagination help but make metaphors of God. The Community and the Tradition must examine our metaphors and our narratives (a narrative is merely a metaphor turned into a plot) to make sure that we have not gone beyond the boundaries of the tradition.

In these chapters, I will use the word "story" in quotes hereinafter to mean any work of culture which attempts to organize experience music and painting and sculpture and poem, as well as play, novel, short story, and film. I take it that any work of art desires to interpret, that is to say, order experience, even the work of art which says that there is no order and that no interpretation is possible. A work of culture is a metaphor and a metaphor is at least potentially a story, an attempt to stretch an ordering experience from one imagination to another imagination.

My theological argument for considering works of popular culture as possible sources for metaphors of God is based primarily on the assumption that if people like a "story," one of the reasons may well be that the "story" helps to order their experiences. I do not see how Catholic theology, given its position on the nature of human nature and the meaning of the Incarnation/Resurrection, can fail to search for illuminating metaphors wherever they are to be found. Moreover, I cannot see how Catholicism can, in principle, reject "stories" merely on the grounds that people like them. If you think human nature is basically depraved and so sinful that most of its works are evil, then you can safely reject that which appeals to large numbers of people.

If grace is everywhere, it seems very likely, if you're Catholic, that it may be where people are.

However, Catholicism does not accept the depravity of human nature and hence must investigate the possibility that the metaphors and "stories" of popular culture may sometimes be sacramental, that is to say, God-revealing.

I will note in the next two chapters that the distaste for popular culture so prevalent in our (still essentially Protestant in its imaginative structures) literary establishment and professorate is focused primarily on two literary genres that are especially prevalent in popular culture—Comedy and Romance. In fact, the quick dismissal of popular culture as trash is based on the assumption that Comedy and Romance are not only inferior literary genres but illegitimate. In the next two chapters, I will challenge both of these assumptions and thus continue my defense of the potential sacramentality of popular culture. Indeed I will take the opposite position: For Catholicism, at any rate, Comedy and Romance are especially likely to be metaphors for God. Grace is everywhere, but especially in Comedy and Romance.

The other three great traditions (Protestant, Jewish, Islamic), each in their own way, are structured on sensibilities that emphasize the radical discontinuity of God and world. God is the "totally other"; the only metaphor we have for God is Christ Jesus and him crucified. While acknowledging that the crucified and risen Jesus is the metaphor (or sacrament if you wish) par excellence of God, the Catholic religious sensibility sees the whole of creation as a metaphor: everything is grace.

All those elements which are peculiarly Catholic—honor to Mary, the cult of saints and angels, statues and stained glass, popular devotions, concern about art and scholarship, emphasis on human institution and human leadership—are manifestations of the prior religious instinct that God's self-disclosing love lurks, intimately and invitingly, in creation.

Admittedly, often in its history, including perhaps especially the present, the institutional leadership of the Church has perceived but dimly the implications of this fundamental intuition. Nonetheless, the Catholic instinct, based ultimately on the primordial religious insight that the enfleshing of God in Jesus confirmed the holiness of creation, persists strongly among the Catholic laity and lower clergy (as my research in the sociology of religion demonstrates). It is the reason why Catholics are psychologically and emotionally able to remain in the Church even though they reject some teachings that, at a given time, the institutional leadership chooses to make important.

As Ellen Foley says in *The Cardinal Sins*, "I want it all back, Kevin—Midnight Mass, May Crowning, the Easter Vigil, First Communion, Grammar School Graduation; I want it for myself and for my kids."

Surely this instinct that God is radically present in the world instead of radically absent is subject to misuse and abuse, especially idolatry, including idolatry of institutions and institutional leadership. However, the instinct that God is radically absent can make the universe a bleak and dismal place. Obviously, there is religious truth in both instincts, but one must choose one's emphasis. Catholicism, particularly in its finest moments, opts for the presence of God, for the world as metaphor. And so do I.

A priest, therefore, is one who preaches the metaphor. Or, since all metaphors are implicitly stories, he is the one who tells the "story" of God's passionately tender love as revealed through creation and as confirmed by the life and death and resurrection and teaching (mostly in stories) of Jesus. As Father John Shea, perhaps the most original contemporary American Catholic thinker, puts it, "A priest calls together the people, tells the 'story,' breaks the bread." In this context, "breaking the bread," celebrating the Eucharist, is indeed presiding over a celebration of the very good news contained in the "story."

The question to be asked of any work of popular culture is whether it provides powerful enough metaphors to suggest sufficiently the presence of grace and thus to illumine the possibilities of life in a grace-suffused world. Are there ordering illuminations in the "story" which serve as a bridge between our initial experiences of grace (stored up in the imagination and touched again by the "story") and cognitive religious reflection? Do the grace experiences in the "story" inform—in the sense of bringing more life and vitality to—our own personal life stories.

The "stories" need not be explicitly theological.

Let me distinguish three levels of religious "story." All stories are in some sense religious because all stories implicitly try to assign meaning, even when they assert that there is no meaning or that meaning is a deception. To quote Ms. Ozick, perhaps on the other side of the question this time, "Every writer is engaged in theology." It may not be so overt, but every writer is engaged in ontology, the nature of being, why are we here, what is the meaning of life. In that sense is every writer a rabbi? Or a priest? Every "story" teller a priest? Every priest a "story" teller?

I contend that there are three levels of "ontology" or "theology" on which a novel may operate. In the first of these three levels, there are what I call the "secular" stories (choose your own label if you wish), the "stories" in which there is no attempt to point at ultimate meaning—the novels of Joseph Conrad, for example—but in which one may find profound, if not always easily explicated, meanings. Let me note that among the secular stories one must certainly count the parables of Jesus. We are so used to hearing them in church and in the context of the allegorical interpretation the evangelists impose on them that we forget that they are without religious content.

The gang is walking along a road, troubled by the slowness of the coming of the Kingdom. They see a farmer sowing seeds. Jesus says the kingdom is like a farmer sowing seeds: many seeds do not produce grain, but still there is a harvest.

End of "story." One point, like all parables, and that not explained. Can you imagine the guys looking at one another saying, Now, what the hell does that mean?

Any attempt to interpret deprives a parable of its full force.

The parable of the sower could mean something like this: Despite all the failure, the harvest comes; there is an inevitable and intrinsic link between sowing and harvest. So cheer up, we're going to win.

You can't be more secular than that. Or more religious, albeit only remotely and indirectly religious.

At the second level, there are "implicitly religious" stories, as I call them, stories in which powerful religious symbols, lurking in the unconscious or preconscious and prevalent in the world religions, abound and create an implicit or preconscious ambience of meaning. The amazingly skillful works of Louise Erdrich, with her rich if implied baptismal and Easter symbols, illustrate this category.

At the final level is the "theological novel" in which questions of meaning and grace are explicitly part of the narrative. As illustrations of this level, one could cite much of the work of Graham Greene and the French Catholic novelists. It is obviously the level at which I choose to work—or perhaps am constrained to write by who and what I am. My point here is that, just as a writer ought to be free to choose his genre, so he should be free to choose his level of religious discourse. The only constraints ought to be internal, the author's vision, the "story" that writes him.

In the next chapter, I will defend Comedy and Romance from the charge that they are trash and contend that while not all comedy and romance in popular "stories" deserve the capital letter at the beginning of the word, some do. It is in such stories that one might especially be inclined to search for grace.

Or Grace.

9

Romance: The Secular Scripture

Romance is about adventure and love, about passion and violence, about ambition defeated and desire frustrated, about coming home and marrying one's love.

If you want a better description than that, read Joseph Conrad and Ford Madox Ford's *Romance*, a narrative definition—and if you're a man, fall in love with the wondrous Seraphina or, a woman, with the determined and steadfast John Kemp (no relation to quarterbacks or congressmen).

Northrop Frye, world expert on Romance, calls his book (based on a series of lectures at Harvard) *The Secular Scripture*. Just as the "myths" (stories) of the Bible are religious attempts to interpret life, so the myths of Romance are attempts to interpret life. In fact, Frye notes, the Bible itself can be considered Romance—the story of adventure and love between God and His people.

A long way from the Harlequin "romances"?

In this chapter, I put the first letter of the word Romance in capital to indicate that I am using the word in the classic sense (*romans* the French would say) to distinguish from the usage you see in the book shops in which it is a category of novels of which the Harlequin series are a part. In principle, I have nothing against romances; for example, I think that because of her skill as a storyteller, Danielle Steele is entitled to her popularity. But the book trade use of the term today is both limited and pejorative.

Frye contends that Romance is the oldest of literary forms. It includes such authors as Apuleius, Philip Sidney, Edmund Spenser (*The Faerie Queen*), Walter Scott, Victor Hugo, Wolfram von Eschenbach (*Parzival*), and Shakespeare.

It is to be admitted, Frye writes, "that popular literature has been the object of a constant bombardment for over two thousand years .... Nearly the whole of the established critical tradition has stood out against it. The greater part of the reading and listening public has ignored the critics and censors for exactly the same length of time."

But Romance is always vindicated in the long run: what is taken to be popular literary form in one era becomes a serious literary form in the next. "Popular literature is neither better nor worse than elite literature. Nor is it really a different kind of literature: it simply represents a different social development of it."

Romance simplifies our life, turns its struggles into adventures, its dreams of fulfillment through sexual love into part of the adventure, liberates the fantasies and the aspirations stewing and steaming in our preconscious and our unconscious, and permits them to surface so that we can face them and put meaning and purpose on them. "The improbable, desiring, erotic, and violent world of romance reminds us that we are not awake when we have abolished the dream world: we are awake only when we have absorbed it again."

In a classic Romance, the hero must fight off enemies and at the same time win the woman he loves. Sometimes it appears that he cannot do both. Other times those who would destroy him seem about to overwhelm him, deprive him of his life and freedom, and deny him the girl, too.

But he perseveres (sometimes with her help), routs his

enemies, wins the girl, and (perhaps after the story is over) beds her, begets children with her, and settles down to home and family and contentment.

We all dream of fulfilling eroticism and of routing the phalanxes of enemies who assault us in our daily life. When we read romance, we are persuaded that if we have courage and imagination and integrity and fidelity, these goals can be achieved, not perfectly perhaps, but at least partially.

> In traditional romance the upward journey is the journey of a creator returning to its creature. In most modern writers it is the creative power in man returning to its original awareness. The secular scripture tells us that we are creators; other scriptures tell us that we are actors in a drama of divine creation and redemption . . . . Identity and self-recognition begin when we realize that this is not an either-or question, when the great twins of divine creation and human re-creation have merged into one, and we can see that the same shape is upon both.

Romance, then, is far better suited for the purpose of creating meaning than other literary forms. It deals quite explicitly with the question of whether human aspirations can possibly be fulfilled.

> The imagination, as it reflects on this world, sees it as a world of cunning and violence . . . .Romance . . . .begins an upward journey . . . .At the bottom is a death and rebirth process, at the top is recreation . . . .Violence and sexuality are used as rocket propulsion, so to speak, in an ascending moment . . . .The end of fable , , , ,brings us back to the beginning of myth, the model world associated with divine creation in Genesis.

My contention here is not that all stories of love and adventure are valuable from either the literary or theological viewpoint. Rather, it is, first, that the Romantic genre ought not to be rejected as a genre merely because its purpose and structure are different from those of other genres and, second, that it is often a more interesting genre theologically because it addresses itself to issues that surge up automatically from the human spirit: can we overcome? can we love?

The serious answer that one draws from Romance is that we can if we work at it and up to a point.

It is a modest enough answer but more reassuring and hopeful than a blunt "no" to both questions (which is what the professors and the book reviewers often seem to demand). It is also the same answer that the Catholic religious tradition gives. Romance, as Ingrid Shafer and Mary Ann Lowry have both pointed out to me, is a peculiarly Catholic genre.

Catholic, I would add, precisely because it says that there are still grounds for hope.

An interesting twist in Romance is that hope remains even when the quest is defeated and the love is denied. One of the most powerful archetypes in the Western World is the Grail legend in its various forms. The hero fails in his quest and loses the girl but still does not regret the effort and would, if he lived, which is often not likely, try again.

Jean Markale, in his *Women of the Celts*, points out that the legend has its origin in a Celtic spring fertility ritual from which developed the narrative. The Grail is the girl is God: the quester seeks all three. Forever in vain.

Not in Ireland, it turns out. In the original myth, Art son of Conn (sounds like a boxer, doesn't he?) finds the magic cup, gets the magic princess, and returns to replace the ailing Fisher King and bring life back to Ireland.

The previous sentence is not altogether accurate: for the Princess Delvacheem (Fair Breast—and that means exactly what it says, the Irish have one of the great breast fixations of all human history, which shows good taste on their part, God (She) knows!) is no fainting Victorian princess. She works her magical spells and pursues the hero as much as he pursues her (Sure, this the way they are, Ah, faith, the girls won't leave the boys alone!). One has the impression that he will never have a peaceful or a dull day for the rest of his life.

James Stephens tells this story at considerable length in one of his collections of Irish folk tales. The story, I believe, is the grandparent of much of Western Romance (Frye seems unaware of it). Moreover, unlike the perversion of the tale which worked its way back up from Southern France and into Thomas Malory, the Irish version is neither life denying nor flesh denying. You can win and you can bed the woman, a marvelously life-affirming and flesh-affirming prospect (and if you're the woman, you can win, too, and bed the man—and make him act right for the rest of his life!)

Moreover, it is a position that Catholicism has to endorse: it is safe to live and safe to love because we are, when all is said and done, held in the loving hand of Life Itself.

Princess Fair Breast is a sacrament for the Hound of Heaven. And don't try to tell me she's not if you're a Catholic.

The Grail story in the form we know it, Christianized and Puritanized, is a genuine Romance—that I will not deny. But the old, pagan, Irish version, I insist, was by far the more Catholic of the two.

Even before they became Catholic, then, the Irish were a difficult and contentious people, claiming to know something that someone else didn't know. No wonder they took so well to Catholicism (even if it required a millennium before they got around to giving up polygamy!).

Romance is essentially and inevitably erotic. You are pursuing a woman (or she is pursuing you). What can be more erotic? The jet propulsion of the story (and much of its hold on the reader/listener) comes, as Frye says, through sexual desire: you want to get the woman's clothes off, carry her off to your bed, and copulate—most tenderly and lovingly—with her. Even if, as in Dante (which Frye considers to be a Romance), you completely repress your sexual longing or at least completely deny the possibility of its fulfillment, it still remains a powerful engine driving the "story."

The girl is bound to be a disappointment, says the literary critic or the book reviewer or the "realist." Soon you'll tire of her and she of you. The kids will get in the way. You'll quarrel often.

You'll both grow old. Eventually, you will die. You will not live happily ever after. You are doomed by the human condition to drift away from one another and to fall out of love just as surely as your hormones forced you to fall in love.

Romance is a lie.

Except that the hungers in the human soul which make love and adventure so attractive might well draw you and the woman together again. If you do not fall in love with each other often, the reason is that you resist the powerful propensity to fall in love again and again and again, with other women perhaps but especially with the woman next to you in bed with whom you share so much in common and who becomes more desirable (though differently desirable) rather than less with the passage of time.

Romance does not end. It runs in cycles. It is not a lie but an invitation. "Living happily ever after," as I will argue in the next chapter, is nothing more than a license to engage in repeated cycles of beginning again.

Or so both the Catholic tradition at its best and human psychology at its best tell us. The Romantics have access to a secret that others do not.

Romance, then, is a literary genre that offers the possibility of renewal of sexual passion. It doesn't promise such renewal but neither does it tell us, as other genres do, that there are no grounds for hope. The Romantic world is not the real world (and readers or listeners don't kid themselves that it is), but it does offer us illumination about the possibilities that may remain to us in the real world.

We can escape from the real world with Romance, but the intent of the genre is to plunge us back into the real world, raring to go, eager for new possibilities of adventure and love.

There is no Romance, then, without powerful eroticism. That makes Romance obscene only if eroticism is obscene—which no Catholic can claim without falling into the puritan heresy. Frye sharply—and nicely—distinguishes between the pornographic and the erotic: the former, he says, is designed to put us to sleep, the latter to wake us up.

All right, you say, Romance is a legitimate genre—one that can properly be called a "secular scripture" because it is explicitly concerned with human life and love—indeed a genre that has some special affinity with Catholicism. But still, it is an inferior genre. Can't we have meaning in life without violence and sex? And is not Realism a superior genre precisely because it does not engage in daydreams but faces life seriously and as it is?

First of all try to live without encountering violence. Secondly try to live and love without sexual feelings. And thirdly, might not the daydreams tell us something deeper about life than the Realism? Might not Frye be right when he says, in effect, that the Real World is a combination of dreams and "reality"?

It is not my intent to argue that Romance is superior to Realism, but only that it is not inferior. Why must we rank them when they both have their function and purpose and truth?

Of course, if we forbade reviewers and other snobs the right to confuse genres and to apply the wrong set of norms to a story, we would take much of the mean-spirited fun out of reviewing.

Why can't we say "both/and" instead of "either/or?" Why can't we say that, for some purposes, Realism is superior and, for some purposes, Romance is superior and that some of the best books are intricate combinations of both? Why do we have to look down on the ordinary person's passion for adventure and love?

In fact, if we are Catholic, are we not constrained to admit the possibility that such passion for adventure and love might be sacramental, might tell us something about God?

And that the sexual hunger that is at the heart of Romance might tell us something about our hunger for God.

And Her hunger for us.

10

In Defense of Comedy

"Begin with violence," Bernard Geis told me, "And end on a note of hope." He paused and smiled, "And have one, better two, sympathetic Jewish characters and one successful woman."

It is not bad advice. My Jewish characters are infrequent— I have enough trouble with the Irish. Some of my novels begin with violence and some do not. But, while some of my short stories end on less than a hopeful note, none of my novels do, less because of Mr. Geis' advice and more because my own world view constrains me to accept the propensity to hope that seems to have been structured into the human organism.

Just as Romance is older than Realism, Comedy is older than Tragedy, the story with a happy ending older than one with a sad ending. Comedy, I propose to argue in this chapter, does not so much mean happiness at the end of a story as it does hope. Thus Comedy, perhaps even more than Romance, is the Catholic story form *par excellence.*

Despite the innkeepers, the Baby is born surrounded by singing angels. Despite the Sanhedrin and Pilate, the Baby, grown to a Man, is not held prisoner in the tomb. Neither will we, or so the story goes.

The only story that matters.

Such a conviction is a matter of religious faith, of course, but also of personality and character and also, perhaps, a surrender to what as a social scientist I am convinced is the nature of human nature—of *animal sperans*, a hoping animal.

Thus I write in defense of hopeful endings. I'm not contending that all novels should end with a touch of hope: a writer must be true to his/her own vision. I am merely saying that a hopeful ending is as valid as any other. A sad ending imposed on a story to please critics (or creative writing professors) is as artificial as a happy ending imposed to please readers. If a writer believes in hope, he should feel free to end hopefully even though such an ending might displease both critics and readers.

The hopeful ending, however, is likely to satisfy most readers precisely because we are creatures who are constrained to hope, even when, intellectually, we assert that we don't want to hope. The propensity to hope, anthropologist Lionel Tiger has argued, is genetically programmed. We must hope even though we know that there are no grounds for hope. Whether we are genetically programmed to hope is problematic—it's probably impossible to prove. Whether there are no grounds on which to hope—in which case we are conditioned to self-deception—is arguable: hope may be a trick or a hint of an explanation, and neither alternative is inherently more tough-minded than the other.

Hope demands effort. Despair does not. The point is that we do hope, even when we don't want to, and therefore a hopeful ending resonates with all the fibers of our being.

In Frank McConnell's illuminating words:

> You are the hero of your own life-story. The kind of story you want to tell yourself about yourself has a lot to do with the kind of person you are and can become. You can listen to (or read in books or watch in films) stories about other people. But that is only because you know, at some basic level, that you are—or could be—the hero of those stories, too. You are Ahab in *Moby Dick*, you are Michael Corleone in *The Godfather*, you are Rick or Ilsa in *Casablanca*, Jim in *Lord Jim*, or the tramp in *City Lights*. And out of these make-believe selves, all of them versions of your own self-in-the-making,

you learn, if you are lucky and canny enough, to invent a better you than you could have before the story was told.

And Stephen King finds at the center of horror fiction, rationale, grounds, compulsion to hope:

> It is not a dance of death, not really. . . .It is at bottom a dance of dreams. It is a way of awakening the child inside, who never dies but sleeps more deeply. If the horror story is our rehearsal for death, then in its strict moralities, it is also a reaffirmation of life and good and simple imagination—just one more pipeline to the infinite. We fall from womb to tomb, from one blackness toward another, remembering little of one and knowing nothing of the other. . . .except through faith. That we retain our sanity in the face of these simple yet blinding mysteries is nearly divine. That we may turn the powerful intuition of our imagination upon them and regard them in the glass of dreams, that we may, however timidly, place our hands within the hole which opens up at the end of the column of truth—that is. . . .well, it's magic, isn't it?"

A pipeline to the infinite? I wish I'd thought of that phrase, but it's what story is all about and that is why there is a powerful propensity in the personality of the reader to resonate with the story that hints that there may yet be some slight reasons, some shreds of evidence, some tiny grounds for hope.

As long as there are grounds for hope, there is room for Comedy. It may be dismissed as trash (though Comedy is not inherently any more trashy than any other genre).

Maybe, just maybe, we will have one more chance.

That's how I would define a hopeful ending—one in which the characters find another chance. Perhaps the most notable hopeful ending in all literature is the end of *Crime and Punishment* in which Dostoyevsky gives Rodion and Sonia another chance (if one is to believe the critics, much against his own inclinations).

However—and this is the core of my argument—we all get second chances. And third and fourth and fifth ones, too. Is not every love relationship in which anyone has ever existed a continuity of new beginnings?

Eventually, of course, we run out of chances—they are

not infinite just as our life is not infinite. But for both me and you, learned reader, there remains another chance. We may not seize it; we may turn away from it in fear; we may, like Lord Jim, blow it again (make the same old mistake but make it differently). We certainly will have only limited success in our new chance. But it's there to be seized, and with its seizure comes a chance for new life—death and rebirth: "For they are twain yet one, and death is birth."

Blackie Ryan remarks of Nick Curran and Cathy Collins at the end of my *Virgin and Martyr:*

> They will live happily ever after. . . .They would have only three or four furious fights each week . . . .At least one day of the week they would not speak to each other. . . .And on five days their life would be ordinary and routine. . . .But on the remaining day. . . .ah, perhaps on that day they would know the love which is reputed to reflect the Love that launched the universe in a vast bang.
>
> Maybe even a day and a half some weeks.
>
> Not much, perhaps. Only a little bit—a little bit of light in the gloom, a little bit of life in the entropy, a little bit of love in the indifference.
>
> Maybe that is enough. Maybe, even, it is everything.

The hopeful ending then is, at best, cautious. As King says of the mother and father in *Cujo:* things improved, not much, but a little. Maybe they can make it together despite their grief, not in a perfect relationship, surely not in one that will ever be able to forget the tragic death of their son, but in one that is still possible and that is still open to possibilities.

Is that not what human life is about? Even if, with Lionel Tiger, you think hope is a self-deception, is it not more satisfying, not to say essential, to live as if there was reason to hope?

Hence the hopeful ending.

Northrop Frye distinguishes four stories, one for each season of the year—Spring Comedy, Summer Romance, Autumn Tragedy, and Winter Satire. All myths are legitimate, all tell us something about life, and all are legitimate myths for the story-teller. But despite the shallow folks who write book reviews for newspapers, none of the myths can claim a monopoly as an illuminating trajectory for life. Is happiness or despair or absurdity or a second chance the most revelatory paradigm?

Who knows? But being who and what we are, the second chance conclusion is the one we like the best because it seems programmed into our bones and is the way we live anyway, no matter what we profess in theory.

Spring and summer storytelling are not fashionable now to the mean-spirited and supercilious people who write book reviews—men and women whose opinions have no influence on anyone but themselves. Annie Dillard explains the puzzle of why book critics are not taken seriously: when art ignores people, people ignore art.

Autumn and Winter stories (and most "serious" storytelling is Satire in the broad sense of that word) are legitimate genres but so are Spring and Summer tales.

I ask no more than the modest concession that there are no data that exclude on *a priori* grounds the wisdom of the hopeful ending. Life may be comic, it may be tragic, it may be absurd, but it may also be romantic, even possibly a Romance.

The Grail myth can be told any of the four ways; it is normally tragic, neither the girl nor the Grail are achieved. One could rewrite it and reward the Knight with both and a lifetime of bliss. Or one could easily turn it into a satire. In principle, Camelot can be a comic paradise, a haunted house, a Kafka castle.

Or it can be a home. A place called Tara on a hill in County Meath, where a magic king, Airt Mac Conn, brings home an even more magic cup and, most magic of all, a Witch/Princess named Fair Breast.

It is no accident—to this writer, at any rate—that such is the Proto-Grail legend from which all others have derived and that, unlike its successors, it is life-affirming and flesh-affirming—hopeful, in other words.

But Airt Mac Conn, as the story makes clear, is never going to have another peaceful day, not for the rest of his life. Fair Breast has a mind of her own and is not at all hesitant about expressing it—at considerable length. Moreover, it is not altogether clear that he captured her instead of vice versa. She certainly wheels and deals in the story, working her own magic spells and giving her own quite definitive instructions, which Airt Mac Conn, like every other Irishman in the history of that strange land, had damn well follow or be in great trouble with his woman.

Never a peaceful day, but never a boring day either. Never a day without conflict and never a day without love.

A very modest conclusion, but not unlike life, isn't it?

It doubtless shows my biases to say that I believe Western culture would be different and much better if the Irish version of the story had triumphed over the sappy, silly Malory/Tennyson/Wagner Grail legend with which we're stuck.

The Tragic theory is that you must seek the Grail/girl forever and never be rewarded. The Comic theory says you can find both and bring them home to mother and live happily ever after. The Satire theory is that you marry the Grail/girl and she makes you unhappy for the rest of your life, because she turns out to be not worth the bother of pursuing.

The stage is littered with bodies at the end of Hamlet, but some folks are still alive and life must go on. Even the tragic ending, in other words, sends some characters and all the audience out into the challenges of "yet a little while," of one more and possibly several more chances. The catharsis at the end of tragedy may leave the protagonist dead but it leaves us very much alive and somehow challenged to continue.

Humankind is born of two incurable diseases: life, of which we all die, and hope, which says that maybe death is not the end. A hopeful ending merely testifies to those twin diseases and raises the possibility that they may be the "Hint of an Explanation" (the title, incidentally, of Graham Greene's best and most Catholic short story). No one is constrained to write stories that end on a note of hope, but neither is anyone who does so to be dismissed as not a serious writer.

As Thomas Patrick Doherty of Tor Books remarked to me once, the horror has been chained, temporarily perhaps, and we still have a little time to keep trying.

Yet a little while.

Catholicism is a Comic Religion (and not in the sense that many of our leaders are unintentional comedians). It believes in hope. It believes that life is stronger than death, love stronger than hatred, good stronger than evil. The Catholic world view can be expressed in any of the four genres. I am convinced, however, that it has a special affinity with Spring and Summer—it is a Spring and Summer religion whose sacramental insight has never been expressed better than in Hopkins' "May Magnificat." But here I merely wish to assert that Catholics must minimally defend Popular Culture against the charge that it is "trash" merely because it has a propensity for hopeful endings. The Catholic world view, more than any other, must defend the right of the storyteller to deal in Comedy.

The Catholic religious sensibility—if not always formal Catholic theology—has always known that the storyteller/God is a Comedian. (She is an Irish Comedienne, I am firmly convinced, but that is another story.)

Yet a little while.

(An earlier and shorter version of this chapter appeared in Writers Digest.*)*

11

The Local Community in Popular Culture

Critic: After all, Chicago is not the center of the Universe.

Me: Actually it is.

Another Critic: I notice there are no Chicago blacks in your stories.

Me: That's right.

Critic: Is that not a sign of racism?

Me: There are no Poles, Slovaks, Slovenes, Lithuanians, Armenians, Albanians, Greeks, Serbs, Czechs, Croatians, Swedes, or Germans either. And only one Italian. And by the way, do you complain because the Prize Winner doesn't have any Irish Catholics in his stories?

Third Critic: Speaking of Saul Bellow, why is your Chicago so different from his?

Me: It's a big city.

These three bits of dialogue suggest the first theme of this chapter: contemporary Catholic fiction tends to be local. Moreover, the locality is not merely a physical place; it is a social structure, a community, an interaction network, a human as well as a geographic environment. This is a specific application of a larger principle of the Catholic theology of popular culture: the "story" (in whatever art form) tends to respect the importance of place, especially local place.

The second theme is like unto the first: while there is no necessity that Catholic storytellers explore the mysteries of local communities, there is something in the Catholic religious sensibility which makes it easier for Catholics, all other things being equal, to write about a local community context that is integral to the story, almost a character in the story.

My argument here is that while my focus may be more narrow than that of other Catholic fiction writers of the time, it is not atypical in its localism. J.F. Powers has his parishes in the St. Cloud (Ostrogothenburg) Diocese; John Powers, the South Side of Chicago; William Kennedy, Albany; Louise Erdrich, the North Dakota/Minnesota border; Elizabeth Cullinan, the Long Island summer resorts; Edwin O'Connor, Boston; Jimmy Breslin, Queens.

If there is one difference between the present generation and its predecessor, it is that writers like James Farrell and, somewhat later, Harry Sylvester tended to be a bit embarrassed by the Irish and their neighborhoods (as Breslin is sometimes) while men like the two Powers and women like Cullinan and Erdrich are not at all embarrassed by Catholic communities.

It seems to me that the differences between Catholic writers and others writing about local community are that (a) the structure of the community tends to be much more a part of the story for a Catholic writer, not merely a backdrop or a context but a positive or negative force and (b) sometimes, at any rate, the local community is more positive than negative.

The reason for this Catholic concern about and respect for the culture and structure of the local community (the neighborhood) is to be found in what David Tracy calls the analogical imagination. Catholicism sees the community as sacrament—as reflection of the order and love with which God presides over the universe. The order may be less than perfect in the neighborhood, and the love may be less than fully generous, but still there is more goodness than evil in the local social structure and hence more sacrament than obstacle.

The very term "old neighborhood" is almost a Catholic theological statement—the community from which we came, where we have our roots, and which we are trying to reconstruct, not as a necessary evil but a positive good.

There is room for debate about local communities, their strengths and weaknesses, but the point here is that the Catholic propensity is to refuse to see person and community as disjunctives. It is not necessary in the Catholic sensibility to choose between them, to respond to the choice "either/or." Rather, the analogical imagination insists on a "both/and" response—person and community organically related to one another, community existing to promote the development of person, person freely working for the development of community.

As Catholic self-hatred ebbs in this country, there will almost certainly be more "neighborhood fiction" that is concerned neither with repudiation or glamorization of the local community but rather with understanding the community, the powerful ties of loyalty which hold us to it, and the great importance of it in our lives.

A man or woman who is both Catholic and a writer has every right, of course, to choose his or her own setting. My argument is minimal: Catholics tend to understand neighborhoods better than anyone else and are more likely to write about them.

Popular culture has no monopoly on local concerns. Some works of popular culture, even reasonably good ones, purport to be set in specific places and yet have no sense of that place. The Reverend Randolph series of mystery stories, for example, claims to be set in Chicago, but its Chicago geography is hazy at best and ludicrous at worst. Yet Randolph, a sometime quarterback for the Los Angeles Rams, is an interesting detective and a challenging theologian, and the stories about him are satisfying puzzles.

Moreover, some works of "high" culture are deeply concerned about place—the short stories and novels of John Updike, for example. Or the North Dakota of Louise Erdrich.

Yet there is a special propensity in popular culture to take place very seriously. The films of Larry McMurtry have to be set in Texas, just as the films of Woody Allen have to be set in New York. Cities like Los Angeles, Miami, New Orleans, and Chicago are sometimes only the backdrop for the film-maker, but with a skilled cameraman, a city enters the story and becomes a character, as did Chicago in *My Bodyguard* and New Orleans in *Cat People*.

The private-eye mystery stories are also deeply "implanted" in their physical environment—Spenser and Hawk in Boston, Marlowe in Los Angeles, V.I. Paretsky in Chicago, Chris Wiltz's stories of New Orleans, Elmore Leonard's tales of Detroit and Miami, John MacDonald's Travis McGee stories in Florida.

Rock music also senses the locale of the singer and sometimes, as we shall see later most notably in the case of Bruce Springsteen, turns the locale into an integral part of the song.

To make a tentative distinction between high and popular culture based on their approaches to place, the former often uses place as a source of poetic imagery which creates an atmosphere for "story," while the latter is likely to be much more realistic in its descriptions of place and to make place a part of "story" itself.

Perhaps the reason for this concern about place in popular culture is that those who produce it are aware that a story does not occur in a vacuum.

Romance and Comedy, in particular, have to be in a specific locale or they can't be at all. Eddings' Belgariad fantasy (about which more later) may be a wild tale of swords and sorcery, but it "takes place" in a very vivid, it totally imaginary world, with which the reader is quite familiar long before he finishes the six volumes (so far) of the story. Indeed most fantasy writers concentrate on elaborate descriptions of their imaginary worlds precisely because (I suspect) they know that their readers require that the implausible take place against a plausible background.

The writer of Tragedy and/or "serious" stories need be less concerned about place because his emphasis is more on character and less on action—although some writers of "serious" stories do indeed re-create place with wonderful skill. Nonetheless, the "place" of high culture is place as it is perceived by the characters impinging on their own agonies and ecstasies. Ms. Erdrich's wonderful North Dakota, for example, or Faulkner's Oxford County, or Pat Conroy's Carolina are less real places than mystical backdrops for tragic drama. You would not read them for literal descriptions of the three states.

The Florida of Leonard and MacDonald, on the other hand, seems to be a place that one would recognize instantly if one made the mistake of going there instead of Tucson for sun in the winter.

I would suggest that popular artists down through the ages have always emphasized place because they are trying to communicate with "locals," men and women who are rooted in one place. High artists, on the other hand, are attempting to communicate with men and women who are cosmopolitans, often deracinated from a place of their own and rootless both in time and space.

I will not attempt to argue here that one audience is better than the other, only that the popular audience tends to be larger because most of us, even if we have moved from somewhere else, value our "place" enormously and cannot understand a "story" that seems mostly independent of place.

Our Indo-European tribe described in earlier chapters promptly consecrated its new space in the forest by bounding it with sacred stones and erecting a monument of sacred stones in its center to link the new bit of cosmos (as College Park, Pennsylvania, was created at the intersection of four diagonals from the corners of the state). With that consecration all of the space became sacred and the center space especially sacred because now the new place was linked to the work of the gods, the task of bringing order out of chaos.

The definition of neighborhood by sociologist Gerald Suttles is not greatly different—that place in the checkerboard of the city where you are safe and where you are accepted (in great part anyway) not because of what you do but because of who you are.

We all come from somewhere. When we tell our story to others we usually say where we are from, what we're doing now and what our trajectory is into the future. We have, in other words, a plot with a beginning, a middle, and a tentative conclusion. It may be theoretically possible to tell your story and leave out your family and your place of origin, but then in your story you appear, almost by definition, to be alienation personified.

One need not like one's family or place. But if one is wise, one acknowledges how much they have shaped one and how important they are to one's story. A psychologist wrote recently that at a certain stage in life young people are willing to forgive their parents! Fair enough, I suppose, though at an even more mature and responsible stage one ought to be able to ask forgiveness from one's parents. Maturity, then, implies a realistic acceptance of origins, neither excusing them or scapegoating them but separating out the good from the bad.

One may maturely and intelligently reject one's place, but in so doing, one should also acknowledge how much of one's rebelling against one's own place is in fact a rebellion against one's own internal problems projected into the place.

Like the creators of much popular culture, Catholicism has always recognized the importance of place. Believing that the Incarnation of Jesus validated the sacramentality of creation, Catholicism knows that space is not only sacred, it is sacramental. God lurks in places, in local communities, in neighborhoods, in groups of friends at the corner drugstore (in days gone by) or at the Mall (in the present).

(I preferred the drugstore, if only because it was more manageable. It was also easier. One had only to lean against the mailbox. In malls, one is required to "crawl.")

In the light of the Incarnation, Catholicism does not reject the human body and does not believe (despite certain errant spiritualities) that spirit is limited by flesh. Therefore it accepts the profoundly local nature of human nature. It comprehends that a body requires that we be "in place." Try as we might, even in supersonic jets, we still are "placed" creatures, limited to three-dimensional spaces, some of which are more reassuring and more attractive and, hence, potentially more sacramental. Catholicism does not condemn the structure imposed on our personality by our necessarily local origins. It warns of the parochialism that results from refusing to look beyond the boundaries of our own place or to consider it critically. But it also understands that one is able to go beyond one's origins only when one is sure of the ground on which one stands.

You may strive to ignore your place; but you are much wiser if you make your peace with it.

And wisest of all if you realize that all subsequent spaces in your life are an attempt (conscious or not) to re-create the spaces of your past, free of the problems and restraints you encountered in it.

The minimal theological position I wish to draw from these reflections is that, since Catholicism believes that God discloses Herself in space, especially in the most loved and most meaningful spaces, it is open to two possibilities with regard to popular culture:

1) The concern with place in popular culture is a constant reminder that humans are placed creatures and that elitist attempts to pretend otherwise are self-deceptive.

2) God may lurk in the places in which the "stories" of popular culture occur. It is therefore possible for the "reader" of popular culture to encounter God in these places. Thus the religion teacher should be sensitive to the possibilities of fa-

cilitating the illumination of the "reader" as s/he encounters the sacramentality of space in products of popular culture.

God is ready to explode out of the space of Depression Texas in *Places in the Heart* and, at the end, finally does so, almost despite the wishes of the characters and the film-makers. (More about this epiphany in a later chapter.)

There is no obligation for Catholic artists and writers to treat place as sacramental. My position here, as throughout the book, is minimalist: there is a propensity for the Catholic imagination to treat space as sacramental (consider Brideshead in Waugh's most famous novel). That propensity is based on the Catholic insight (on which we have no monopoly but which our sensibility tends to stress) that we are placed creatures: we all come from some place and are in some place. And God is in both places, lying in wait for us, on a tree, perhaps in Richard Wilbur's words, as "the Cheshire smile which sets us fearfully free."

As Blackie Ryan would put it, "The risk is that, if you're not from somewhere, you may not be someone. And if you are from nowhere, you certainly are no one."

It is a not unimportant contribution to literature.

If we don't make it, who will?

12

TV: Cosby as Evangelist

In the controversy over TV evangelism, no one seems to have noticed that the most influential religion teacher in America is not Jim Bakker or Jerry Falwell or John O'Connor or Joseph Bernardin.

Rather, it is Bill Cosby.

Every week his program and its clones present vivid and appealing paradigms of love to vast audiences. This love is disclosed by the resolution of family tensions in the lives of characters who have become as real as your next-door neighbors—Cliff, Claire, Jason, Maggie, Sondra, Denise, Vanessa, Theo, Rudi, Alex, Andy, Jenifer, Malory, Mike, Carol, Ben. So we learn, without even realizing it, how to live lovingly in families.

We laugh at the familiar pattern of conflict and tension created by apparently trivial family crises like the double promotion of a studious young woman, an engagement announcement, a fiftieth birthday, a big telephone bill, a fight between young lovers, a decision by a boy that he wants to take flying lessons, a wedding anniversary of grandparents, a divorce between friends, an assault of "flu" on the family. As we laugh, we see the virtues required for conflict resolution: such frequently honored but difficult qualities as patience, trust, sensitivity, honesty, generosity, flexibility, and forgiveness. The shows rarely draw explicit moral conclusions for us. Usually they do not insist on hammering home ethical principles. Rather, they hint lightly at the skills and traits which sustain love and, their work done, skip off quickly to the commercial.

A modern version of the medieval morality play has slipped into prime time television almost without anyone noticing it.

There are exceptions to the general restraint about moralizing and preaching: In an episode of *Growing Pains*, Kirk Cameron, who plays Mike, talks directly to the young people in the audience after the final commercial and emphasizes the importance of saying "no" to cocaine. In the hour-long drama of *Family Ties* in which supernerd Alex—Michael J. Fox—mourns for a dead friend, he faces squarely problems of life and death, meaning and belonging, faith and despair. The Cosby program rarely attempts to preach on the need for family love. It doesn't have to.

While the morality play genre is evident, University of Arizona sociology Professor Albert Bergesen, a student of popular culture, argues that the appeal of the Cosby program (and to some extent its clones) is to be found in the intensity of family love "into which we slip when the program begins. It is like a Franklin stove radiating warmth around which we crowd on a cold winter night. We know about rising divorce rates, single-parent families, abortion, incest, wife beating, and teenage pregnancy, but when the Huxtables are on screen, we absorb the affection of a functioning, intact family and feel good. When the program is over, we are more hopeful for families and for own family. It isn't merely the gentle moral lesson. It's the appeal of love."

An escape?

When I listen Sir Georg Solti and the Chicago Symphony, it's an escape, too. But it's also a renewal. *The Cosby Show* is number one because it has mastered the art of renewing hope for the family. Your family.

The Cosby Show delights kids because they can identify with the various characters, particularly the well-meaning but frequently inept Theo. It also delights parents because, feeling as they do that they are oppressed by their kids, they rejoice in Heathcliffe Huxtable's triumph over his kids. Parents particularly enjoyed the episode in which Theo was given money and charged with living on his own in the family house. Just how much does it cost to pay people to do for you the things that your parents do for free?

I confess that in that episode, I liked best the marvelous little girl, Rudi, playing a harsh bank president who refused to extend credit to Theo. Rudi is my favorite of all the kids on the various programs, even more adorable than Andrew on *Family Ties*.

The Cosby show, then, provides moral paradigms and displays warm and renewing love. Does that make it religious?

"Sure it does," Professor Bergesen shrugs, "family love is one of the tiny windows through which the Good or the Possible or God, if you want to use the term, peeks at us. It is in the little things of life, isn't it, that we often find the meaning of the big things?"

Having watched a couple score of tapes from *Cosby, Family Ties, Growing Pains, Mr. Belvidere,* and *My Sister Sam* in a few weeks, I am prepared to propose that anyone who can certify that they have viewed two of these programs during the preceding week can be dispensed, if not from Sunday church attendance, than at least from listening to the Sunday homily/sermon. They do it a lot better than we do it.

I also think I collected enough homily ideas for the next two years (including this year's Holy Week sermons—based on the *Family Ties* story in which Alex's friend dies and Alex himself must die to his old self to put on the new man).

How many clergy, I wonder, see the family programs as

sermon material? Very few, probably. Too busy being relevant. And too blinded by ecclesiastical and ideological concerns to see religion where the Founder saw it—in the ordinary, daily lives of people.

Their congregations certainly watch, however. In a parish in Tucson, I recently proposed, half-fun and full-earnest, that we think about the *Martha, Mary, and Lazarus* show in which these three young people (if they were not young, they would have been married) who were unofficial foster children of Jesus would be imagined as not much different from Denise, Vanessa, and Theo. The point was that the love among those four was as authentically human love as portrayed (however simply) in the Huxtable clan.

The people thought the series was a great idea.

Then, moved by my success, I noted that the appealing love between Michael J. Fox and his little brother was another template for family life.

I couldn't remember the name of Fox's role. "What's he called?" I demanded.

"Alex!" the congregation answered with more vigor than they normally use in the official responses of Mass.

"And the little brother?"

Every kid in church looked at me like I was crazy. "Andy!" they shouted.

(What kind of a geek doesn't remember a character whose name is the same as his own?)

I bet that not one in twenty members of the congregation could tell you the name of the president of the American bishops.

Are these ethical (though not moralistic) and religious (though not ecclesiastical) themes intended by those who produce the programs?

Family life has been the raw martial of much of Cosby's humor from the beginning of his career, and it has always been a humor of love. Perhaps his doctorate in education has made him more reflective about what he is doing, more conscious of the moral and religious issues he is tackling; but he has always been, in his own way, a minister of the word.

The other programs are based on the insight that implicit ethics and religion in a matrix of humor are highly commercial in a country where meaning and belonging are as important as they have ever been and where those institutions traditionally charged with meaning and belonging—churches and schools—are failing to deliver sufficient amounts of either.

So ministers of religion condemn television; and television does the work that they are not doing. There are many ironies in the fire.

The most vivid of the tapes I watched was the *Family Ties* episode about the death of Alex's close friend, a young man as kind and as humble and as self-effacing as Alex is just the opposite. A friend from the earliest days of grammar school, he died in an auto accident at a time when Alex was supposed to be with him. Alex had refused to join him because of pure selfishness. Hence he felt guilty not only because his friend had died and he hadn't but also because his life was purchased by the selfishness of which his friend seemed incapable.

After the funeral, Alex returns to the Keaton family house but continues to see his friend whenever the rest of the family leaves the room. Typically, the friend is perfectly willing to forgive Alex. Just as typically, Alex is as hard on himself as he is on others.

The hour-long program provided much more room for character analysis and development than the ordinary half-hour shows do. Michael J. Fox's brilliant acting made all that development come out of the Alex we already knew. Nothing new was added to Alex, but we had much deeper insight into his character than before. We came to understand the complexity of a very bright, quick-witted young man with talent and ambition who grows up in a family in which his parents are superannuated hippies and his brother and sisters are typically laid-back members of their own generation. We'd always known Alex as the supernerd, the reader of the *Wall Street Journal*, the conservative admirer of Richard Nixon, the canny investor who wants to become rich.

We had also known him through his wonderful affection for his little brother Andrew (got it right this time!). We were aware that if his heart was not exactly made of gold, it was at least made of silver.

Now, in the unwrapping of his character as he tries to cope with death and the meaning of life, we understand how this complex young man has come to be who and what he is. And Alex, in an agonizing and honest reappraisal of himself, realizes how his quick wit and quicker tongue cut him off from other people his own age and how much he hides behind his mask. He also realizes that he loves each member of his family dearly and has let each of them down badly, one way or another.

Finally, he must ask himself whether he believes that life is stronger than death and whether he really believes in a Love that overcomes death. Tentatively, he decides that he does and that he must undergo a change (a *metanoia*).

At the end of the story, he is still the same old Alex and yet not quite the same. He has learned a little bit about what life means and has become, therefore, a little bit different and a little bit better.

We who have watched perhaps know ourselves a little bit better, too, and have recalled our own experiences of bafflement, anger, guilt, and despair because of the death of someone we loved. We may have recalled, as well, the subsequent experience of reintegration and new beginning when we went beyond guilt and anger to a death and resurrection in which we put off something of our former self and reappeared a little wiser, a little kinder, a little more aware of our own weaknesses, and a little more determined to try to be the kind of person of whom we are capable of being.

Compared to the leaden Holy Week program a few years ago when Cardinal Bernardin bored audiences on the superchannel, that episode of *Family Ties* was a practically perfect Good Friday/Easter story. The advantage that the producers of the program had over the Cardinal is that they were required to tell a story while he was constrained by inept advisers to preach.

When in doubt always tell a story.

I wonder how many homilists and catechists in America comprehend what wonderful instructional resources these programs are.

Not very many, I suppose. I was not one of those who saw the possibilities until a commission from the *New York Times* forced me to watch programs that my nieces and nephews told me I shouldn't miss.

Critics of both the right and the left have been jumping on the family comedies lately, as they will do when something is extraordinarily successful. The programs, it is said, are shallow and superficial. They do not depict the anguish and suffering of many families or the discrimination against many black families. They ignore the misery and unhappiness that plague many husband/wife and parent/children relationships. They deal only with intact, upper-middle-class families. They are mushy and sentimental. The acting is gauche and exaggerated. The men are wimps, never wanting (as a Chicago critic observed comparing these programs unfavorably to the new Fox Broadcasting series *Married with Children*) to get away from the family and go to a Bulls game.

Like much media criticism, these comments are the result of the fallacy of misplaced genre. A half-hour TV program is not a three-hour Broadway production. A miracle play is not a sociological report or an ideological indoctrination. It paints with quick, broad strokes and says to us not "this is the way all families are" or "this is what you must do" but rather "these are the skills needed to make intimacies work."

In fact, *My Sister Sam* is not about an intact family: Sam is a single, woman photographer in San Francisco who has a "relationship" with a man who dwells in New York. Her teen-age sister Patty shares Sam's San Francisco loft, a much more hip setting and situation than the Huxtable house and environment in Philadelphia. But the conflicts, the problems, and the love are similar to what we see in the other programs. Indeed trust is the virtue unremittingly extolled in the episodes I have watched of this show.

The warmth in the Huxtable family is as expressive as it is, I suspect, precisely because the family is black. Not only do white Americans see the inside of a black, upper-middle-class family (often for the first time), they see one where the black tradition of explicit affection is permitted to flourish.

Would they dare display such intense affection between husband and wife if the family were white?

So much cuddling between husband and wife might not seem natural in a white family. (It sure wouldn't if they were Irish.)

Those who demand that Cosby be more "militant" fail completely to understand the subtle boundaries that separate genres and the damage you do when you blur these boundaries. Should The Cosby Show be turned into an ideological platform, its fragile magic would destroyed.

Sometimes the acting in these programs is very sensitive. In an episode of *Mr. Belvidere*, Kevin, weary of his virginity, decides to "make it" with the football team's "whore." But Kevin's natural respect for women—opening doors, helping her on with her coat, giving her flowers—persuades the girl that she need not be "easy" to be loved. Kevin fails to "make it," but he helps the girl to acquire self-esteem and transform herself. The subtle interplay between the two young people (Rob Stone and Debbie Barker) is one of the most touching and skillful scenes I've ever watched on television.

The scripts are normally well written and effectively paced (and on the *Cosby Show* almost always deft). The jokes are frequently very clever: Sam's agent, about to give her advice about trusting Patty and still imposing limits, says, "I don't have any children of my own, but I do watch A.M. television . . . ."

But there is more to religion, is there not, than mere family love? What about peace and hunger and the third world?

Social concern that worries about the distant neighbor and ignores the intimate neighbor is likely to be neither healthy nor durable nor successful. Religion that has forgotten the importance and the difficulty of the most intimate of relationships is not likely to be taken seriously when it pontificates on other relationships. Surely religion ought to have immense social implications. But these implications will not be recognized unless religion also provides satisfying paradigms for the meaning of life and the healing of the wounds acquired and imposed in trying to love the intimate other.

The basic objection to *Cosby* et al. is that they are about intact, middle-class families, a social institution that many Americans in the cultural elite (and this includes not a few clerics) think (or would like to think) is obsolete.

What's wrong with a few programs about intact families?

It turns out, on the basis of the success of the family programs, that most Americans, including many who are not in intact families, disagree. Sometimes it may be necessary to break up a family. But the public apparently believes that an intact family is, on the whole, better than an unintact family. Sometimes it may be necessary to be a single parent, but on the whole, it is better to be a married parent. Because single parents and broken families are increasing numerically (though recent data say the increase has stopped), it does not follow, the public seems to think, that the intact and affectionate family is any less the ideal or that familial love, even in deviant situations such as illustrated by *My Sister Sam*, is any less important.

So at any rate enough people feel to keep The *Cosby Show* on the top of the list and to keep NBC with Cosby and *Family Ties* number one in the rating game.

The subject matter and the content of American TV is

determined not by what the elites think appropriate but by what people like—in the case of Cosby et al, fortunately both for people and for religion.

"Love comes alive on that program," says Professor Bergesen. "Sure sometimes it's mushy. Sure it ignores some big problems. Sure no family is so perfect. Still they make love real. Not many people can resist that."

And in my fantasies for the future (after the *Martha, Mary, and Lazarus Show*), I wonder if some day William Cosby, E.D., might be hailed not merely as a doctor of education but as an *Ecclesiae Doctor*, as the television era's first Doctor of the Church.

(An earlier and shorter version of this chapter was published in the Arts and Leisure section of the New York Times.)

13

Born in the USA: Springsteen, Blue-collar Prophet and Catholic Troubadour

If the voice of social prophecy is heard in the land today, it does not come from the *Pastoral Letter on Poverty* of the Catholic bishops; it comes, rather, in the voice of a parochial school graduate from Asbury Park, New Jersey, who is a reader of Flannery O'Connor's stories and a member of the Catholic, ethnic, blue-collar community that the Bishops sold out in that pastoral.

No one listens to the Bishops. Millions listen to Bruce Springsteen, not including, one assumes, bishops.

Rock music is adolescent protest.

There is nothing wrong with that. There is much about which adolescents should protest (including the failure of their schools and their churches to help them prepare for life). Moreover, if maturity means integrating earlier phases in our life cycle so that we are able to call on their insights and experiences when appropriate, a component of the mature person should be the capacity to cry out with adolescent outrage when it is appropriate in adult life. There is then room for adults to enjoy adolescent protest music, too (not that they have to).

The adolescent does not want to grow up; he resents being forced to leave behind the playful world of childhood. On the other hand, he wants to be grown up all at once. He hates being suspended in the amorphous stage between childhood and adulthood. He finds himself tormented by passions that he did not know only a year or two before and yet forbidden to do anything about those passions. He is fascinated and terrified by his sexual longings and wants both instant pleasure and instant love. He detests the foolish rules that family, school, church, and society try to impose on him and abhors the hypocrisy of those who make the rules but refuse to keep the rules themselves. He dreams great, wonderful, romantic dreams and finds these dreams and even the possibility of them ever coming true denied to him in his daily life.

From his point of view, he has reason to protest. And if he loses his outrage about stupid bureaucracies, corrupt institutions that don't practice what they preach, and the blighting of dreams, then he may have grown up, but he hasn't matured.

Rock-and-Roll, its origins in gospel music and rhythm-and-blues, is appropriate musical rhetoric for protest. The protest, however, does not have to be either political or countercultural, a fact that seems to have been overlooked in the late sixties and the seventies.

The cry of such early Rock greats as Elvis and Chuck Berry was in some sense a Peter Pan cry, a protest against growing up, a scream of adolescent frustration in search of true love. Rock music antedated the counterculture and was appropriated by it. The drugs, violence, political radicalism, social protest, sexual perversity, and crazy dress—the whole Woodstock syndrome— were additions to the original Rock impulse, not essential elements in it. As Springsteen himself admits, he did not become a musician because he wanted out of American society but because he wanted in.

The alliance between Rock and the counterculture was not, however, illegitimate. For the counterculture spread in opposition to the Viet Nam war, and Rock was an ideal medium for young people to assert their protests against the war. The voice of the Rock musician as political and social protest, however, is something less than completely authentic. The musician is not quite part of the group in whose name the protest is issued. And the "mainstream" is quick to appropriate the counterculture artifacts as fashion and as products to sell. As Jon Landau, then a Rock critic and now Springsteen's manager, remarked in the seventies, "We say we are a counterculture, yet are we really so different from the culture against which we rebel?"

If that was an appropriate question ten years ago, it is all the more appropriate today when Wall Street brokers run cocaine rings.

One of the things the "mainstream" (Wall Street, Midtown, Hollywood) and the counterculture have in common is contempt for the hard-hat, the white, blue-collar worker who is portrayed as a male chauvinist hawkish pig in the films and books and songs the latter produces and the former consumes.

The older tradition of protest songs of the twenties and thirties and forties was protest in the name of the same blue-collar workers. Joe Hill was not a long-haired drug user shouting obscenities at ordinary citizens. Rather, he was killed and then immortalized in song for trying to organize citizens into a union to fight the mining bosses.

Both the liberal left (whether in its counterculture manifestation or not) and the "mainstream" despise unions and union members and rejoiced when George Meany was thrown out of the Democratic convention in 1968. The liberal left conveniently forgets that the industrial unions (USWA, UAW) and the American Federation of Teachers have done more to improve the wages of black and brown workers than all the affirmative action programs in the country put together.

If there is one enemy in the liberal left demonology for whom there is no tolerance, it is precisely the white, blue-collar union member who, in the liberal left mythology, is the opponent of all good things—racial and sexual justice, peace, concern for the poor. Archie Bunker is the villain.

The myth has little connection with reality. The white working class (particularly the Catholic white working class) turned against the war long before other Americans. Small wonder, their sons were doing the fighting and the dying.

In his "Bruce Springsteen and the E Street Band Live" album, Springsteen tells how his mother and father rejoiced when he was turned down for the draft. It was a typical reaction, its typicality supported by every survey taken at that time. The liberal left has never been able to give up its myth to the contrary.

You gotta hate someone. And if you can't hate Jews or blacks or gays, who's left to hate?

Ethnic hard-hats, that's who!

There is a nice irony, then, in the fact that the most popular Rock musician in America is from a Catholic, ethnic (part Italian-American) family; wears working-class clothes; cuts his hair reasonably short; does not use drugs (or even smoke), maintains gentle order at his concerts; lives in a privacy so intense that he is rarely recognized on the streets; is obviously heterosexual; and cries out in protest for the white worker whom everyone else in America seems to detest or ignore.

Both the left and the right want to claim him. George Will, in a ploy of intellectual dishonesty shocking even in him, tried to link Springsteen to the Reagan re-election campaign. The President himself endorsed "Born in the USA" as standing for the same things he stood for—perhaps his hearing aid was off. Springsteen gracefully ducked away from endorsement and from the request that he appear with the President.

The left quite properly sees the most recent Springsteen

songs as social criticism and laughs delightedly at the President's misperception. But it wonders why he didn't repudiate the President, why he is still an American patriot, and why his generous donations go to organizations like the steelworkers and not to more "revolutionary" causes. Some of his critics on the left suggest that he is a Rock version of the ineffable Sylvester Stallone, a musical Rambo.

They must not have heard his song "War."

"Born in the USA" is a song everyone would like to claim but with which both the left and the right are uneasy. It is critical of the war and also of the treatment of the blue-collar whites who fought in it and were repudiated by society when they came home. He defends the American dream, rages against its failure for so many of the vets, and still honors the flag and hopes that the dream can be realized for them.

Inconsistent?

I confess I don't think so. It is a position which a very large minority of Americans share, and certainly a majority of those "white ethnic blue-collar (some of whom are white-collar) workers" who have traditionally voted in overwhelming majorities for Democratic candidates and still do. If you grow up Catholic in Asbury Park, New Jersey, and your father is a factory worker, what other political and social position makes sense?

Springsteen's social protest is not sophisticated. He is a musician, not a politician, characteristic of the humility that seems to natural to him, he does not think his success in one area of life makes him an expert in another. His protest comes from his heart and his gut and not from any more clearly thought out ideology. His political thinking may grow more precise and nuanced as he matures. We hear now a man wrestling with social injustice—described in terms of a broken dream—and wondering what to do about it. "You're really not free," he tells his audiences, "until everyone has been as lucky as you."

Yet it seems unlikely, given the kind of man he apparently is, that his solutions will ever harden into rigid ideology. It will be interesting to watch his progress as a musician and as a social commentator, especially since he seemingly works very hard at keeping himself open to further growth in every aspect of his life.

"The E Street Band" record is a deliberate autobiographical self-revelation of a man conscious of his own struggle for maturity and fully intending to continue the struggle.

The distinction he sees between himself and Elvis is flat, "But I grew up and I didn't want to be just like that no more."

One of his biographers (there are at least eleven biographies) sums up what this maturation means:

> In the time of punk and disco, however, Bruce's music not only seemed to be a throwback; in some important ways it really was one. It could be argued, on the evidence of his rockabilly rhythms and persistent optimism, that he hadn't a radical bone in his body and perhaps far too many conservative ones. Yet in another way, he represented the most radical of all threats to juvenile hegemony within rock and roll. He represented the idea that performers and audiences could grow up, assume adult responsibility, and tackle serious themes, without abandoning rock and roll's kernel of joy . . . Bruce Springsteen, all but alone among the post-Beatles pop singers, seemed immune to nihilism. Despair was a familiar companion in his recent songs, but dark portents were almost always overwhelmed, if not dispelled, by cascading affirmations of the tenet succinctly summarized in "Badlands": "It ain't no sin to be glad you're alive." What he learned from Elvis was the importance of that principle and the potential price of ignoring it. (Dave Marsh, *Glory Days*, page 41).

Am I saying that this hopefulness comes out of his Catholicism? You bet I am. Where else did he get it and sustain it against all the trends and fashions in his profession?

My contention is not that his hope and resiliency and his ability to say "both/and" in preference to "either/or" is the result of explicit reflection on Catholic doctrine. There is no trace of that in his lyrics. I am saying, however, that at the level of imaginative instinct, he is profoundly Catholic, perhaps without realizing it, and that the Flannery O'Connor influence is no accident.

There are almost no Catholic symbols in his music; but at a deeper level, the more recent songs display a powerful instinct that one can begin again and that the dreams of the past need not be abandoned but can be reclaimed and reformulated for the next phase in life. Maybe you can't exactly go home again, but you can take home with you—a profoundly Catholic sentiment.

Perhaps his wife Julianne, if not exactly the "Jersey Girl" he thought he loved as a teen-ager nor the Rosalita of that rollicking song, is the kind of woman he dreamed of at the Jersey shore and a promise that dreams can indeed come true.

The young people with whom I water-ski in the summer insist on playing "Rosalita" every day. It is a charming love story, totally adolescent, unalterably romantic, and incorrigibly hopeful. My fellow skiers don't even seem to notice that in its hope it is utterly different from almost all other Rock love stories. I suspect, for these young friends, it would not have mattered if the "Boss's" social instincts had not suddenly and powerful surged into his music. But they find the message of his protest completely compatible with their own world view.

In his early songs, Springsteen was a teen-ager with great dreams of love and happiness, though without any clear notion of how the dreams would be achieved. In the middle songs ("Born to Run," "The River," "Nebraska") he cries out in anguish at the frustration of the dream for so many people—criminals, yes, but also for those who have lost their jobs; those who live in the decaying old homes; those who drive the run-down cars; those whose shops on Main Street are boarded up; those like his father who worked all their lives for a dream and did not, despite their hard work, ever quite see the dream come true. Then in the "Born in the USA" album, there is shift not so much away from anguish as away from despair, an edging towards renewed hope where he promises his love that they will finally find their place in the sun, no matter how long and how far they must run.

Thou has made us for thyself alone, O Lord, and our hearts are restless till they rest in thee.

Hope that strong will never tumble over the precipice to despair.

There are, then, two protest themes of Springsteen in his middle thirties: one is against the society that permits its own best dreams to be blighted for so many of its people and the other, more profound but not unrelated, is against the anguish of the whole human condition—even if the dream does come true it is not enough. The former cry may be the louder just now, but the second, deeply religious, is the more important.

If we are to judge by Bruce Springsteen's efforts so far, the answer that will evolve in time will be the same one that is inchoately given already: it is safe to hope and to renew the hopeful energies latent in our remembered dreams.

No one ever said that you had to find the Jersey Girl in Jersey.

The answer, even in its still ragged form, is incorrigibly romantic and incorrigibly Catholic.

I don't see how his music can help but become even more religious than it already is. In his mid-thirties, a husband now, Bruce Springsteen is asking serious questions about what life means. As he works out his answers he will doubtless share them with us. One can be sure that they will not be nihilistic; and he will become an even more important religious prophet than he is today.

I contend that his Church has failed him on two grounds. First of all, in its enthusiasm to embrace the "preferential option for the poor" (which does not include its own employees, of course), it has written off completely the social group from which Springsteen comes. Most blue-collar workers are still employed and, like Springsteen's family, are therefore not "poor." Indeed the preferred "poor" are non-white and "third world." Everyone else, even if their dreams have been blighted, their neighborhoods are falling apart, their towns and cities ruined, is "middle class" and hence the enemy, the "middle class Catholics," whom Archbishop Weakland, in fine display of unconscious Marxism, denounced for opposing the teachings of the *Pastoral*. The available evidence showed that the Catholic middle class, which pays the bills for the Church and even for the bureaucrats who drafted the pastoral, supported the general orientations of the Pastoral long before the bishops started to think about such things.

The elitist ideologues who do the bishops' thinking for them had decided, along with the rest of the liberal left, that the "white middle class" had to pick up the tab for help to the "poor." Therefore, by definition, the woes of the people about whom Springsteen agonizes did not matter. The important suffering, you see, is "minority" suffering. And the white ethnic middle class/working class is not a "minority."

I wonder if any of the people who wrote the Pastoral or the bishops who signed it ever listened to the Springsteen songs.

The point is not that the "minority" groups are unimportant. The point is, rather, that if one person or group's suffering is written off as unimportant, then no suffering is important—an excellent Catholic principle.

Our leadership just doesn't seem to understand that anymore.

This is not a Michael Novak objection, based on the assumption that American capitalism is just fine. Novak is dead wrong. American capitalism has many serious problems—inferior products, corrupt management (more interested in "acquisitions" than in productivity), and terrible labor-management relations—none of which seemed to concern the bishops.

My objection comes from the other side: the bishops have sold out to the left liberal fallacy that human suffering in a socially fashionable "victim" group is worse than the same suffering in a socially unfashionable group.

The judgment of Springsteen's songs is not likely to move them.

The Church's second failure is that it has apparently done nothing to help or sustain Springsteen in his search for meaning and for a clearer articulation of his grounds for hope.

He is a major religious prophet, a Catholic with a profoundly Catholic viewpoint. He was married in Church to another Catholic. Their children will undoubtedly be raised Catholic. Yet as with so many other Catholics in the performing arts, the Church has no ministry to him and no sign of any understanding of what he is up to. Nor, sadly, would it ever occur to him that the Church, as he knows it, could help him as he "runs."

Why should the Church, as he knows it, be expected to tell him why it is safe to hope, why there is reason to dream, why it "ain't no sin to be glad you're alive"?

Why indeed?

The release of Springsteen's album "Tunnel of Love" may be a more important Catholic event in this country than the visit of Pope John Paul II. The Pope spoke of morality using the language of doctrinal propositions which appeals to (or repels) the mind. Springsteen sings of religious realities—sin, temptation, forgiveness, life, death, hope—in images (implicitly perhaps) from his Catholic childhood, images that appeal to the whole person, not just the head, and which will be absorbed by far more Americans than listened to the Pope.

Troubadours always have been more important than theologians or bishops.

Some Rock critics contend that Springsteen has turned away from the "positive" music of "Born in the USA" to return to the grimmer and more pessimistic mood of "Nebraska" or "The River." It might be debated how optimistic "USA" really was. But, while there is tragedy in "Tunnel of Love," there is also hope. The water of the river still flows, but now it stands for rebirth. Light and water, the Easter and Baptismal symbols of the Catholic liturgy, the combination of the male and female fertility principles, create life in "Tunnel of Love."

Unlike the other religions of Yahweh, Catholicism has always stood for the accessibility of God in the world. God is more like the world than unlike it. Hence Catholicism, unlike Protestantism, Judaism, and Islam, permits angels and saints, shrines and statues, stained glass and incense, and the continuation of pagan customs—most notably for our purposes here, holy water and blessed candles.

The point is not that the Catholic sensibility is better or worse than other religious sensibilities, but different. Nor is the point that any of the sensibilities can survive unless they are integrated with the others. Finally, the point is not that Catholicism has any monopoly on light and water symbolism, but rather, that it emphasizes them more strongly than other traditions. No one else has holy water or blessed candles.

Religion is more explicitly expressed in "Tunnel of Love" than in any previous Springsteen album. Prayer, heaven, and God are invoked naturally and unself-consciously, as though they are an ordinary part of the singer's life and vocabulary (and the singer is the narrator of the story told in the song and not necessarily Springsteen). Moreover, religion is invoked to deal precisely with those human (as opposed to doctrinal) problems that humankind in its long history has always considered religious—love, sin, death, rebirth.

On the subject of human sinfulness, Springsteen sounds like Saint Paul, who lamented that "the good which I would do, I do not do; and the evil which I would not do, that I do."

In "Two Faces," the singer complains that he is two men, one good, one evil; one sunny, one dark; one that says "hello" and one that says "good-bye." He fears that the evil face may deprive him of his love. He tells us that, at night, he gets down on his knees and prays that love will make the other man go away, but he admits that the other will never leave.

For a couple of thousand years in Western culture, that experience has been called Original Sin, the only Christian doctrine—as the Lutheran church historian Martin Marty has remarked—for which there is empirical evidence.

Springsteen returns to this theme in "One Step Up." The singer and his wife are alienated. She is no longer the girl in white outside the church and the church bells aren't ringing.

The singer doesn't know who is to blame, but he is caught

in his own guilt. He is not the man he wanted to be, somehow he has slipped off the track. He's trapped, moving one step forward and two steps back.

In "Cautious Man," the singer (Billy) imagines that on one hand is tattooed the word "love" and on the other "fear." In autumn he marries his spring lover because he always wanted to do what was right. But alone on his knees at night, he prayed, "for he knew in a restless heart the seed of betrayal lay."

One night the fear tattoo got the better of him, and he stole away from his marriage bed and strode down the highway—the road that in the symbolism of earlier Springsteen lyrics is always the way to freedom. Now, it's only a road.

And in the title song of the album, the singer realizes how difficult married love is: It ought to be easy when a woman and a man fall in love, but they live in a haunted house and the ride in the tunnel of love is rough, rough, rough.

In all these songs, the singer discovers the tragedy of life in the conflict between the two men that Saint Paul described nineteen hundred years ago. Tragedy, however, is not pessimism, not despair. It's still possible to fight back. Possible, but not easy. Love dies. When it goes, it's gone. When you're alone, you "ain't nothing but alone."

Despite his "Brilliant Disguise," the singer knows "in the wee hours" that he is not the good husband he swore to be at the altar but a harsh doubter whose bed is cold. He invokes God's mercy on the man who doubts that of which he ought to be sure. And he knows he's a fool. He may have all the riches in the world, but he lacks his beloved—he "Ain't Got You."

If Springsteen left us there, the charge of despair might be appropriate. Theologically, he might well be characterized as a Manichee, one who believes that human love is perverse and evil. But he does not stop either at sin or the difficulty in fighting sin. He sings of renewal, using each time the Easter/Baptismal renewal symbols of light or flowing water, usually both of them.

In the song "Spare Parts," a young mother deserted on her

wedding day by her child's father bemoans her fate: she is young and misses the party lights. She hears of a woman who has put her baby in the river "and let the river roll on." She is tempted to do the same, so she kneels before his crib where she "cried till she prayed."

Then, despite her prayer, Janey brings her son to the river. As in every case where he sings of hope, Springsteen becomes poetic: Waist deep in the running water, with the sun shining brightly above her, she lifts her son up to the sky and then carries him home. She lays him in his bed, takes her wedding dress and ring to the pawn shop and returns home with good cold cash.

The young mother holding her son in the waters of the river under the bright sun and then lifting him up and carrying him home, now sanctified for life, is surely a baptismal image. How could it be anything else? Could someone not raised in the traditions of blessed light and holy water, not exposed as a child to the light and water of Easter, have produced such a scene?

Sure.

But the point here is that Bruce Springsteen did acquire this imagery in his Catholic childhood. Even if he is not aware of the Catholic symbolisms of light and water (and I suspect that he may know what he is doing but not quite know that he knows), he is using in Catholic fashion these profoundly Catholic symbols of his youth: he is using light and waters as symbols of rebirth.

Billy doesn't desert his wife. Knowing that he'll always be caught between fear and love, he returns to his marriage bed and brushes the hair from his sleeping wife's face, which the moon has turned white. Her glowing face fills the room with the beauty of God's fallen light.

The light now becomes quite explicitly God's light—it is a sacrament, a hint of a power that, together with his wife's beauty, enables him to fight his fear.

And the singer who knows that he has two faces will not give up his woman. He defies the evil man he would not be. He won't deprive the singer of his love. Let him go ahead and try!

Why such confidence? The most "liturgical" of all the songs in "Tunnel of Love" mentions a saint—"Valentine's Day," the Catholic feast (abandoned by our own prudish liturgical purists) of the renewal of romantic love.

The singer is driving home, pondering the truth that in independence there is freedom, reveling in the excitement of the road. Yet he has just spoken to a friend of his who has become a father. The friend's voice sounds like the light of the skies and the rivers and the timber wolf in the pines. Maybe, the singer admits, he travels fastest who travels alone, but tonight, as the big car rushes down the highway, he misses his girl and he misses his home. Now that might not be quite your man Seamus Heaney, but it's not bad poetry either. And it also has light and flowing waters.

In the final verses of the song—and of the album—Springsteen closes the circle of sacramentality: light (God's light again) and the river and the bride and God become one, an irresistible symbol and story of the rebirth and renewal of life and love.

He wakes up from a nightmare and finds God's light has come shining on him. He's scared and terrified and also born anew. The water rushing over him isn't the cold river bottom; the wind rushing through his arms isn't the bitterness of a dream that didn't come true. No, the wind and the water and the light is you. So he quietly asks her to be his valentine. If that's despair, I'm the Dalai Lama.

Are these songs the story of Springsteen's marriage? Such a question is none of our business. An artist creates out of his experiences and does not necessarily describe them autobiographically. Surely the new maturity, the new sense of tragedy, and the new feeling of light and water and rebirth and hope in human love must come out of his experience of marriage, encoded in the fictional narratives of his lyrics. To leave no doubt, the last words on the jacket are "thanks, Juli."

Rock critic Steve Perry notes that throughout his career,

Springsteen has been obsessed with the themes of community (which is what one would expect from a person steeped in the Catholic imagination). On the one hand, he laments the death of his communities of origin, and on the other, he strains for the freedom of the river and the road. The advantage of such a position is that one can combine nostalgia with freedom from intimacy. Now, in marriage, he finds that he has created a new community of his own with its demands and its frustrations and its disappointments. He can still escape from it to the road. He can still flee from complexity and intimacy and human frailty to the power of the high-speed car.

Only mostly he doesn't want to, not for long, because it is at home with the beloved that one finds healing water and God's holy light. And the Valentine.

Is Juli the Valentine? Well, again that's none of our business. But if she is, she has much of which to be proud.

The piety of these songs—and I challenge you to find a better word—is sentiment without being sentimental, an Italian-American, male piety not unlike that to be found in some of the films of Martin Scorsese (especially *Mean Streets*). It is not perhaps Sunday Mass piety, but it is, if anything, much richer and deeper and more powerful. It is the piety of symbol rather than doctrine.

Most of the Rock critics, by the way, admit that in terms of lyrics, music, and singing technique, "Tunnel" is the most important stride in Springsteen's career. Marriage can do that for you.

In a conversation reported in the May 5, 1988 issue of *Rolling Stone* Springsteen confirms this interpretation of "Tunnel:"

I wanted to make a record about what I felt, about really letting another person in your life and trying to be a part of someone else's life. That's a frightening thing, something that's always filled with shadows and doubts and also wonderful things and beautiful things.

. . . . I don't believe that you find something and there it is and that's the end of the story. You have to find the strength to sustain it and build on it and work for it and constantly pour energy into it . . . . You gotta write that new song every day.

I have no desire to claim Springsteen as Catholic in the way we used to claim movie actors and sports heroes. I merely observe that this is (not utterly unique) Catholic imagery on the lips of a troubadour whose origins and present identification are Catholic. I also observe that the Catholic origin of the imagery serves to explain them. I finally observe that the critics seem to pay no attention to the images, perhaps because without a Catholic perspective you have a hard time understanding where they come from and what they mean.

(It is the same implicit but rich liturgical piety that is to be found in the stories of Louise Erdrich.)

So if the troubadour's symbols are only implicitly Catholic (and perhaps not altogether consciously so) and if many folks won't understand them or perceive their origins, what good are they to the Catholic Church?

Surely they won't increase Sunday collections or win converts or improve the Church's public image. Or win consent to the Pastoral on Poverty.

But those are only issues if you assume that people exist to serve the Church. If, on the other hand, you assume that the Church exists to serve people by bringing a message of hope and renewal, of light and water and rebirth, to a world steeped in tragedy and sin, then you rejoice that such a troubadour sings songs that maybe even he doesn't know are Catholic.

(Note: as this chapter is being prepared for publication, there are press reports that Springsteen's marriage has broken up. This personal tragedy does not weaken the singer's message; it merely indicates how difficult it is to live up to the vision in the message.)

14

Ronstadt and Mellencamp: The Search for Roots

The air in Centennial Hall was tense with expectation; a current of restlessness swept back and forth among the well-dressed Mexican Americans who were at least half the audience. But it was not an anxious electricity nor an angry one. On the contrary, the anticipation of *Los Tucsonenses* was joyous. One of their own was coming back to perform in the University's hall—not only a third-generation Tucsonan who had made good in the big world but now someone to sing *their* own songs, the songs her father taught her.

And she was to *sing* their songs in the heart of a University that, for all its recent good will and honest effort, has never been able to relate to the Mexican-American middle class that has been in Tucson much longer than the century-old University.

Then the show began, "a romantic evening in old Mexico" with the Mariachi Vargas; the Ballet Folklorico de la Fonda; and their darling, Linda Ronstadt, a shy, almost frail woman with an enormous voice. *Los Tucsonenses* cheered wildly after each number. When her father, Gilbert Ronstadt, walking with the help of a cane, joined her on the stage, they all rose in respect to one of their heroes. So did the rest of us.

We *Anglos* (an appellation bitterly resented by the Celt in me, but, for the moment, let it pass) cheered with them, profoundly moved by the music and by the enthusiasm of the Mexican Americans. It was a special night for Tucson and perhaps for the whole country. Linda Ronstadt's search for her roots had offered to the rest of the country a slice of the wonders of Mexican-American culture. The success of her tour and her record *"Canciones di mio Padre"* indicated that the rest of the country was interested. Mexican Americans were no longer perceived merely as a social problem; they were now *seen as* what every ethnic group in fact is: a cultural resource.

Frederico Ronstadt, son of a German engineer who had migrated to Mexico, came to Tucson in the eighteen eighties. A successful businessman, he was involved in both politics and music. He and his brother founded the *Club Filharmonico*— which *Tucsonenses* will tell you was the first symphony orchestra in the city. His daughter Luisa was a popular singer in the Mexican-American community. The family has kept the traditions alive. His grandson Pete is the chief of police, and his granddaughter is probably the most successful and certainly the most durable and most gifted woman Rock singer of her era.

To reach that success, however, she had to leave behind Tucson and her Mexican-American heritage (though, be it noted, never in opposition to her family, who always supported her). Moreover, as one pieces together from interviews and profiles the story of her life during the two decades after she left Tucson, one is appalled at the physical and emotional toll the Rock music circuit takes from the lives of its celebrities, especially if they are women. Must a person go through such alienation and privation to be a success in American popular music? Is it necessary to leave home?

For Linda Ronstadt it surely was. There was no room for her in the Tucson of twenty years ago. Even though she attended

SS. Peter and Paul grade school and her family was close to Bishop Francis Green (to whom Fred Ronstadt left his flute), sixteen-year-old Linda was expelled by the pastor of her parish from a parish high club dance for playing Rock music. It was pagan, evil music, he told her. Once again the Church missed a chance to embrace one of its gifted children.

Is it possible to "go home again"? John Cougar Mellencamp (about whom more shortly) argues that it is. When asked why he lives in Indiana near his home town of Seymour, he replies that he doesn't want to live anywhere else.

For Linda Ronstadt, a permanent return to the Tucson of her youth may be impossible, in part because that Tucson has been overwhelmed by waves of Anglo immigrants and doesn't exist anymore. But in Canciones, she does return to her musical roots and shares them with the rest of the country. At the level of symbol and story, if not of literal history, she has already gone home again.

Theologically, *Canciones* imposes on us two subjects for reflection—the celebratory nature of the Mexican-American world view and the inescapable importance of roots in our life. I shall attend to the first here and postpone the second until after a consideration of the Hoosier music of John Mellencamp.

Ask a literate *Tucsonensis* about Mexican-American religion and s/he will tell you about festivals—birthdays, baptisms, name days, rites of passage. The calendar, you will learn, is very important because you need to have available a list of which saints are being honored every week so that you can send presents to those who bear the names of the saints. Press a Mexican American about what all this means and you are likely to hear about yet more festivals and parties. Indeed, you will probably have to ask three or four times before it dawns on your respondent that you are interested in content and not form.

One of my graduate students gave the perfect answer: "Well, I suppose it means that we believe that God is part of our family and that he comes and joins us in all our festivals and celebrates with us like a member of the family."

Then she added, "Of course we don't know all the rules like you Irish do. That's why my children are in Peter and Paul school, so they can learn the rules and grow up to be good American Catholics just like the Irish children."

SS. Peter and Paul, you will remember, is the parish that ejected Linda Ronstadt for playing Rock music. At the time my student spoke those words, the same man was pastor.

I did not plead that there was a time when the Irish knew how to celebrate too. I merely said that the exchange ought to be in both directions and that the Irish could learn from the Tucsonenses the festivity of the Catholic tradition.

I did not even add, for which I expect points from the recording angel, that the pastor of SS. Peter and Paul might especially benefit from a little joy and celebration in his rigid, punitive, shanty-Irish life.

Linda Ronstadt's *Canciones* are almost all love songs, many of them, Tucsonenses will tell you, sad and melancholy songs. But the Mexican-American culture resolutely refuses to permit melancholy to triumph. With the Mariachi Vargas playing enthusiastically in the background, joy exorcises the melancholy themes every time. Joy—and faith—are victorious even in the beautiful and poignant *Dos Arbolitos* in which the singer observes sadly that the two trees are inseparable companions but that s/he has no companion. Sitting under the tree at the end of a tiring day, the singer is going to ask God, who makes companions even for the trees, to send a human companion.

It is the resolute joy of her songs, rather than explicit reference to God which makes them theologically important. In a fascinating interview reported in American Airlines in-flight magazine, however, she shows that she is quite self conscious about the religious function of her music:

"But *joy*," said Linda Ronstadt, "is a combination of despair, fear, fatalism, anger, triumph — it's all those things. You know Joseph Campbell, author of

Hero With a Thousand Faces? He was a very good friend of mine, the neatest man I've ever known. He said to me once, 'Life is basically intolerable.' He said music is the only way we have of dealing with and music is myth. Music is oral dream. It's a way of triumphing over despair. The Catholics [she is one] say, 'life is a vale of tears. Help me here in this vale of tears.' It's a myth. The metaphor of life is the vale of tears. So . . . "

She broke into a glorious grin. ". . . if you can triumph over it, that's cause for joy. This music has got that in it. It's mythology. It's a triumph over a situation that is basically intolerable."

Even at their most melancholy, they are joyous. For the Celts, the opposite might be true: even at our most joyous we sound melancholy.

Those priests and religious who are engaged in "Hispanic work" are often immune to this rich dimension of Mexican-American culture. Indeed the "Hispanic Caucus" of clergy and religious that has appeared in many large dioceses (made up almost entirely, be it noted, of people with Celtic and not Hispanic names) often are the most joyless collection of celebrants that one could possibly imagine. They have "iden-tified" with the Mexican Americans often to impose on them their own political agenda and are outside redeemers who have come to save and not to listen and learn.

They should be made to listen to Linda Ronstadt's *Canciones* every day and thus perhaps to come to understand that festival and celebration are essential to the Catholic tradition. The Mexican Americans have it and we don't. We must learn joy from them, much more than they must learn political strategy (not to say "liberation") from us.

I'm not saying that the cause of political and social justice is invalid. On the contrary, Mexican Americans have been cheated and continue to be cheated. I am saying, rather, that those who align themselves with *La Raza* will only be exploiters and manipulators themselves (no better in their own way than the pastor of SS. Peter and Paul) until they are ready to learn as well as to teach.

You won't find much joy in John (Cougar) Mellencamp and his return to his small town, Hoosier roots. You encounter, rather, in his most recent music, especially the two albums *Scarecrow* and *The Lonesome Jubilee*, resignation and acceptance. If Linda Ronstadt represents the Catholic imagination (that which David Tracy calls "analogical," the awareness of God everywhere), John Mellencamp represents the Protestant imagination (the dialectical imagination in Tracy's terms which emphasizes the emptiness of creation). While he may not yet attend the Church of the Nazarene regularly as his family did, Mellencamp's search for roots—or more precisely his acceptance of the roots he never really left—requires the absorption of the stern Protestant theology of his own tradition.

His return also involves the rediscovery of such traditional Hoosier instruments as the penny whistle, the mandolin, the banjo, and the dulcimer—to his work what the mariachi are to Linda Ronstadt.

His acceptance of the "dialectical imagination" is never more clearly stated than in the quote from *Ecclesiastes* on the jacket of *Scarecrow*:

> There is nothing more sad or glorious than generations changing hands. Generations come and go but it makes no difference. Everything is unutterably weary and tiresome. No matter how much we see, we are never satisfied . . . So I saw that there is nothing better for men than that they should be happy in their work for that is what they are here for, and no one can bring them back to life to enjoy what will be in the future, so let them enjoy it now.

What must one do in the face of that grim news? How does one cope with the sad truth that like "Jack and Diane" most of us are doomed to loss and frustration?

"You realize that this is pretty boring shit here. This is what we all do. So once you realize that life is boring, then you can really deal with it, and you can make the best of it."

You live with the truth that "family and friends are the best things I've known"; you celebrate the small town in which you and your wife and kids live, the memories of the simple years of your teens (and a dance hall called the Cherry Bomb), and the ordinary events and responsibilities of life which provide us humans with dignity and honor. You realize that life is like "paper in the fire," doomed to turn brown and blow away, but still you also understand that, just as at a fast-food joint you can choose between "hotdogs and hamburgers," you have a choice in life between "right and wrong," between "giving in or holding on."

And make no mistake about it, "holding on" is a difficult task. The most you can hope for is that you do it more often than not.

Like Bruce Springsteen, to whom he has often been compared, Mellencamp is painfully aware of human sinfulness. He also is much less hopeful about our capacity to overcome it.

Mellencamp's return to Hoosier, Protestant roots came quickly. His anarchist period of rebellion did not last long. While he still swaggers and still revels in foul language and still sounds angry some of the time, his world view has shifted to that of a small town, German Hoosier Protestant—which is what he always was, just as Springsteen always was an Italian Catholic from Jersey and Ronstadt a Mexican-American Tucsonan (with German roots on her father's side and Dutch and Irish on her mother's).

All three have come, each in their own way, to appreciate both the value of roots and their inescapability. Ronstadt laments publicly that when she was growing up, bilingual education was unthinkable, so she never really learned the language of her father's songs. Mellencamp likes the Atlantic and Pacific coasts, but what really matters are the family and friends, the people with whom he grew up in Hoosierland. Springsteen laments for the lost communities of the past (more poignantly than the other two) and agonizes over the new communities he is trying to build.

Mellencamp's Hoosier world may not be yours. (It surely isn't mine!) Ronstadt's Tucsonan world may be one you find attractive. (I certainly do!) Springsteen's Jersey may remind you of folks down the street in the neighborhood in which you grew up. (It does so remind me.) The point to be learned from their return to roots is not that one should want the world that they seek, each in their own way, to re-create. Rather, the lesson of their most recent music is that whether you can go home again is hardly the question.

The issue, rather, is whether you can ever really escape from the culture that formed you and indeed whether you should even try. If Rock singers, among the most alienated people in America because of the nature of their lives and work, are forced in the middle years of their life to make peace with their past, then who can escape that difficult, poignant, pleasurable, and agonizing peace initiative?

Elite American culture assumes that roots are not really important (for all the hoopla about the black quest for roots). The universities and the national media both take for granted the necessity and the virtue of alienation. Indeed elite university faculty members often assume that one of their sacred roles is to wrench young people out of their roots, to deracinate them and alienate them from their families, their local communities, and their heritages.

(They usually don't succeed but not for want of trying.)

The Catholic Church, which because of its sacramental sensibility has a vested interest in localism and sacred places, is so preoccupied with distant and mostly empty concerns about which it can do very little (the "third world") that it does not celebrate anymore its neighborhoods, local communities, and ethnic roots (I was the only cleric at the Ronstadt concert in Centennial Hall). Rather, it agrees with the assumption of the cultural elites that the human person is infinitely mobile and can be picked up and placed anywhere in the world with little pain or cost.

Physically, we can be moved anywhere (though the rhythms of our many body clocks will protest). Psychologically and religiously, however, mobility extorts an enormous price on the personality and its relationships. It is possible but not good for humans to live at great spatial distances from their origins.

For many of those who have left home, it is impossible to go back, if only because home might not be there anymore (destroyed by expressways, urban renewal, housing projects, or resegregation). But it is adolescent to remain fixated in rebellion against the energies and perspectives which have shaped you. To go home again emotionally and spiritually is essential for adult maturity. One must make peace with one's origins, one's family, one's culture, one's religious imagery. To a very considerable extent, what one is has resulted from the these dynamisms. To make peace with them is to make peace with the self.

By making peace, I do not mean an uncritical acceptance of the childhood and adolescent influences in one's life. Rather, I mean that the adult comes to terms with both the good and the bad, both the right and the wrong, both the limiting and liberating aspects of one's origins—and hence of one's self.

You might bitterly resent the fact that you have been shaped by West Side Chicago Irish Catholicism (in which case you would be a fool, but for the sake of the argument I yield the right to such resentment). But for weal or woe, that's what you are and always will be. In Paul Ricoeur's word, the second naivete is a critical acceptance of what is both good and bad in that heritage, a rueful acknowledgement of what might be bad and a celebration of what is good.

That's what adults do.

The elite society thinks that such critical but sympathetic reexamination of one's origins is both unnecessary and wrong (unless perchance you are a member of one of the fashionable social groups—which middle-class Mexican Americans, German Hoosiers, Italians from Jersey, and West Side Irish Catholics are certainly not). Elite society is wrong. The music of Ronstadt, Springsteen, and Mellencamp tells us how wrong.

Popular culture both shapes society and is shaped by it. The roots-seeking Rock musicians are reflecting a broad cultural discontent as well as articulating and shaping it. If one reads the literature and listens to the music of the two singers discussed in this chapter (and Springsteen), one is almost overwhelmed by their passion for roots. They express one of the most desperate yearnings of modern humankind, a religious and human need which cannot long be denied.

One puts aside the tapes and the compact disks, the articles and the interviews, and wonders how long elite society can continue to pretend that such needs do not exist or are "conservative" and hence can be safely ignored or dismissed as "nostalgia."

And one also wonders how long the Catholic Church and its official theologians (of the right or the left) can continue to be indifferent to the hungers of humankind for responses that it is uniquely equipped to offer.

Probably for a long, long time.

15

Desperately Seeking Madonna

Hard line Feminists don't much like Madonna Louise Veronica Ciccone, the upper-middle-class, Italian-American woman from Pontiac, Michigan, who is—at the present writing—the most popular Rock performer in the world.

A Feminist columnist has called her a slut. Others have said that she has set the cause of women back thirty years. Still others have condemned the "pro life" stance of her song "Papa Don't Preach," in which the singer rejects an abortion for her unborn child. (The pro-life side did not rally to her support because they probably think she's a slut too; and anyway, those folks don't listen to rock music.)

Madonna herself is not sure about Feminism. As she said in an interview with Mikal Gilmore in *Rolling Stone* magazine:

> To call me an antifeminist is ludicrous. Some people have said that I'm setting women back 30 years. Well, I think in the '50s women weren't ashamed of their bodies. I think they luxuriated in their sexuality and in being strong in their femininity. I think that is better than hiding it and saying, "I'm strong, I'm just like a man." Women aren't like men. They can do things men can't do.

It is an answer that one would expect from a woman who attended Catholic grammar schools, never takes more than two drinks at a time, does not use drugs, was a virgin longer than most, and proposes to raise a family. It is, nonetheless, a feminist answer (note the small "f") and one that appeals to the teen-age women in her audience because it is their answer too.

As Madonna herself puts it, she is telling young women that they can be sexy and still be strong and in control of their lives: "I'm an implicit feminist."

> Those people are afraid of their own sexuality. I like the fact that men appreciate my voluptuous body. But that doesn't mean I would be subservient. I stand for the things feminists stand for because I do what I want to do and I'm in control of my own life and I'm very happy.

But, young woman, don't you understand that no self-respecting, Hard line Feminist wants men to appreciate her voluptuous body?

> I think that women who are strong or women who wanted to be strong or be respected were taught this thing that they had to behave like men or not be sexy or feminine or something and I think it pissed them off that I was doing that. Also I think that for the most part men have always been the aggressors sexually. Through time immemorial they have always been in control. So I think sex is equated with power in a way and that's scary in a way. It's scary for men that women would have that power and I think it's scary for women to have that power—or to have that power and be sexy at the same time.

A better one-paragraph description of the contemporary situation of men and women you'll not find.

Madonna is a powerful spokesperson for the only kind of feminism that has a chance of winning widespread support among the young women who listen to her music—the feminism of having it both ways.

Men complain to me often that "women want to have it both ways. They want the rights of men and the privileges of women."

Me: It's always been that way in my ethnic group.

Men: They can't have it both ways.

Me: Yes they can. And they will. Men have had it both

ways for a long time. Now women want it both ways, too. That's what feminism means.

That's what Madonna, called not inaccurately by *Time* an outrageous blend of Little Orphan Annie, Margaret Thatcher and May West, is about: she demands for women, especially for young women, the right to be what their bodies demand of them—simultaneously virgin and siren.

Or to state the case in explicitly Catholic terms, Madonna is arguing in her songs and in her public persona for both the unity of human nature and the equality and diversity of the human genders.

Three cautionary comments are in order:

1) Much of Madonna's performance is a comic put-on. Thus the song "Material Girl" is greeted with laughter by the teen-age girls who listen to it. The present writer, an aging cleric, laughs at it too; it is clearly meant to be funny. A lot of "grown ups" don't get the joke, quite possibly because they are parents and do not remember what they were like when they were teens. Any responsible search for grace in Madonna's songs, however, must begin with the understanding that JudyHoliday is her great heroine and that Madonna is comedienne (as is God). If her film *Desperately Seeking Susan* does not prove that, then nothing can. When you can't laugh at and with this outrageous but funny young woman, you cannot even begin to understand either her or her appeal: "If people don't get the humor in me or my act, they then don't want to get it. If ten-year olds can get it and laugh, then surely an adult can."

Not necessarily, Madonna; an adult who has trapped herself into the role of disapproving parent can't possibly get it.

A typical example of her humor: at the end of "Papa Don't Preach" (a song which pleas for understanding and does not confront Papa, who may, according to one Madonna interpretation, stand for Il Papa — John Paul II), an offstage voice cries out, "Madonna, Get off that Stage!" Once, when her father, to whom she is quite close, was at a concert, she persuaded him to come out on the stage and drag her off—causing great hilarity to the two of them and to the audience when it discovered that he was really her father.

2) To find grace in a popular artist does not oblige one to accept all the paraphernalia of the artist's style. The multicolored assortment of lingerie which Madonna affects—early in her career with a crucifix thrust in the top of a camisole or bra—may seem offensive to many, especially to those who don't like to see God linked with sex. This is an issue, I would submit, of taste and not of either morality or religion. I don't find it particularly offensive. In fact, possessing the usual amount (and perhaps more than the usual amount) of male hormones, I find Madonna in a black corset attractive (or at least "cute"), indeed more attractive than the usual Las Vegas performer because she always manages to keep a touch of her primal innocence in such array. Those who find this dimension of her show offensive must bracket it if they wish to search for an underlying message that might be graceful.

3) The innocent, waif-like aspect of Madonna's style cannot be ignored. If you are so obsessed by the sexy clothes and gyrations and facial expressions that you miss this innocence, then you cannot understand either her appeal or her message.

Let me state the heart of my argument this way: Happy is the woman who can be both wanton and modest; a great blessing is she for herself and for her man. Happy is the woman who can be both wench and virgin, both sensual and vulnerable, both experienced and innocent; a great blessing is she for herself and her man. Such is the nature of integrated womanly sexuality: the biological programming of a woman inclines her to be both (without determining her behavior) modest and wanton.

Indeed such is the nature of human sexuality; the two sentences above would be just as true if the genders were changed. But in this essay we are talking about the sexuality of a woman as portrayed by a woman artist.

Rock music, as I have indicated previously, is protest

music. Madonna's protest—profoundly feminist in its convictions and implications—is against the bifurcation of womanly eroticism. The world tells young women (as it undoubtedly told little Madonna Ciccone) that you must be either a virgin or a slut, either naive or knowing, either a "good girl" or a "bad girl." The organism of a young woman tells her powerfully that such worldly wisdom (in Madonna's case as in the case of so many others promulgated with fierce determination by Catholic school teachers) is wrong, that her body is designed to be both inviting and cautious, that she is biologically programmed to both attract men and keep them at a distance.

Hard line Feminists find this biological fact profoundly offensive. Sexual attractiveness is a dirty trick God or evolution or someone has played on women. In the world of the Hard line Feminist the models of human relationships are same-sex intimacies.

Whatever the ideologies say, such a line will never sell among ordinary men and women. Anyone who associates with teen-age women knows that they alternate between siren and nun. (Of course Madonna wanted at one time to be a nun. She went to a Catholic school, didn't she?) Such alternation is a natural part of the maturation process as a young woman discovers and comes to terms with her sexual potentialities. Madonna's stand, profoundly if perhaps only implicitly Catholic, is that both dimensions of a (young) woman's sexuality are good and that in a mature, self-possessed woman, they can and indeed must be integrated.

> People have this idea that if you're sexual and beautiful and provocative, then there's nothing else you could possibly offer. People have always had that image about women. And while it might have seemed like I was behaving in a stereotypical way, at the same time I was also masterminding it. I was in control of everything I was doing and I think when people realized that, it confused them. It's not like I was saying "Don't pay attention to the clothes— to the lingerie—I'm wearing." Actually the fact that I was wearing those clothes was meant to drive the point that you can be sexy and strong at the same time.

Which is what every teen-age woman wants to be. Every woman, indeed.

The argument for this interpretation of Madonna can be made from her most popular song, "Like a Virgin." The singer, beat and incomplete, has made it through her wilderness but did not realize how lost she was, how sad and blue, until the touch of a lover made her feel "shiny and new"; he touched her like she was a virgin and suddenly she felt that she was a virgin again. His respect and affection healed and renewed her.

It's very difficult for me to see how those lyrics can be misunderstood. A woman who is no longer a virgin physically encounters a man who treats her with so much affection and respect that it seems like she is a virgin emotionally. She is not a used-up, discarded thing but rather someone shiny and new.

It seems evident that we are hearing the timeless cry of the human heart for renewal. Is not the gentle care with which the singer's lover treats her the way God alleges that He treats us? Is He not the lover Hosea of the Jewish scriptures? Is He not the gentle and relentlessly pursuing Hound of Heaven? Does not the song repeat the traditional Catholic teaching that spiritual virginity is important, not physical virginity?

Does not every woman wish that, no matter how many times she has experienced sexual intercourse, this particular night her man will treat her as someone shiny and new and surprising and wonderful? Does not every man wish the same thing? Does not the song repeat the traditional Catholic teaching that human passion is the sacrament of Divine passion, that the most gentle and tender of human lovers is a hint of what God is like?

Why don't we Catholics celebrate this brilliant catechetical presentation? Beats me. Maybe the lingerie gets in the way. Listen to Madonna on the subject:

> At first, I mean, I was surprised with how people reacted to "Like a Virgin," because when I did the song, to me, I was singing about how something made me feel a certain way—brand new and fresh—and everyone else interpreted it as "I don't want to be a virgin anymore. Fuck my brains out!" That's not what I sang at all.

Indeed not. She sang about a sacramental experience (without calling it that) and watched in dismay as it was distorted beyond recognition.

To the prurient, all things are prurient.

Madonna again: "People thought I was saying I just wanted to have sex, when it meant just the opposite. It celebrates the idea of feeling the opposite. It celebrates the idea of feeling untouched and pure. I like having the secret knowledge that what it said was good."

Ah, say the murmurers, but have you seen the videotape? Yeah, she says she feels like a virgin again, but that's a pretty sexy tape! And the wedding dress she wears may be white, but it's a pretty sexy wedding dress. Doesn't that negate everything the lyrics say?

Only if feeling like a virgin in the presence of your lover is not and ought not to be an overwhelmingly sexy experience. But in fact, is not the experience of being a vulnerable, shiny, brand-new person in the presence of a gentle and masterful lover a powerful erotic fantasy and, when it happens, a devastating erotic reality?

Isn't this the way we are in the presence of God?

Wedding white is not designed to be sexy? Who you trying to kid?

And if you think the wedding dress on the cover of "Like A Virgin" (with the crucifix between the bride's breasts) is dirty, then you should complain to God about Her bad taste in designing women in general and brides in particular.

(The womanly breast is a masterpiece of design for which puritans will never forgive God, especially Catholic puritans.)

The Catholic imagination, the analogical imagination, says God is like creation, not radically different from it. It says that the human body is beautiful, that human eroticism is good, that human beauty and human passion are a hint of God's love. It sees no contradiction in the presence of a crucifix between two shapely (and quite adequately covered) breasts. It does not say "either virgin or siren"; it says, rather, "both virgin and siren" because it understands that such is the way God designed the human species.

Those aspects of the Madonna persona which the dialectical imagination thinks are opposed, the Catholic imagination sees as different aspects of the same integrated reality.

In a sensitive and perceptive article in the *New Republic*, Professor Joel D. Schwartz argues that on the one hand, Madonna is a sweet-sixteen Connie Francis with old-fashioned, hand-holding romance. On the other hand, she is also a hard-driving rock singer with an image of vulgar sexuality with "her penchant for blurring the distinction between clothes and underwear."

"On the concert stage the tension is unmistakable. Is the message of recovered purity and chastity just a kinky put-on, as her lurid squeals and raunchy dances would imply or is it genuine?"

Professor Schwartz notes that neither Debbie Boone nor Tina Turner could perform "Like a Virgin" but only a performer who is an amalgam of the two. Only a performer who in the depths of her personality imagines it is possible to be both? Only a performer who, surely without realizing it, possesses the analogical imagination? In Schwartz's words:

> Everyone seems to agree that there is something puzzling and inscrutable about Madonna and it is this quality that goes a long way toward explaining her cult appeal. My suggestion is that much of this is owed to an ironic dialogue that she half-consciously creates between two visions of human potential which are deeply rooted in American popular culture. What is the "real" American self struggling for survival in contemporary society? Is it Pat Boone or Little Richard? Karen Carpenter or Janis Joplin?

Such questions are perfect expressions of the "either/or" paradigm of the dialectical imagination. The almost automatic Catholic (analogical response) is to demand why both can't be real.

> One unmistakable message that is transmitted to the audience is that there is an intense and necessary complicity—between these two utopian

visions. Virtue would lose its pristine luster if there were no vice to overcome and the libido would quickly lose its prurient appeal if there were no rigid moral code to defy. The saint and the sinner nourish one another . . . By internalizing both innocence and license within the same persona and by turning them on like faucets, Madonna suggests that they too are mere appearance, mere affectations . . .

Or perhaps different aspects of the same ingeniously created reality? Why must the opposite of innocence be license? Why is the libido equated with the sinner? Why is the luster of the moral code equated with the denial of eroticism?

Would not the married woman saint be sexually wanton with her husband?

And vice versa?

Cannot a woman (or a man) be innocent and wanton at the same time? No, put the claim of the analogical imagination more strongly, is not the nature of human nature such that, at its perfection, human sexuality is simultaneously innocent and wanton? Is it not at such a time that human eroticism is most sacramental?

The analogical imagination denies the validity of Professor Schwartz's neatly stated dilemmas and understands what Madonna is about.

Is not innocence powerfully erotic? Are not chastity and wantonness correlatives? What is more pleasurable than calling forth the wantonness that lurks in the most chaste of partners? Is there anything that is more fun than falling in love again with and then seducing anew the familiar mate? Is not the best of sexual partners both fire and ice? Both passive and aggressive? Both fragile and strong?

If the human experience is analogical in the sense that it combines both sets of characteristics, why is it necessary to oppose them intellectually? Why say "either/or" when our experience tells us that really it is "both/and"?

Does not the teen-age woman, listening to her newly discovered woman's body, who wants to be both a siren and a virgin, understand the nature of sexual reality better than the professors and critics and theologians who try to oppose the two realities?

Some women complain that they are expected to be both wife and mistress. Despite the difficulties of combining the two roles, would they, in fact, really want to choose one or the other?

(And *mutatis mutandis,* cannot the same be said for men? Sure it's hard to be both the protector and the seducer, but isn't that better than being one or the other or neither?)

Is it not a grave weakness of the contemporary official Catholic approach to marriage that it does not encourage more wantonness between married lovers? More crucifixes between lace-covered breasts?

Madonna is the perfect test case for whether we really accept the analogical imagination. I suspect none of the other essays in this series will so offend "official" Catholic reviewers as this one. The paraphernalia of the Madonna persona has blinded them to the message behind the mask.

Yet she is one of us—still identifies as Catholic, still praises the strength and backbone Catholicism provides, still carries a rosary even if she doesn't say it much.

She is one of our own who is preaching effectively a component of our tradition of which we are afraid—the sacramentality of human eroticism. Instead of celebrating her, we ignore her or condemn her. The problem is not with Madonna nor with the analogical imagination but with us, with our blind, rigid, prudish paradigms that cannot and will not distinguish between taste and morality, our approach to reality in which propriety is more important than parable.

And what will happen to Madonna Louise Veronica Ciccone from Pontiac, Michigan? She is a tough, resilient, shrewd, ambitious, Italian-American woman. We should know her well because she is to be found in most of our parishes. Will she survive the celebrity challenge? It won't be easy because those whom the media make, they strive to destroy.

She surely won't get any help from her Church.

But she is too tough, too smart, I think, to be destroyed: "Marilyn Monroe was a victim and I'm not."

You'd better believe it.

It would be unwise to bet against her aging like her counterparts in our parish and being, at forty, the equivalent of the president of the woman's altar society (and a president who accepts no nonsense from the pastor).

I only hope that, at that age, she is not embarrassed by the message of the crucifix in her cleavage, as powerful a symbol of the analogical imagination as is currently available in popular culture.

16

Fantasy: the Modern Fairy Story

The fairy story is not dead. It lives on in the "Swords and Sorcery" subgenre of Fantasy, which in turn is a part of SF (Speculative Fiction as it is now called), and that, in its turn, is a division of Romance.

The brothers Grimm are alive and well and writing under such names as David Eddings and Stephen Donaldson. There is, however, a critical difference between the multivolume sagas of these Fantasy (I will use the term throughout this chapter, though strictly speaking, I am discussing the Swords and Sorcery sub-genre) writers and the older fairy stories. In the latter, magic worked automatically: if you had the power to cast spells, you cast them and that was that. Moreover, it was mostly luck that the hero and the heroine had the right spells available to them at the right time.

In the Fantasy sagas, sorcery is not automatic. It requires enormous effort of the will, must be used sparingly, and cannot be counted on to work perfectly all the time. In contemporary fairy stories, then, much more depends on the character, the effort, the sacrifice, and the determination of the wizard.

Hence the Fantasy sagas are almost always quest tales, variations on the legend, monumental struggles between good and evil. They are the purest of Romantic forms because their structure requires less of "reality" than do other varieties of romance. The Fantasy reader (unlike the critic who says the stories are implausible, an obvious but irrelevant comment) is willing to suspend his requirements for plausibility almost completely precisely because he knows he is plunging deeply into his own and the author's unconscious.

The Fantasy tale is the purest form of Romance. The adventures are the most violent, the loves the most passionate (though rarely described in detail), the quests the most arduous, the forces of good and evil most clearly delineated. Every Fantasy is a war in heaven and, as usual, good almost loses.

The world of Fantasy, then, is utterly unlike the world in which we live daily. It is the ultimate, if you will, in "unrealism." But it corresponds faithfully to the world of our imagination, the world of "what if," the world of "once upon a time, long, long ago" ("in a galaxy far, far away"). The Fantasy is not only pure Romance, it is pure story.

The story usually occurs in a medieval-like environment in which most, if not all, modern technology does not exist (either because it has not been developed or because it has been lost). People ride horses or walk; fight with swords and daggers; contend with a vast variety of dukes, princes, counts, kings, emperors, and other petty monarchs; sail in wooden boats; honor feudal commitments; and work magic.

Especially work magic—some of them in the service of Light and others in the service of darkness.

There are also, almost by definition, dragons. Good dragons, bad dragons, indifferent dragons, smart dragons, dumb dragons, clever dragons, stupid dragons.

Where did they come from?

Want to bet that if it wasn't for the St. George story, we

wouldn't have dragons in our Fantasy? Other monsters, even Cookie Monsters perhaps, but not dragons.

The St. George legend tells us a lot about the meaning of fantasy in the Western World and particularly about what cultural and religious influences have shaped it.

We have, of course, thrown St. George out of the calendar of saints for the totally prosaic reason that he might not have ever lived.

And certainly never slew a dragon, right?

Unlike the fairy story, however, contemporary Fantasy focuses on the internal development of the characters of the questers, particularly the protagonist. He suffers, he learns, he grows. He descends, in other words, before he is able to ascend; he tastes defeat before he is able to savor victory. He wins finally not because of his magic (though he needs the magic too) but because of the strength of his purified character.

Because the struggle between good and evil is so sharply drawn, the Fantasy is, willy-nilly, explicitly theological. Normally, however, the theology is, if not Manichaean, at least Zoroastrian: light and darkness, good and evil, are locked in a centuries-long battle. The forces of Evil—Torak in the *Belgariad* of Eddings, Lord Foul and Sunbane in the *Chronicles of Thomas Covenant the Unbeliever*—are equal to the forces of good until the very last minute. Moreover, since Fantasy readers like their favorite sagas to be repeated in follow-up sagas, Evil has a way of bouncing back for the beginning of the first volume of the next series.

Fantasy readers apparently demand multivolume sagas. The *Belgariad* required five volumes and now a sequel saga is in the works. The Covenant Chronicles run six volumes so far. I have lost track of how many volumes there are in Katherine Kurtz's *Deryni* chronicles or the Margaret Weis/Tracy Hickman *Dragon Lance* legend or in Anne McCaffrey's stunning *Dragonholds of Pern* chronicles. Individual volumes in each of the series are not so much read, I think, as gulped down like popcorn.

Fantasy reading is even more addictive than mystery reading;
Fantasy readers eagerly scout the paperback racks, waiting for
the latest volume in the series they are following, much like in
the old days we used to flock to the neighborhood movie theater
on Saturday afternoon to see what happened to Jungle Jim or the
Lone Ranger. Or like several generations of kids have rushed to
the TV every week to see what happens to the crew of the
Enterprise this week.

Pure escapist entertainment, you say, kid's stuff, no
relevance, trash?

Only if one has become so jaded that the little child's plea
"Mommy, PLEASE tell me a story" no longer vibrates in your soul.
And only if you no longer have the hunger for meaning in your
soul from which that wild cry of longing surges.

The Fantasy, as I have said, is pure story. But the best of
the contemporary Fantasy writers can be said to produce trash
only if everything not written by someone associated with the
New York Review of Books is trash.

Story, not character development, holds your attention in
the Fantasy sagas, but the writers are skilled professionals. The
plotting is adroit, the premises usually ingenious, the suspense
compelling, the characters believable, the descriptions often
brilliant, the atmosphere impressive.

Are they escapist? Of course they are. All cultural works
are escapist in some fashion. Are they entertainment? Certainly
they are entertainment; no one finally continues with a story that
is not entertaining. "Story," as I have said before, fascinates so
that it can illuminate, takes one out of one's own world and into
another world.

The difference between Fantasy and other forms of
"story" is that the fantasy world is utterly different from our
own—Romance drawn to its purest and most logical conclusion—and the fascination particularly intense. The difference
between a Fantasy addict and one who tosses the book away in
skeptical disgust is that the former is able to suspend his re-

quirements for plausibility more readily than the latter. The former is not more childish but more childlike than the latter.

There are two sets of theological implications of Fantasy, one, I think, to be found in the stories themselves and the other in our addiction to them.

The death and resurrection themes pervade Fantasy. The quester is almost always a Christ figure as well as Everyman. Sometimes, as in Donaldson's Covenant Chronicles, the protagonist must literally die to bring salvation to his world—and in the case of Thomas Covenant, leave his bride to continue his work. Only through suffering can the protagonist attain to new life. In the end it is the good man's character, not his magic, which triumphs over evil: the young Belgarion triumphs over the one-eyed God Torak (and wins the fair Ce Nedra, one of the all time great little bitches of Fantasy, albeit a young woman whose courage you are constrained to admire) not because he is more experienced or because he has better magic but because he is braver and better disciplined.

The cosmology of the Fantasies, no matter how convoluted and ingenious, almost always postulate an ultimate goodness beyond the gods who roam the stories. In the *Belgariad*, this goodness (Tillich's God beyond the gods?) sometimes impatiently whispers orders directly to Belgarion and even to Ce Nedra. The wizards may be condemned and rejected by the official religions, but they know that they serve a higher and better Goodness. There is irrationality, malice, blind evil, black magic in the fantasy world and terrible violence and death. But Goodness wins, just barely, but it still wins; and the quest, as for the Orb in the *Belgariad*, is for a pure symbol of Goodness.

Fantasies may indeed be among the purest literary output we have of the untrammeled imagination. Significantly, that imagination in the Western World today seems to be shaped by Catholic themes even if the storyteller and the reader are not explicitly aware of that fact. The theological content of Fantasy may not be particularly elaborate. It may not require a theologian of the first magnitude to analyze, but it's there and functioning more or less explicitly.

St. George and the Dragon written time and time again.

The more important theological observation is the resonance that the Fantasy genre excites in its readers—a hint that the writers of Fantasy may know more about the nature of human nature than the elite critics who ignore them or the supercilious academics who dismiss them (or the puritan clergy who dismiss such entertainment as a "waste of time").

If we are able to suspend our requirements for plausibility long enough to let our imagination flourish and frolic, then we display an imagination that passionately believes that the can be found, Love won, Evil turned back, Goodness obtained. Fantasy is one more proof that it is in the nature of human nature to hope.

In some sagas, Donaldson's and Barbara Hambly's *Darwath* Trilogy, for example, the protagonist is lifted out of the present world and carried off to another world, perhaps to return to our world when the work is done. This technique seems to me to be an explicit acknowledgement of the dreamlike nature of Fantasy. It begins in the dreams of the author and appeals to the daydreams of the reader. Pure romance, pure story, pure dream, pure meaning.

To daydream, we now know from psychology, is as natural and as necessary to human nature as to dream in our sleep. Fantasy, I contend, is of considerable theological interest because of what it reveals about the daydreams of modern, supposedly unreligious Western humankind. To criticize the daydream because it is not "real" or not "socially concerned" is to completely misunderstand the function of the daydream in human nature. To repress our fantasy dimension is, in effect, to try to pretend that we are not a blend of body and spirit, limited by our own finitude but still possessing a hunger for absolute goodness, perfect beauty, enduring love.

There is little moral complexity in Fantasy. Good is good and Evil is evil. There is temptation; indeed the appeal of the temptations is awesome, but there is no confusion between temptation and wisdom as there often is in life.

As Northrop Frye points out, "The popularity of romance, it is obvious, has much to do with its simplifying of moral facts. It relieves us from the strain of trying to be fair-minded, as we see particularly in melodrama where we not only have outright heroism and villainy but are expected to take sides, applauding one and hissing the other. . . . The lack of plausibility does not matter, because the formula holds the attention like a bright light or color."

One does not look to Romance, however, for moral paradigms but for a vision of the struggle between good and evil in the cosmos and in our own character. No child hearing a fairy story, no adult reading Thomas Covenant's adventures in "the Land" looks to find moral teaching in them. (When you get explicit moral or political teaching in Romance, as you do in the Travis McGee stories, you quickly become bored.) Romance, "story," Fantasy, are about meaning not morality; about descent into the pit of evil (and into the core of the self) and ascent from it; about finding, losing, and reclaiming true love; about death and resurrection. About religion, in other words, not about morality.

Those who write fantasy have more ready access to their own fantasies than the rest of us do. Those who are able to read it and to enjoy it also have considerable honest openness to the currents of their own imagination, currents of anger and passion, of fear and determination, of desire and frustration.

Everyone's imagination would like to choke goofy little Ce Nedra. And so too everyone's imagination would like to embrace and caress the flaky, sexy, gutsy little redhead.

And surely, when her baby is stolen, everyone wants to use all the powers, natural and magical, at his/her command in our fantasy world to find her kid and punish those who have stolen him. And then, perhaps, take her home to bed to produce yet more children.

And that's what Fantasy is all about.

Some Fantasy is poorly done. There is no obligation to like it or to read it, although there is perhaps an obligation not to ridicule those who do. And if we are Catholic, that is to say if we believe in saying "both/and" because we believe God lurks everywhere, we ought not to ignore either the revelation of the nature of human nature in its appeal or the revelation of the pervasiveness of Christian symbols in its content.

Fantasy is the purest continuation of fairy story and legend, St. George alive and well and living in your bookstore if not your church calendar. Odd, isn't it, that they have St. George and we don't. And they also have, one way or another, St. Valentine, the patron of romantic love, and we don't.

He was tossed out of the calendar too, if you remember.

The Church has given up story, and as I write this chapter, there are four Fantasies (five if you count Stephen King's *In the Eyes of the Dragon*) on the Times best-seller list. Theologians flee from story because stories are not true; they are unhistorical myths, not suited for modern secular man living in the secular city and searching for secular relevance. Modern secular man turns for illumination to Anne McCaffrey, Katherine Kurtz, Stephen Donaldson, and David Eddings. They have stories to tell, you see, and we don't. Moreover, their tales of Death and Resurrection, of descent and ascent, are clearly and patently our tales, which somehow we are afraid to tell.

The problem for theologians and church leaders, including parish priests, is the same problem that afflicts shallow book reviewers: genre confusion. There are many different language games, many different models for describing reality, many different styles of storytelling. Science is surely one, critical history another, social concern a third. The point is, however, that no single model has a monopoly on truth. Each tells the truth, limited and partial, which it is able to understand in the language that it properly uses. No one looks to Fantasy for solutions to the rising waters of Lake Michigan (Heaven knows I wish that

Belgarath the wizard or his tart-tongued daughter Polgaria would show up and make the waters go back. Or even Moses). And no one—at least in his/her right mind—looks to microbiology for an explanation of the purpose of human life. Critical history can tell you a good deal more than historical fiction about the facts of monastery life in eleventh-century England, but it cannot give you the imaginative feel of such a monastery the way Ellis Peters' *Cadfael Chronicles* do (about which more later).

Religious truth is passed on in stories before theology and catechetics can begin. Contemporary Catholicism has not only lost its own storytelling tradition, it has failed to recognize the components of that tradition when they appear elsewhere.

And if you don't believe that, let me propose that at next Sunday's Mass your priest (or you, if you are a priest) begin the homily by saying, "Can I tell you a story? Once upon a time, long, long ago . . ."

Watch every kid in the church sit up and listen, including the kid inside every adult still searching for narrative explanation.

Once upon a time, you see, there was this witch Xorinda, a good witch who had been captured by evil men. And a young duke named Ranlaf was sent to take her prisoner and bring her back to be executed because there was a witch hunt in their world at that time. And he swore the most solemn oath that he would bring her to the authorities so they could kill her. And on the way back, their ship was chased by a big pirate ship with blood-red sails, and all the tourists (they had tourists in that world too) including even the little kids would be killed by the pirates unless the pious and holy young duke asked the witch (whom he feared but had begun to like, if you know what I mean) to destroy the pirate ship. And . . .

Ranlaf the young duke is the "chosen" one, a character who is usually the protagonist in the Fantasy chronicles. The "chosen" person—someone who must carry on the quest whether s/he wants to or not—is a figure who crosses the boundaries of all the "wonder" genres.

The Special Person with unique powers is a familiar figure in SF, Fantasy, and Horror stories. Whether the Person wants the power or not, s/he is stuck with it and must use it for the good of others.

The protagonist, in other words, has a vocation. The wonder genres frequently deal with the vocation theme.

Sometimes the boundaries among the genres are blurred. Anne McCaffrey vigorously insists that her dragons are science in the world of the planet Pern and not fantasy. Roderick MacLeish's *Prince Ombra* can probably be called a horror story, but it also could be described as heroic Fantasy.

Charles L. Grant's *The Pet* is certainly horror but with touches of Fantasy. While Orson Scott Card's *Speaker for the Dead* and *Ender's Game* are pretty clearly Science Fiction—though of a very lyrical and mystical variety—his new series, which begins with *Seventh Son*, is more Fantasy and Horror than SF. Anne Rice's scary vampire stories are Horror, if ever there is horror, but she provides a fascinating historical and scientific explanation for the origins of vampires (and only someone with a Catholic background could have produced such sensual and, if one may say it, incarnational horror). John R. Maxim's dazzling *Time out of Mind* is a Horror story but with a scientific base in the premise that genes have memories of past events.

Most books in the wonder genres are not so difficult to classify as these. The reason why some seem to participate in several genres is that certain authors are less concerned about specific genre distinctions than they are about the Wonderful and the Special, about Surprise and Vocation.

The distinctions, in fact, are more important to publishers and reviewers than they are to authors and readers. The reader is attracted by the wonderful and identifies with the Chosen One. The author is delighted with his God-like ability to create surprise and to impose a vocation on his protagonist.

Two theological themes, then, pervade the wonder megagenre: wonder and surprise.

In *Seventh Son*, Alvin Maker is the seventh son of a seventh son and hence the recipient of special powers about which he has no choice. He lives in the "Wobbish Territory" (Wabash territory?) of early nineteenth-century America. It is a rather different America, however. The New England States are ruled by a Lord Protector and the Southern States are three Crown Colonies, the Duchies of Jacobia, Carolina, and Virginia. The Cavaliers and Roundheads are still fighting one another. George Washington has been beheaded for treason. Tom Jefferson has created a separate nation in the mountains called Applachee. Ben Franklyn has brought together in a compact the six United States of New Amsterdam, New Orange, New Holland, New Sweden, Pennsylvania, and Suskwaheny (capital at DeKane) and the Indian state of Irrakwa. In addition to Wobbish, the new territories are Huron, Hio, and Noisy River (Michigan, Ohio, and Illinois).

Here already we have surprise, an America different enough from that in our history books to make us wonder what happened (and by the end of the first book, we are only beginning to understand) and, in addition, the marvelous and dread powers of Alvin Maker, the Seventh Son of a Seventh Son. His special abilities—which offend both the Devil and the Un-maker, the principle of chaos in the universe—are a concentration of the magical powers of American folklore (about which Orson Scott Card has done considerable research). His opponent is water, primal chaos; his allies are Taleswapper, an elderly wandering storyteller, and Little Peggy, a "torch" or "seer." One doesn't know what is the great evil that the Un-maker plans (or whether it has to do with different political configuration of America) or what is the precise vocation of the magical little boy, Alvin. But one does know by the end of the first volume that (a) there is great evil to be resisted and (b) Alvin is the elected one: he and he alone must resist and defeat the evil.

The reader is hooked, as s/he is supposed to be hooked.

Bentley Ellicott is a nine-year-old boy in the New England

town of Stonehaven, like every other such boy except for the minor fact that he is the heir of David and Arthur and all the other great warriors who must do battle in the course of history with the Power of Evil, Prince Ombra (Bentley, in fact, is hero number one thousand and one). If he loses, there will be a nuclear war. If he wins, humankind gets another chance. His allies are a police chief, a bossy little girl named Sally, and an improbable red-neck, jade-eyed angel called Willybill. Bentley wins his battles, as an anointed hero must, and he wins only just barely, as is inevitable since evil is never a push over, not even for an anointed hero.

In *The Pet*, Don Boyd is a seventeen-year-old boy in Ashwood, New Jersey, a town already plagued by horror: six teens have been brutally murdered. Don has all the troubles of a confused, late adolescent male—he doesn't get along with his school or his parents or his friends or his girl. Moreover, he is a dreamy lad who identifies, perhaps too much, with animal posters on the walls of his room, especially the poster of a big, angry stallion.

One night the murderer attacks Don. Out of the fog comes a real stallion that stomps the killer. Then horror for Ashwood really begins. The animal, conjured up unintentionally by Don, attacks anyone who angers Don—including his mother and his girlfriend—even if Don does not want the person harmed.

How can Don undo the evil he has created? How can he change his magical powers that he doesn't want?

He learns that the evil is inside himself as well as in the world beyond himself. The killer "pet" is his own anger run wild. If he chains his anger, the pet is chained.

So he begins to mature and to control his anger, conscious that the demons he can create lurk always outside his window as well as inside himself, waiting for the self-control with which he chains them to dissolve.

Like the world of *Prince Ombra*, the world of *The Pet* is utterly ordinary: a town in New England, a suburb in New Jersey, a gutsy nine-year-old boy, a troubled seventeen year old. The wonder comes not from the oddly different America and the magic-permeated Wobbish territory but from the contrast between the serene surface of ordinary life and the seething horror just beneath the surface. In all three stories, however, the young male is a vessel of election, a man with special powers and a special mission, who must learn to control and discipline himself before he is able to battle titanic evil.

Jonathan Corbin also lives in a perfectly ordinary world of 1980 New York with one interesting exception: whenever it snows he becomes someone else and lives in the New York of a century ago, somehow involved in a murder and a monumental theft. Then, suddenly, someone in his own world is trying to kill him. And he is in love with two women, Margaret from the last century and Gwen from this century, who may or may not be the same woman. If he is to save the life of these women and, incidentally, his own, he must solve the murders from a century before and set right in the present the wrong done in the past.

Neat challenge, huh?

Again there is surprise, wonder, special power, vocation, and a struggle against evil, this time thoroughly human rather than supernatural evil. Again there is no choice: like Boyd and Ellicott and Maker, Corbin does not want to be the Chosen Vessel of Goodness, but he's stuck with the job, like it or not. And like Boyd, if he wins, he'll also get the girl, the Magic Princess!

I do not propose that the four writers, Card, MacLeish, Grant, and Maxim, are telling the same story nor that they are writing variations on the same formulae. Rather, I argue that each of these four stories not only cuts across genre lines but touches, each in its own way, on two key themes of the wonder genres and, indeed, of all the Western literary tradition: astonishment and election, wonder and vocation, surprise and calling.

Tom Doherty of Tor books has suggested that American readers are more attracted by Horror than by Fantasy because the Horror myths of demons and ghosts are a derivative of Christian mythology while the Fantasy myths originate in Celtic and Teutonic antiquity. The Grail story, Celtic originally, has been thoroughly Christianized, though as I have remarked earlier in this book, it has been adapted by the wrong kind of Christianity and is much more Catholic in its ancient pagan form (or in its modern Woody Allen form).

All four stories I have just described are more Horror than Fantasy and all are profoundly Christian. The theme is dominant only in the one Catholic story, Maxim's *Time Out of Mind.* The other three are Protestant in the sense that the individual hero must fight the forces of evil by himself with little in the way of community support and no particular woman ally. Jonathan Corbin has a network of allies who support him and sustain him and the marvelous Gwen who invites and attracts him.

In each of the books, the ultimate enemy is not the evil without but the weakness and fear within. In each, the hero must sacrifice to win, must give up something of himself in order to triumph.

He must, in other words, put off the old man so as to put on the new. He must die in order to be reborn.

Each protagonist, then, is, at the level of symbol, a Jesus figure, a person called to death and resurrection, a man whose Election is for Good Friday and Easter Sunday.

I do not know whether any of the four authors had this symbolism consciously in mind. I presume that they did not. However, in our cultural tradition, permeated as it is by two thousand years of Christian storytelling, narratives of the battle between good and evil easily take on a Holy Week shape, Vessels of Election easily become Christ figures, the Wonderful easily appears first as Incarnation, then as Resurrection.

There may be other ways of describing wars in heaven. It would be interesting, for example, to compare such stories in the Parsee (Zoroastrian) tradition with those in the Yahwistic tradition. But our tales of horror and fantasy are told by men and women in the latter tradition and for readers in the same tradition. Without any need for conscious reflection, writers and readers alike slip into Biblical paradigms; Moses figures, David figures (Bentley Ellicott is told that David is one of his predecessors in the fight against Prince Ombra, as is the Fisher King, Arthur Pendragon), and Christ figures almost automatically appear.

The question is not whether one can find signs of grace in such stories, the question is rather how one can possibly avoid seeing them as religious and theological novels.

If one enters into lands of wonder and fights wars in heaven against evil, one has entered the literary imagination of the Bible, perhaps not explicitly, as does R. A. Lafferty, but none the less effectively. Such stories are, in a special way, Secular Scriptures in Northrop Frye's sense of the word. Not only are they myths to parallel the scripture myths, but they are in fact the same myths, the Jesus story (which, at the level of myth, retells the Moses and David stories) told again with some alterations in detail but very little change in structure.

Bethlehem is Surprise; Golgotha is Vocation; the Empty Tomb Very Early in the Morning the First Day of the Week is Surprise reborn. Christmas, Good Friday, Easter: not the paradigm for all speculative fiction, but a pervasive paradigm nonetheless, one which readers especially enjoy and quite possibly the secret of the attraction of these genres. Bentley Ellicott, Alvin Maker, Don Boyd, and Jonathan Corbin are not only Moses and David and Jesus, they are Everyman. And everyone.

Most readers do not turn to the wonder genres for self-consciously religious purposes, in part because their religious teachers and leaders are incapable of instructing them on the religious paradigms latent in such stories. Yet the wonder genres come, in substantial part, from the fact that they reinforce the basic imaginative structures of the reader's personality, those templates which s/he has inherited from his/her cultural tradition and which s/he routinely uses to order and interpret the phenomena of life. Unself-conscious Yahwist that the reader is, committed in the depth of his/her preconscious to the conviction that wonder is possible, that good is stronger than evil, and that the individual person—either alone or with a network of allies—can overcome the evil forces that swirl around, the reader delights in the confirmation of these nearly instinctive response patterns that shape his/her world view.

We interpret and direct our lives through the myths that are templates living in our imaginations. Many of these myths, especially the most basic ones, originated in the Sacred Scriptures, even if we are no longer conscious of such origins. Harmony between the patterns of these myths and the patterns of the stories we read, even if this harmony is on the preconscious or unconscious level, is a deeply satisfying experience.

A religious experience? If that which confirms our religious paradigms can be said to be religious (and how can it not be said to be religious?), then most certainly a religious experience.

"Escapist entertainment," sneers the critic.

In response, one must say that all culture is designed first of all to be entertaining. Whether the confirmation of myths as valid paradigms is escapist or not depends on whether one thinks the myths are valid. If there is no wonder, no surprise, no special vocation, no romance in human life, then obviously stories from the wonder genres are escapist. If, on the other hand, there are grounds for hope, reason to expect surprise, and justification for wonder, then the "escapism" is rather a hint of an explanation, a confirmation that the parallelism between the structures of the imagination and the structures of the story is a valid sacrament of the universe.

The wonder genres, then, may be dismissed only by the argument that there is no reason to hope, no valid expectation of surprise, no wonder to be found, and no special vocation for any of us.

If the genre is valid, then a given book must be evaluated on how skillfully it lives up to the demands and constraints of its genre and is not to be dismissed (as it often is by critics) either

because it is of a certain genre or because it is "escapist entertainment."

The purpose of story, according to John Shea, is to attract
us into another world, illumine us with possibilities, and then
return us to our own world with a broadened perspective on who
we are and what we might do with our lives. Such an effect is
only possible if we enter the world of the story with certain
preconceptions about what is possible, preconceptions that need
less to be changed than to be strengthened and enriched.

A wonder story will enthrall us only if we are hungry for
wonder. A story of vocation will send us back to our own
vocation with an awareness of new possibilities only if there is
already a sense of vocation, however vague, weary, and tenuous,
existing in our preconscious.

The great fantasy sagas all tell about the implacable
demands of vocation. Camber of Culdi, Kelson Haldane (in
Kurtz's stories), the elf monk Alfred (in the *Hound and Falcon*
tales of Judith Tarr), and the various heroes and heroines of
Dragonlance (Tanis, Caramon, Laurana) do not want to be
vessels of election; they do not want to be the saviors of their
peoples; they do not want to be special men and women. But
they come to realize—and this is their character development,
their maturation—that they have no choice. They are special,
they are called, they do have vocations. Without them all is lost.

The stories appeal precisely because those who read
them understand, perhaps very dimly, that every man and
woman is special, that everyone has a vocation to do that which
no one else can do.

Stories of wonder and vocation, of the special self called
upon to do that which no one else can do, have powerful and
seductive appeal to us because our formal religion has been
denuded of such paradigms. Who is special? Blacks, women,
gays, third world peoples—certainly not the ordinary laity in the
Sunday congregation. What wonder is there in the world? Only
secular wonder, the wonder of a battle against oppressive ruling

classes. The only actions of which we are capable are the confession of guilt and the abandonment of our class privileges.

Such appeals (and I do not think I exaggerate their theological or homiletic prevalence) have little impact, mostly because the laity in the congregation know that the models and the ideologies behind them are not accurate or useful depictions of reality. Obviously there must be social justice for all; but just as obviously theologians and homilists have no special insights about the policies and programs necessary to achieve such goals.

Our daily lives often seem unbearably dull and routine. Our own self often seems intolerably commonplace, one more social security number in the big government computers. Our love is often agonizingly ordinary, devoid of mystery and challenge and allure. The stories in the wonder genres suggest what formal religion no longer seems to suggest: that such interpretations may be premature; that we still may be surprised; and that there are still works of virtue which, if we do not do them, will never be done.

They are more religious than either the theology book obsessed with (Marxist) politics or the empty Sunday sermon about birth control or abortion or Central America or money.

For we know in the depths of our soul (partly because we are Yahwists and partly because we are human) that we do live in a cosmos dense with wonder and that each one of us is a unique and special vessel of election with a vocation to which no one else is called.

And that there is a person around some place and that s/he is a marvel of enchantment.

The wonder genres, then, not only provide raw material for homilies and for theological reflection. They reveal to us, more powerfully than does most formal religion, the yearning of the human spirit for surprise, mystery, excitement, challenge, calling.

For, in other words, Herself.

And our hearts are restless till they rest in Her.

17

L'Amour and Le Carre: the Western World and the Shadow World

Did the West create the late and lamented Louis L'Amour or did he create the West?

It's a fair question. While L'Amour inherited a Western mythology from his predecessors, he has preserved it, refined it, developed it and, with his 180 million books (90 million-copy best sellers that take two columns to list in the introduction sections of his books), his screen plays, and his short stories, he has carved a definitive model of the mythological West from which all other models are likely to seen as deviants.

It is not the *real* West of course; no myth is like the reality that spawned it (Lincoln was a great and good man but the Lincoln myth transcends the man and is different from him). But neither is it totally unlike the *real* West either.

L'Amour is a careful researcher; the locales, the details of dress and armament, the customs, the physical settings, the laws, and the government forms are all accurate and precise. He is not writing realistic fiction (in my book that is praise), but you can count on his details. The simplification, the Romance of L'Amour's stories, is that they are accounts of "wars in heaven," epic struggles between good and evil. Doubtless such conflicts did occur in the Old West but rarely with the paradigmatic clarity of L'Amour's stories. His books are peopled by good men and bad men and weak men and strong women. Ambiguity and moral uncertainty are absent, as they must be in myths.

The Old West probably lasted no longer than twenty years—from the end of the Civil War to the last of the great cattle drives in 1885. The epic battle (in myth if not in reality) between the Earps and the Clantons at the O.K. Corral in Tombstone took place in 1881. Doc Holiday died in Denver, a convert to Roman Catholicism because of the prayers of the only woman he ever really loved, a Daughter of Charity who was his cousin. The Old West was won by then; the day of the cowpoke and the gun-fighter was over.

To some extent, it was already a myth in its own time because of the efforts of the magazines and the Wild West Show of Buffalo Bill Cody. The first Western films were made while many of those who had "tamed" the West were still alive. William Barclay "Bat" Masterson died a sportswriter in New York in 1921. Wyatt Earp died in my lifetime (1929). His wife, Josephine Marcus Earp, died during the Second World War at the time that the film about her and her husband, John Ford's *My Darling Clementine*, was being planned—a film that would contribute mightily to the Myth (even if it had rather little to do with the facts of the life of the Earps).

The Wild West myth, nonetheless, became the dominant "story" in American culture, easily routing such competitors as the Revolution, the Civil War, and the Coming of the Immigrants. A mere two decades of activity, involving relatively few people and far fewer gunfights than one can see in reruns of, say, a dozen Western films, is the archetypical American story.

You can try to debunk the myth if you want. You can argue

that there was much in the Old West that does not fit L'Amour's paradigm. But myths are never successfully debunked. They operate on a different level of "story" than does *real* history. Many of us who devour L'Amour know full well that the *real* West was substantially different, but we still enjoy the myth because it is a paradigm that purports to give meaning to the struggle between good and evil, a template that shows us how to conduct ourselves in that struggle.

If L'Amour is the great storyteller of the Old West, so Clint Eastwood has replaced Tom Mix and Alan Ladd and Gary Cooper and John Wayne as the prototype of the Western *persona*. Every time I read a L'Amour story, I think of the protagonist looking like the sometime Mayor of Carmel, especially in his roles in *High Plains Drifter* and *Pale Rider*, the latter role a brilliant performance that stops just that fraction of an inch short of self-satire which marks great acting (the sort of thing Sir Alec Guiness does routinely).

More about Eastwood later.

Another major influence in preserving the Western myth is Western Art, founded, for all practical purposes, at the turn of the century by Frederick Remington who progressed from "Romantic Realism" to Impressionism. I had considered a separate chapter on Western Art—pop culture art—but there would be nothing more to say that has not been said in this chapter. Western Art is enormously popular; despite that fact, some art critics seem prepared to admit that it is "serious." In fact, Western Art is less a specific art form than a specific subject matter that seems open to many different artistic styles.

The classical Western—and every one of L'Amour's stories as well as every one of Eastwood's films is by definition classical—is a morality tale spelling out the myth of good triumphing over evil through honesty, resourcefulness, integrity, respect for women, and courage.

"Do not forsake me, O My Darling!" Some of us remember that theme from *High Noon*, another Western classic. It said it all.

Imagine it playing in the background as this chapter continues.

But why does the myth have such an enormous and inexhaustible appeal? Most of us were neither born nor raised in the West. We do not come from Western families. We have not experienced life on the frontier. The Wild West did not directly shape our personal or familial or ethnic group cultures. Why is it our favorite American myth?

Why do people who grew up in Columbus, Ohio, come to Tucson (which, alas, has little of its Wild West ambience left); buy four-wheel-drive vehicles; mount rifles over the windows; and wear boots, cowboy hats, and bolo ties?

Why, in my Tucson manifestation, do I possess boots, a cowboy hat, and a bolo tie?

Frederick Jackson Turner, the great American historian, argued many years ago that the Frontier had shaped American life from the beginning and that the closing of the last frontier (say, when Arizona entered the union) might have a profound effect on American life. Turner's thesis has been challenged and will not stand any longer as literal and demonstrated historical truth. But as story, as symbol, as myth, the Turner theory is dead right. We are a "people of plenty," a nation whose character is permeated by expansiveness. We still believe that there can be plenty for everyone in our society. And as a result, we also believe that the moral code of the West, as reflected in the myth ("Smile when you say that, Pampas!") is one by which, with some modifications, it is possible to live.

When the people of our so-called allies describe the present incumbent of the White House as a "cowboy," they think they are insulting him. They don't understand that to most Americans, the lonely figure of the saddle bum is the hero in our formative saga, our Ulysses, Our Aeneas, our Finn MacCool.

My friend Jim Harkin, a specialist on Tombstone, suggests that the Tombstone saga is an epic because all the conflicts in American society were played out in that tiny cattle and silver town (none of the films, by the way, dare to describe how small it was and how unimpressive the O.K. Corral really is): conflicts of city versus county, North versus South, newcomers versus old-timers, federal government versus local government, Democrats versus Republicans, WASP versus ethnic. The Earps were WASPS, Republicans, newcomers, city, and North. Johnny Behan—with whom Josie Marcus had been living—was Irish, Democratic, county, old-timer, and South. Even though the Clantons and the McClurgs lost the gunfight, Behan's faction won and the Earp group had to leave town in a hurry and eventually the state.

The West, then, is in our blood, not necessarily the historical West but the mythological West that is both like and unlike the historical West. The moral code enunciated in the classical Western is not quite the code by which men actually lived, but it is not completely different either.

Thus the principle of respect for women was generally honored by the most murderous of the gunfighters and the most dissolute of cowpokes. Indeed a young woman would, in all probability, have been much safer in a frontier town than she would be on a state university campus today—where fifteen percent have been raped and another thirteen percent are victims of attempted rape.

Jungles are where you find them.

Rules of fairness, honor, and keeping one's word might not have been followed all the time (what code is?), but they were still the standards, which are, be it noted, considerably higher than the standards that seem to be in effect among the young rustlers on Wall Street these days.

The cowpoke may not have been a medieval knight, but then most medieval knights weren't either.

The Western Morality Play, then, presents men living out a stern, principled code of individualistic morality (very Protestant indeed) in which lonely men fight their way back into social acceptance without sacrificing their integrity or their honor. It is not a bad code as far as it goes. And if it doesn't go far enough (there was little sense of social justice or ecological concern until the more recent L'Amour books), it goes a lot farther than many of the codes that seem to be operating in America today.

Why do we identify with L'Amour's heroes?

There are two questions in that sentence: Why do we identify with protagonists in any story? and Why do Americans have a special predilection for the cowpoke on his "ole paint"?

The first question, I think, goes to the heart of the nature of human nature: we identify with the people in stories from the very first story we hear as children and we continue to identify all our lives. If we can't identify with a protagonist, we toss the book aside, unless it is required reading of one sort or another. The character has taken on reality in the imagination of the storyteller, and by the storyteller's skill, the character leaps into our imagination, where we cooperate with the author to bring the character to life. The author and the reader (listener) are co-creators of the protagonist and immediately become deeply involved with him. If there were not the almost irresistible urge in the depths of our soul to so cooperate with the author, there would not be stories. No one would bother to write them or read them.

Why this impulse, this almost God-like impulse, to create our own beings and live for a time in and through them?

At one level, that's a question to ask God. If we knew why God enjoys telling stories with our lives, then we would know why we do the same thing with the stories we tell and hear. My guess is that She does it because He falls in love with His creatures as we also do, writer or reader, teller or listener.

At another level, the almost compulsive search for "story" is part of the effort by which we try to chart paths of meaning through our lives, to work out with the protagonist the problems and dilemmas we ourselves encounter. This effort is not self-conscious and certainly not arduous; rather, it is something we do naturally and spontaneously as part of our nature as creatures who need meaning and experience and express meaning in narratives before we do it in rational theories.

Sometimes the "story" only reinforces our own biases and prejudices, our patterned responses, our self-deceptions. But for some people, the well-told tale can be and often is an illuminating and redirecting experience—although not necessarily in every case and not even usually anything more than a mild, transforming experiences.

But that's what stories are for.

Why then the Western Hero? Messrs. Mix, Cooper, Ladd, Wayne, and Eastwood?

In part, I think, because we are a people of a new land who spread across a continent in less than a century and are both awed and optimistic because of that experience and in part because the definition of the "good guys" and the "bad guys" is very sharp, even if you can't tell them by the color of their hats anymore. We may know that the templates for living in these morality stories are far too simple. But it's nice to know that the templates are there just the same.

Villains are much more problematic, I will be told, in the real world. No one is quite as evil as a Western "bad guy" (even if he isn't wearing his hat, a fancy vest is usually the tip-off). Men and women do bad things mostly because of emotional disorder or social oppression. They are not (fully) responsible for the evil they do.

Well, perhaps not. But . . .

Stalin? Hitler?

That five percent of male collegians who have already raped or tried to rape women?

That forty percent of the same population who say they would rape women if they were sure they would not be caught and have to pay for it?

Child molesters and murderers?

Wife beaters?

Muggers who kill for a couple of dollars?

Drug dealers?

The extent to which such folk are morally responsible for their evil we can leave to God. Their human responsibility may well be appropriate matter for psychology and sociology. But when a mugger has a knife at your throat, when a rapist is attacking your wife, when a relative molests your daughter, when a drug dealer sells your kid crack, you think he's a villain even if you are a psychologist or a sociologist.

The university world is filled with predatory males who prey on women students and now a whole new crop of potential slaves on the block—women junior faculty. Routinely, they promise to vote for promotion and tenure if the woman grants them "sexual favors." Just as routinely, they then vote against her. Some of them get caught occasionally and are astonished to be told that the rules have changed.

I exaggerate? Ask young and attractive women assistant professors or graduate students whether I exaggerate.

Do such men need psychologic counselling? Sure. Would it do any good? Maybe. But do either of these facts make their behavior any less evil to the exploited woman?

In the West, such men would be dealt with in more direct fashion. Sometimes I'm not altogether sure that our way is better. A woman was safer on the frontier than she is in the faculty room of many a university department.

There are lots of villains on the front page of the papers every day.

At this moment, I know of three people whose careers are in jeopardy because of plots against them by men and women in their professions who resent their success. If you don't know of any such phenomena in your circle, if you have never been unfairly accused by those who hate or envy you, then call these people paranoids. Otherwise, acknowledge that ordinary, respectable, middle-class people (especially in bureaucracies) are, when they are in the grip of ravenous envy, capable of the most vicious psychopathic behavior or of savage acts of evil.

Oh, there are villains around all right, and whatever their motivations might be, they are dangerous. The Western myth provides paradigms and templates for dealing with them—of which the most important is not to lose your cool and not to overreact because that usually plays into the bad guys' hands.

And the next most important is to fight them whenever and wherever you can.

Back in the good old days of Eric Ambler and Helen MacInnes, I used to enjoy the "spy" novel as a kind of European or Asian Western. The forces of good and evil were similarly arrayed. The people in the white hats were Americans. (There even was a character named Col. Hugh North in books by an author whose name, alas, I cannot remember.) I did not take the books seriously, however, because I could not believe in the "shadow world" they described. More recently, with the Watergate mess, the Iran-Contra repeat, the attempted assassination of John Paul II, the unexplained death of John Paul I, the Banco Ambrosiano scandal, etc., etc., I have stopped reading such stories because the real world, it would seem, is much scarier and much crazier than the fictional world of the spy story.

There is certainly a "shadow world" made up of the intelligence agencies of the great nations (and of Israel), the Mafia, the international drug trade, the munitions merchants, the various terrorist groups, rich Arab businessmen, Islamic fanatics, Bulgarian smugglers, Turkish gangsters, and folks who work in the White House basement. They are out of control and no one seems able to stop them. Alas, the Vatican does not seem hesitant to play in this game on occasion, as ineptly as it does everything else.

The major chronicler of the "shadow world" is a man who once played in it, David Cornwell, who writes as John LeCarre. In the paradigms of his stories, the distinction between good and evil is very thin indeed. George Smiley may be superior to his Russian counterparts but only just. And Circus, the British espionage agency, is shot through with treason, corruption, and mindless bureaucratic ambition of the sort the Russians would not tolerate. Smiley's best friend is a traitor (one has the impression that, like the American Communist party at one time, M.I. 5 had as many traitors as it had loyal agents). His wife sleeps with the traitor. The bureaucrats are out to get Smiley and finally do. Even though Smiley and his "people" finally aid his enemy on the other side to defect, Smiley is still thrown out of the agency, and the victory over the Russian is a sorry, tainted, and finally senseless victory.

Which seems to be an appropriate verdict on the whole shadow world enterprise. In T. S. Eliot's words, when good does evil to fight evil, it becomes indistinguishable from its enemy.

LeCarre poises always on the brink of nihilism and despair, most notably in his last (and most intricate, not to say convoluted, book) *The Perfect Spy*—a book apparently about his own father.

If we are no better than they and probably not nearly so smart, then what difference is there between good and evil?

I gather from occasional explorations of paperback racks that there are many imitators of LeCarre, not as elegant in their literary style but making up for stylistic deficiencies by even greater cynicism.

The perfectly good Romantic genre of the spy story has been corrupted and almost destroyed not by realism, alas, but by reality.

I often wonder whether fact has imitated fiction and hence destroyed fiction. Watergate conspirator Howard Hunt wrote spy stories. Did he act out the roles he had created? Do those folks who work in the White House basement read the same kind of stories? Did they take Helen MacInnes' characters as their models? Does anyone in the Vatican read LeCarre?

LeCarre's stories, in truth, are reverse romanticism. They provide their own paradigms and myths, perhaps more appropriate for the world of corporate irresponsibility in the large bureaucracy: When it doubt, get out.

Not bad advice, as a paradigm if not as a literal rule.

On the other hand, in some organizations (including, I would note, the Roman curia) it might be wise advice to take literally: when the corruption oozes down the corridor towards your office, take your cue from Alan Ladd or Clint Eastwood, get on your horse, and ride over the mountain.

18

Anne McCaffrey: "Romance" as Talent User

"**Why,**" I asked Harriet McDougal, editor-in-chief of Tor Books, "does Anne McCaffrey use her own name on her 'romances?'"

"You know Anne?" Ms.McDougal replied.

"I've corresponded with her but never met her."

"She's the kind of woman who does not tolerate baloney. She is no less proud of her 'romances' than she is of her science fiction."

It was the answer I had been hoping to hear. Unlike other writers who produce "romances" under pseudonyms for fear of ridicule, Anne McCaffrey was not ashamed of books like her *The Year of The Lucy*.

Ms. McCaffrey is at the very top of the Science Fiction profession. Her brilliant series of stories about dragons on the planet Pern has won almost universal acclaim. The later volumes in the series have enjoyed long periods on the *New York Times* best-seller lists. She was not about to be apologetic for her "romantic" writing. In my judgment, that was the perfectly proper attitude. She had nothing for which to apologize.

Of all the popular genres, none are more condemned than

women's "romances." They are regarded, even in the book trade, as cheap, escapist stories written for neurotic, overweight, frustrated women who consume them without taste or sensibility the way an addict consumes drugs and for the same reason—a search for brief oblivion.

These "romances" are, critics will tell you confidently, nothing more than literary soap opera.

These critics would often have been compulsive viewers of the TV series *Hill Street Blues,* which was prime-time soap opera (in the sense of a continuing series of stories featuring plots and subplots, many of them artifical, about many characters which were designed to bring you back each week to find out "what happens next"). They would reply that *Hill Street* was different because of the writing and the stories and the characters and the acting and the "realism."

Leaving aside the question of how really "realistic" *Hill Street* was, such critics were implicitly accepting the genre argument I have used throughout this book: a genre should be judged by its best efforts, not its worst. If soap operas are not always worthless and if women's "romances" are soap operas, does not it follow . . . .

But arguments like that have no impact on supercilious critics. Of all the trash in popular culture, there is nothing more trashy than "romances."

Walk into the "romance" section at your local Walden or Dalton, look at the covers, read the jackets, consider the titles, and begin to glance at a chapter. Do you really believe that there is any merit in such junk?

For the most part, the stories have little merit—the plots are predictable, the characters two dimensional, the writing flat, the settings contrived, the conclusions obvious from the first page of the book. They are hastily produced, formula-derived productions for an audience that has almost no standards other than a demand for a story that will hold their attention for a few hours.

I would add, however, that the same observation might be made of many mystery, adventure, spy, western, and science fiction stories. To single out "romances" for special attack seems to mean that the contempt is for the readers more than the genre.

At least the "romance" novels are readable stories, which is more than can be said of many of the pretentious exercises in "serious literature" which emerge from the small presses. Better a predictable story than an impenetrable one.

Moreover, while it may be true that the genre has a lower proportion of novels that can be described as well written, it is also true (though little noted) that the era of the machine-tooled "romance" seems to be over; the "romance" audience is making more demands on its writers for plot and character and style than it used to. Certainly the enormously popular Danielle Steele, the Queen-Empress of the "romances," is a skillful and ingenious writer. One need not be a fan of Ms. Steele to admit that her stories are presentable exercises of the storyteller's craft.

My concern here, however, is not to defend the genre from criticism but to explore its central myth and examine a case in which the myth is skillfully presented—Anne McCaffrey's *The Year of the Lucy*, which is written with the same command of storytelling, the same skilled characterization, and the same themes as her science fiction. If these skills are commendable when applied to the myths of science fiction, why are they not commendable when applied to the myths of the "romance?"

As Tom Doherty puts it, why should a story be judged by its setting?

The fundamental myth of "romance" is woman triumphant, woman overcoming the insensitivity and stupidity of man, woman protecting herself and her own, woman taking care of others at risk to herself, woman becoming herself and achieving happiness despite enormous odds.

It's not a bad myth, especially because it resonates with many women's experiences; it reinforces the paradigm with which they (are forced to) organize their lives; it offers the possibility that there is yet hope to squeeze some happiness and some fulfillment out of the difficult situations in which a woman find's herself.

Make no mistake about it, "romance" is part of the Secular Scripture. The desperation in some of the incarnations of the "romance" myths is an indication of just how desperate the lives of women can become.

The men in these stories are universally dolts, almost always childish, insensitive boors who, under the influence of a good and determined woman, can become (with considerable difficulty) nothing more dangerous than appealing, if unruly, little boys.

This is a view of the male half of the species which is not limited, by the way, to "romance" novels. In the "serious literary" work by women (from Margaret Drabble to Margaret Atwood), men are portrayed in equally unflattering colors.

I asked a friend if that's the way women really view men. "Conceited vulnerability," she smiled.

Well, that settles that.

The central myth of the "romance" (and perhaps of all fiction written by women) is that men are so busy blundering through life with their aggressive, achieving, possessing goals that women, with their superior sensitivity to emotional nuance and to the needs of the species to be nurtured, must provide the tender care for themselves, their children, and everyone else, the blundering male fools included.

Moreover, in this era of feminism, the woman must do all these things and, at the same time, wrest success for herself in the men's world of business or profession.

It is not a model whose utility for organizing the data I would care to dispute.

The man may think he is superior; the woman knows that she is but, under normal circumstances, is too clever to tell him.

(Among the Irish, I add parenthetically, the last paragraph does not apply. We Irish males know from the earliest moments of life that our women are superior and that, you'd better believe, is that.)

In the sexual dance, the pawing, sweating, heavy-handed male rushes blindly towards the quick and triumphant release of orgasm heedless of his partner's need for affection and tenderness and heedless, too, of his own suppressed or ignored vulnerability, which requires loving tenderness even more than the woman does.

He thinks he's a great, powerful lover. The woman knows that she has to teach him how to love, for her benefit indeed, but even more for his own.

It is again a model whose capacity to organize data I would not dare to deny.

Men should read a couple of novels written by women each year. They provide useful raw material for an examination of conscience.

These mythological themes are the context for Anne McCaffrey's *The Year of the Lucy*. Within that context, the thread that holds the story together is provided by the words of Lucy Farnol to Mirelle Martin: the parable of the talents is not only about money, it is about the special abilities each of us is given.

It is not an unusual exegesis of the Scriptures, though it is perhaps unusual in any contemporary novel to observe a scriptural text that explicitly quoted.

Lucy is dead when the story begins in 1961. Mirelle is wrestling with the problems of a marriage in which passion is cooling; a typically doltish husband; three children; the demands of suburban motherhood; a dominating and interfering mother-in-law; another man who is as sensitive as her husband is insensitive; troubled friends who lean on her for support; and her own illegitimate birth, which husband and mother-in-law use constantly against her—and which provides an excuse for shying away from the artistic talents (as a sculptor) that she has apparently inherited from her parents.

Caught up in this mass of troubles (not untypical of those

that assault any woman in "romantic" stories and perhaps not all that untypical of woman's lot in general), Mirelle begins a statue of Lucy to recall her friend and the challenges her friend represented. In the course of the story, she finally routs her mother-in-law, helps her friends, decides for husband and family instead of lover, makes peace with her past, and makes a definitive commitment to her artistic talents.

Woman, in other words, triumphant.

Ms. McCaffrey's story is distinctive not because its myths differ notably from those of other books in the same genre but because the plot, atmosphere, characterization, and dialogue are so skillfully done *and* because the agony of unused talent is so brilliantly depicted.

The demons tormenting Mirelle are finally inside her. She could easily cope with her husband (who, while a dolt, is a tractable dolt) and her mother-in-law if she could come to terms with her own talents. The argument used against them is that they will call attention to her illegitimate birth, but she knows better than that even at the beginning of the story. She is afraid of her talents because she is afraid to reveal herself in the use of them. If she can make peace with her talents, then the demons without can easily be tamed.

The problem, little lady, says Ms. McCaffrey, is not your husband. It's you. Blaming him is a dodge, a cop-out, an escape.

This twist on the myth is unusual because, one suspects, women don't really want to hear it. As a woman theologian remarked to me, "Women of my generation wake up in their late thirties or early forties and realize that they haven't done very much with their lives. They look around for the target and the first one who crosses the firing range is their husband. So even if he has been smart enough to sustain and encourage the development of her talents, he is the one on whom they open fire. They announce that they want to be their own person, by which they mean that he is the reason they are not their own person. Often they shed him and still don't become their own person. Only a few are willing to admit that the problem is not their husband, but themselves and that getting rid of him will not solve anything."

Mirelle's husband is certainly not opposed to her sculpting. He does not object to the money it occasionally brings in, though he is now proud that she doesn't have to work for the money. He even seems to like and appreciate (in clumsy male fashion of course, nothing more sensitive than that would be permitted a husband in this genre) what she does. He really does not value it as something very special, but then neither does she seem to value her talent all that much. If she had insisted on taking her art more seriously, he would certainly have accepted such a decision, not with good grace perhaps but without major opposition.

No, the problem is fear of herself. Only when she accepts, however tentatively, the implacable demands of her own talent can she become herself and create some cosmos out of the chaos in the world outside herself.

This is the myth turned to prophecy in the Old Testament sense of a challenging call for personal moral responsibility. I like it so much probably because, in my years of trying to be a priest for upper-middle-class Irish-Catholic women, the biggest single spiritual problem I have encountered, one for which I have no answers, is the reluctance of very gifted women to use their gifts.

My failures in the face of this problem are legion, my successes I can count on the fingers of one hand.

Men waste their talents, too, but they bury the waste in a blind charge towards occupational success, doubtless at considerable psychic cost. Women didn't use to have such a handy escape. They can plead children for a few years, but that excuse slips away as the children grow older—which does not mean that the excuse will be abandoned. Now that women have careers, too, they can use the same excuse as men for suppressing their talents, but somehow it doesn't work quite so well.

Mirelle Martin's case is typical of many in that the support and encouragement for her work in her personal environment is mixed, some people aware and encouraging, some indifferent, and some opposed. But in many cases of which I have had experience, the support was universal—husband, kids, family, friends, clergy. Yet somehow the women not only refused to risk themselves in their work but made it a high moral principle not to take the risk. (Novels by women rarely describe the extraordinary skill with which some women can transmute their fears and biases into the most exquisite moral principles.)

Talents denied inevitably become demonic; they turn in on the one who refuses to use them and destroy. When this happens, when the woman convinces herself that it is "too late" (another cop-out because by definition it is never too late), then scapegoats are sought in whom the accumulated guilt can be discharged—husband, family, friends, parents, psychiatrist, and poor parish priest (please pity poor parish priest).

Not a pretty sight.

And one, by the way, which is utterly destructive for the kids, particularly the girl kids, who happen to be around.

Mirelle in *The Year of the Lucy* does not deteriorate that far, but if she should, she would probably engage in the same laying-on of blame, all the time hating herself for a failure that she knows deep in her heart is her own and not anyone else's.

Poor Mirelle.

Fortunately, at the end of the story, she seems to have averted such an end, though realistically we know (as she does) that even when woman is triumphant (as they tend to be in such stories), woman has a lot of hard work, rough ups and downs, and repeated temptations to loss of nerve ahead of her. The important lesson of the story, however, is that Mirelle now knows and acknowledges that the problem is within herself. She has achieved the beginning of wisdom. She knows that she does not use her talent because she is afraid of the self-revelation, of the undressing of the self, of the psychic stripping and the spiritual nakedness that artistic creation requires.

I conclude from *The Year of the Lucy* that, in the hands of a skilled storyteller with deep insight, the myths of the "romance" genre become powerful theological stories, stories that not only illumine new possibilities (which I have been insisting in this book is what stories are supposed to do) but impose a personal moral responsibility, a prophetic demand to seize the possibility.

"Romance," like other story genres, holds that new beginnings are possible. It tells women that if they are willing to take the chances involved in change, they can notably improve their lives. Such a theme, granting all the limitations of one's own context, is a powerful spiritual challenge to what is difficult but possible.

The theme cannot be faulted, not if one is a Catholic and believes that in the Resurrection of Jesus, renewal is always possible. If the genre does not make the case for personal responsibility of the challenge to rebirth powerfully enough to disturb the consciences of those who read its novels, perhaps the reason is that those who believe in the Resurrection, those who are supposed to be the custodians of the Catholic sensibility, do not perceive the possibilities in the "romance" genre. And perhaps don't perceive the possibilities in their own tradition.

There is much meaningless babble about "Evangelization" in current Catholic clerical circles. The only output I see from this babble is the organization of diocesan offices, the mailing of newsletters, and the holding of conferences.

If one really wants to evangelize, one would be hard put to find a better medium than women's fiction.

211 / GOD IN POPULAR CULTURE

19

Stephen King: Things That Go Bump in the Night

"You're writing religious stories," I accused Stephen King at a Literary Guild cocktail party in New York.

"Of course I am," he agreed. "Most people don't believe me, but that's exactly what I'm doing."

"Anyone who writes about hope," I continued, "is writing about religion."

"Absolutely. Sometimes I wish I was Catholic like my wife. You people have great images of hope. But you almost have to be raised with them."

Thus my theory of sociology of religions was summarized and validated in a brief exchange of dialogue.

King writes stories of hope, maybe only a little hope—as in *Cujo* in which things got better, not much, but a little better—but still hope. In his non-fiction study of horror literature, King contends that the appeal of the field to readers is that they are scared stiff but still survive and thus experience a hint that one does survive, no matter how great the terror.

Pet Sematary is the only one of his stories which ends in pure despair: everyone dies a horrible death. Yet it is also one of King's most moralistic stories: the destruction is caused not by pure accident, as in *Cujo*, but by a profoundly unwise and even "sinful" attempt to use the powers of darkness for a good end. They are there to scare us, King seems to be saying, and to threaten us but not for us to, Faust-like, make pacts with them.

King is surely the most popular storyteller in America today and hence fiercely hated by the small-minded, mean-spirited folk who write book reviews or preside over book review sections in newspapers and magazines. Moreover, he is quite capable of turning out three or four books a year, all of which make the best-seller list. How can he be a "good writer," much less a "serious writer," if he writes so much?

Hard on Agatha Christie, Mozart, and G. K. Chesterton, isn't it?

And how unwise of God to have produced writers with different styles and paces of work.

I often wonder whether King's success is less attributable to the "horror" of his stories (his friend Peter Straub writes with more gore and more sheer terror) and more to the fact that he is such a marvelously skillful craftsman of suspense. When people tell me they want to learn how to write fiction, I tell them to outline one of King's novels. For sheer, raw talent and disciplined skill at the telling of tales, King is hard, indeed just about impossible, to beat.

He has been threatening to turn away from Horror and write in other genres. I hope he does, not because I dislike the genre (on the contrary, I love it—when my nephew told me that a line in one of my novels made him jump out of his chair, I was inordinately pleased) but because I'm sure that he will be equally skillful and equally successful. Those who try to write him off as a Grand Guignol hack will be proven wrong, not that such proof will still their envy of his success.

Nonetheless, the Horror story is his genre at the moment, and there is no better author to study to learn what the power and the attraction of the story is. Why do we (well, some of us anyway) like to have our wits scared out of us?

If Fantasy Romance is written out of the world of our dreams, Horror Romance is written out of our nightmares. In Fantasy, we struggle with enemies of flesh and blood, albeit ones with remarkable powers. In Horror, we struggle with demons, ghosts, and creatures that go bump in the night—enemies that are subhuman or superhuman, vampires, monsters, ghosts, haunts, devils, and all the other weirdos that populate human storytelling as the storytellers try to explain the existence of evil that cannot be attributed to human evil alone.

Are there such beings? Do they exist in a secular, scientific, mechanistic universe?

The late Everett Hughes used to tell us in sociology class about an old woman in Quebec who told him that ghostly presences no longer appeared but "in the old days, when I was young, they did appear." Have the creatures that go bump in the night disappeared from the earth because people no longer believe in them?

There are three questions tied up in that single sentence, and they must be untangled before we can attempt an answer:

1) Are there paranormal or parapsychological phenomena?

2) Are there evils or terrors that lurk in our own souls, which scare us, and which we can deal with in Horror stories? Do these evils sometimes generate themselves outside of our imagination?

3) Are there evil energies in the cosmos which are beyond human understanding?

I tend to answer "yes" to all three questions, but it seems to me that a "yes" to the first part of question (2) and to question (3) is enough to explain the fascination of Horror stories. And much of King's popularity.

To the first question: the evidence the parapsychologists have gathered is of such weight that if evidence of similar weight existed to support other theories, the theories would not be rejected. A vast number of Americans, forty-two percent in a recent NORC study, report "real" contact with the dead, as do sixty-six percent of widows and widowers. The paranormal then seems to be "normal." I make no metaphysical or theological judgment about such phenomena. Sociologically, I judge that they are sufficiently common to require that we learn more about them.

Incidentally, as I warn my students, no one who is not well grounded in his or her own religious tradition should mess with the paranormal much less the occult. There seems to be a strong propensity for folks to become more than slightly flaky when they permit the pursuit of such phenomena to become a substitute for religion.

The answer to the first part of the second question is an obvious "yes." Our nightmares are the raw material of the Horror story. They are also the attempts of the preconscious and the unconscious to process symbolically the fears that preoccupy us. Horror fiction takes these lurking terror images out of the unconscious and puts them in the preconscious where we can respond to them.

We like Horror stories, I believe, mostly because we fight through Horror, are terrified as we are by nightmares (most of which are not terribly scary), and then survive to live another day. It is useful to experience narrative that assures us that good is stronger than evil, especially the vague, nameless, monstrous evil that lurks in the dark basements of our souls.

And which occasionally—on dark roads at night for example—floods up out of the basement to scare the living daylights out of us.

(In passing, I have learned from my personal interviews with those who have had contact with the dead—usually very sane, sensible, and normal people—that they do not consider these experiences to be scary at all.)

Much more difficult is the second part of question (2)—do we sometimes project these fears out of ourselves and give them some kind of transient and apparent substance in the world outside of our imagination? I am inclined to think that we do and that many of the "manifestations" that fascinate psychic researchers are the result of such phenomena—unintentional and unconscious (or mostly unconscious) projections. Some may also be the result of lingering psychic memories that can attach themselves to some places. I have no proof that such things happen and no explanation of how they can happen, but such a model seems to fit some of the data.

Thus the other day a woman met me at my office at the University of Arizona to show me some pictures of an "ectoplasmic" cloud that had appeared in her family recreation room at home (not in Arizona). She and some other members of her family (not all of them) had seen the phenomenon but only in a fraction of a second. The camera had caught it and held it. Then she showed me the same thing in a picture of an Arizona sunset taken on the porch of a house her family had rented for a month.

The woman, I hasten to add, was not the kind who would be capable of faking such a shot, and there seemed to be nothing wrong with the negative to account for it.

I suggested, as I usually do in such circumstances, that when she returned home she ask a family friend to say Mass in the house.

That usually is enough.

What do I make of such things? Like a good Catholic cleric, I'm profoundly skeptical of them. I don't doubt the reality of the event; I merely doubt the need of any supernatural or preternatural explanation. There are some people, I have learned through the years, with remarkable psychic sensitivities who pick up things that no one else catches or can cause phenomena without intending to do so. That would seem to be sufficient explanation. As a scientist, however, I do not want to exclude other possibilities.

My case here is not that such experiences generate our love for Horror fiction (they may generate ideas for Horror novelists, however) but that they are sufficiently prevalent to confirm the fact that we live in a world in which much remains to be explained.

Stephen King tells interviewers that he looks under the bed at night to make sure there are no monsters there and that the creatures who appear in his stories are beings that he is actually afraid might be lurking in an unused closet or at a dark crossroads on a moonless night.

I think he's putting the interviewers on. I would guess, rather, that he has an extremely active imagination, immediate access to his preconscious, and a vivid awareness of how fragile life is.

Maybe it comes to the same thing.

The most powerful technique King has for scaring us is his ability to contrast Horror with the most ordinary events of daily life and especially the ordinary events of domestic life. King's children and teen-agers are utterly believable in their thoughts, their actions, their fears, their hopes, and their conversations. Then, unannounced and unexpected, Horror erupts.

I get a little scared even writing about it. In the King stories, the survivors continue to hope. But what if you're caught in a Stephen King story and you're not one of the survivors?

What if God is writing a Stephen King story and you're one of the characters that gets carried off by the monster and gobbled up in the third chapter?

Think about it.

Which brings us to the third of my questions: are there demonic energies at work in the cosmos and in our lives? Is there really a war in heaven? Are there really demons, titanic, intelligent powers of evil with whom we must war endlessly, always about ready to lose?

Don't laugh that one off.

As my seraph Gabriella points out in *Angel Fire*, the assassination of the Archduke Franz Ferdinand at Sarajevo was tragic as all deaths are but, on the global stage, a seemingly minor tragedy—an Archduke killed (as many others in Franz Joseph's family had died tragically) by a crazed member of an obscure Serbian nationalist group in a small city of which very few people in the world had ever heard. Sad, yes, but who would have believed that it would launch forty years of war in which some two hundred million people would die (of war, famine, and disease), as many as the species had produced in all its history up to the beginning of the eighteenth century.

It was a war no one wanted, for which no one was quite ready, and which no one thought would last very long. Yet by the end of September of 1914, Gabriella notes accurately (Seraphs in general are pretty good at history, though occasionally they juggle so many scenarios in their minds that they get a little confused), the world was locked into forty more years of war and the bright, confident expectations of the turn of the century—not unreasonable expectations of peace and progress and prosperity and democracy and vast improvements in the quality of human life—were utterly destroyed.

The modern world died in August, 1914. In the United States, it probably lasted till 1968.

Don't say there are not diabolic energies at work in the cosmos when such things can happen.

Or when a distasteful African practice of eating live monkey brains (apparently) launches the horrendous AIDS pandemic.

As Charles Burton Russell in effect observes in his comprehensive four-volume work on the Devil, the existence of such a being is a model that fits the data very well indeed. Our ancestors postulated a devil as an explanation for the cosmic evil that we experience in our daily lives and in the world around us (and even in our own personalities).

My purpose here is not to argue whether the cosmic evil energies need to be personified. In fact, I don't think they do. Once you have personified them, you are no closer to an explanation of why God tolerates such energies. Rather, my intent is to observe that there are plenty of reasons for being scared. If King is truly scared (and I think that he does scare more easily than most of us), the only legitimate conclusion is that he may well be wiser than the rest of us. He may be more aware than the rest of us how fragile life is and how many things can go wrong.

Naive Lockean optimism, buttressed by easy faith in scientific progress, is part of American humanism, and we all believe it in part no matter what our religion. We tend to think that anything can be fixed, given time and money and effort.

Murphy's law is a much better description of reality.

What's the answer to Northern Ireland? I'm often asked.

There is no answer, I respond, and thus prove myself very un-American.

We live in a disorderly cosmos in which at any time almost anything can go wrong and we are well advised to be scared. Only a fool would think differently.

There are balancing arguments (life was probably built into the cosmos when it was one-tenth-to-the-minus-forty-second-power old), but the thesis here is that even if our discursive mind, our propositional intellect, our conscious self thinks there's very little to worry about in this day and age, our preconscious and our unconscious know better: there's a hell of a lot to worry about.

It is precisely those fears that we confront in Horror stories, the fears of all the terrible dangers that lurk around us, of all the things that could go wrong, of all the terrible evils that might very well occur.

I'm not sure whether Stephen King really sighs with relief at the end of the day and announces to his wife, "Well, they didn't get me again today." But it's not a bad prayer of gratitude to utter every night.

What if the Spanish Influenza should return? It killed forty million the last time.

What if the bacteria responsible for the bubonic plague (still lurking here in Arizona, harmlessly it seems) should suddenly mutate and no longer be subject to the controls that have held it in check since, as The Black Death, it carried off a third of Europe?

What if AIDS should change so that the virus is acquired by breathing?

What if . . .

Think about it.

Are there angels? I'm not sure what the theologians say anymore, but I sure as hell hope there are and that the one assigned to me is as clever as my fictional Gabriella.

There is an impulse in the human personality which says that it will all still work out for the best, an irresistible impulse, very much like Springsteen's rejection of nihilism discussed prviously. All these defiances of evil can be subsumed under one label: "Hope."

The classic Horror story is based on this impulse, instinct, intuition: we are embraced by a protective *umwelt* (envelope, but it always sounds better in German) which will take care of us and is the ground of our hope.

It is this "loving embrace" (Anglo-Saxon erotic images are even better than scholarly German images) which we sense, as it were, out of the corner of our eye, which produces our hope renewal experiences; it is both the ground of religion and the source at which we direct the name God with the instinct that it is not improper to consider that source to be a "thou."

Horror stories fascinate us, then, because they enable us to face the most terrible things that "might happen" and yet end with an almost instant (if not very profound) hope renewal experience.

So the conversation between Steve King and me, he from his literary analysis of Horror and I from my sociological theory of religion, converged on one important fact: it is in our nature to hope. The Horror story challenges our hope in the most, you should excuse the expression, horrible fashion. We continue to hope.

Therefore we conclude that we will continue to hope, that it may be safe to hope, and that the source of our hope will take care of us.

She'd better. So many things can go wrong.

20

Varieties of Apocalypse in Science Fiction

The science fiction "little magazines" (*Analog, Galaxy*, etc.) are distinctly ambivalent about films like *Star Trek, Star Wars*, and *Close Encounters of the Third Kind*. On the one hand, they are delighted to see science fiction forms appeal to a broad range of consumers of popular culture. On the other hand, like all cultists, the SF purists who review for the science fiction journals are appalled at how disrespectful such films are of the solemn and sacred Forms that currently reign in "authentic" science fiction. Heroic sagas of the *Star Wars* sort, particularly those with reasonably happy endings (living happily ever after for Han Solo and Princess Leia must mean at least several fights a week and maybe several every day), were abandoned by the SF purists long ago; the thought that the wee folk in the flying saucers might be benign (even Cherubic) is enough to send the canonists of SF off to the local office of their Inquisition to demand that Orthodox Doctrine be enforced.

One knows that the saucer folk are either callously indifferent to us lesser mortals here on earth or ultimately impatient with our stupidity and bent upon either reforming us despite ourselves or simply eliminating us from the universe as a dangerous lower life form that does not deserve to exist. The smiling little fellows from Close Encounters are not apocalyptic visitors at all.

Apocalypse, ah, that's the word! Science fiction was born from an apocalyptic vision and currently flourishes on another apocalyptic vision but does not seem to understand what apocalypse really is.

It is Comedy: a story of Hopeful Endings.

And Romance: a story of New Beginnings.

In the Christian scriptures, one reads the Book of Revelation (once called by papists such as the present writer, "Apocalypse"), which is filled with falling stars, suns going out, moons disappearing from the heavens, blasting trumpets, and the general dissolution of the world. The book represents, in a sense, an extended reflection on the descriptions of the final days of the world given by Jesus in the gospel stories.

The apocalyptic literary style was the most popular religious literary form in the Middle East, particularly in Palestine during the Second Temple era. If you wanted to communicate religiously with Jews and proselytes (fellow travelers of Jews who did not practice the full rigors of the Mosaic law)—who may have been one quarter of the citizens of the Roman Empire—the apocalyptic religious mode of expression was almost essential. Hence its popularity with the writers of the Christian scriptures.

It is very difficult for those of us who live in a different era to penetrate back into the minds of the apocalyptic writers and preachers. Were they speaking "literally" or "poetically"? Did they really think the stars were going to fall from the heavens and that the world was going to be consumed by fire? Or were they rather describing in striking imagery the human condition and particularly the human religious condition? The best answer to that last question seems to be that, if we asked it of an apocalyptic preacher or writer, he would not have the faintest notion of what we were talking about. If we could explain our terms, he would probably say that his style was somewhere between poetry and literal description and would be baffled as to why anybody would be interested in a question such as ours.

Later Christians' piety, however, became quite literal and rigid in its interpretation of apocalypse and identified the apocalyptic imagery with the "end of the world" or "Judgment Day," a specific event with which history was to terminate and at which all the imagery described in the apocalyptic literature would physically occur. The medieval Latin hymn *Dies Irae* is the epitome of the extreme literalization of apocalyptic imagery as it has found its way into the Western imagination (think, for example, of the wild music of Verdi's *Dies Irae* in his *Requiem*). The end of the world and its possible renewal, then, is a major theme in the Western creative imagination, although destruction of the cosmos has always seemed far more important to popular Christian piety and to elite artistic and literary imaginations than has the renewal that may come afterwards. One need only think of the Horrors of Michelangelo's *Last Judgment* in the Sistine Chapel (Horrors that never seem to terrify the College of Cardinals all that much when it assembles to elect a new pope) to realize that what fascinated Michelangelo's genius was destruction, not reconstruction.

One of the curious anomalies of the development of the apocalyptic/eschatological imagery in the Western imagination is that those literary scholars who have very skillfully attempted to reconstruct the style and the imagination of Jesus himself are now pretty well persuaded that he personally avoided almost entirely apocalyptic imagery and that apocalypse in the New Testament is an adaptation of the message of Jesus to a popular literary and oratorical style carried on by his followers. Jesus himself, it would seem, much preferred to shatter people's preconceptions with parables instead of with falling stars, exploding suns, vanishing moons, and great conflagrations sweeping across the earth.

If we wish to understand the importance of the apocalypse in the Western imagination and in the science fiction segment of popular culture, we must go back beyond the Christian scriptures to the origins of apocalypse in the post-exilic, pre-Second Temple era of Judaism. As good a place as any to start is the fourteenth chapter of the book of Zechariah:

> See, a day is coming for Yahweh when the spoils taken from you will be divided among you. Yahweh will gather all the nations to Jerusalem for battle. The city will be taken, the houses plundered, the women ravished. Half the city will go into captivity, but the remnant of the people will not be cut off from the city. Then Yahweh will take the field; he will fight against these nations as he fights in the day of battle. On that day, his feet will rest on the Mount of Olives, which faces Jerusalem from the east. The Mount of Olives will be split in half from east to west, forming a huge gorge; half the Mount will recede northwards, the other half southwards. And the Vale of Hinnom will be filled up from Goah to Jasol; it will be blocked as it was by the earthquake in the days of Uzziah king of Judah. Yahweh your God will come, and all the holy ones with him.
>
> When that day comes, there will be no more cold, no more frost. It will be a day of wonder—Yahweh knows it—with no alternation of day and night; in the evening it will be light. When that day comes, running waters will issue from Jerusalem, half of them to the eastern sea, half of them to the western sea; they will flow summer and winter. And Yahweh will be king of the whole world. When that day comes, Yahweh will be unique and his name unique. The entire country will be transformed into plain, from Geba to Rimmon in the Negeb. And Jerusalem will be raised higher, though still in the same place; from the Gate of Benjamin to the site of the First Gate, that is to say the Gate of the Corner and from the Tower Hananel to the king's winepress, people will make their homes. The ban will be lifted; Jerusalem will be safe to live in.

Leaving aside the references to Yahweh, and the bizarre Middle-Eastern names, the images are not all that foreign to the addicted reader of science fiction. Indeed, Zechariah might be giving a brief synopsis of *Lucifer's Hammer* by Larry Niven and Jerry Pournelle (an account of a comet colliding with earth). What did Zechariah have in mind?

Contemporary researchers on the apocalyptic literature (see, for example, Paul D. Hansen, *The Dawn of Apocalyptic: The Historical and Sociological Roots of Jewish Apocalyptic Eschatology*, Fortress Press, 1975) are reasonably persuaded that the apocalyptic literature is fundamentally Jewish in its origins and influenced only very slightly by the neighboring pagan literary styles. Jewish literature of the immediate pre-exile era was prophetic, heavily concerned with moral striving, humanist in obligation in Yahweh's name to create a just and moral society. It would remain free and powerful not by force of arms but because of both its fidelity to him and the moral excellence that characterized the lives of its people.

The moral and religious visions of the prophets, of course, are the core of the Jewish and Christian religions and represent one of the major breakthroughs in religious consciousness of all human history. However, the prophetic vision of a just and religious messianic age was not achieved, and later prophets such as Jeremiah wrestled with an explanation.

Had Yahweh's promise been misunderstood or had the people been faithless? In any event, the kingdom was destroyed, the people carried off into captivity, and the messianic hopes dashed. Upon return from exile, the Israelite elites, discouraged, disheartened, and oppressed, fell back on the older creation symbols that their religious heritage shared with the rest of the Middle East—images of the struggle between cosmos and chaos, between good and evil, between light and darkness. Creation was the ordering of the universe by Yahweh (or by demigods in other Eastern religions). The fires were put out; the darkness was illuminated; disorder and conflict were held at bay; and life became possible in the world, though sometimes only tenuously and barely possible. If the first creation had not inaugurated a process that led to fulfillment, so argued some of the post-exilic elite, most notably Zechariah and the author of the second part of Isaiah, then perhaps what was needed was a dissolution of the old world back into its primal chaos and a re-creation of the cosmos by a new and decisive act of the Ordering Principle.

The notion of a new beginning, of the destruction of the old and the creation of the new, was apparently widespread in ancient times—widespread in the era after the exile. The old kingdoms and empires were breaking up and new were being born. It was, for those who followed the stars, the end of Taurus the Bull and the beginning of the Age of the Fish. If the apocalyptic literary style was Jewish and even prophetic in its formation, it reached backwards into the creation images of the Middle-Eastern nature religions and sideways into the conviction that a new era was beginning—a conviction that was prevalent in Mediterranean Hellenism as well. (When the Emperor Augustus closed the door to the Temple of Mars, the event was hailed as the beginning of a new era of peace, not totally dissimilar to the messianic eras hailed in the Jewish scriptures. Given the enormous influence of Judaism in the Roman Empire at the time of Augustus, of course, it is quite possible that most of the inflow of imagery was from Judaism to Roman Hellenism instead of vice versa.)

The apocalypse image, as such, is unique to those cultural environments where Yahwehism—in its Jewish and/or Christian forms—has had an impact. Both eschatological themes are muted or nonexistent in other religious traditions.

We so take for granted the apocalyptic theme, it is so much part of the unconscious cultural environment, the literary air we breathe, that we hardly distinguish it and are hence quite unaware of its special impact, particularly on the Western imagination. Still, it is not unreasonable to assert that if it were not for apocalypse, there would not be science fiction because there would not be a vision of a future that is better than the past nor of a decisive intervention of a saving force which leads to a re-creation, a reconstruction, and a renewal of the world.

In the nineteenth century, philosophy believed that science could eliminate human misery and suffering, and the literary imagination strove to construct scientific paradises in which the good life, guided by a benign (if mildly totalitarian) science, was possible. The work of the American Ignatius Donnelly and the Englishman H. G. Wells testified to that bright scientific vision. It was science as a reconstructing agent inter-vening in a more or less gentle apocalypse to renew the earth.

The vision has faded, killed in Europe by the forty years of war that began in August, 1914, and in this country by Dallas and Vietnam.

We are now in post-exilic times and the Second Temple has yet to be constructed. It is an era of pessimism, not to say fatalism, which makes Zechariah seem like a naive optimist. The SF imagination no longer constructs scientific utopias but either partial or total apocalypses in which the bad we know is wiped out and replaced by something worse or, alternatively, some-thing every bit as bad. The positive component, then, of the apocalyptic imagination has been lost, and the science fiction writer of the day has more in common with Thomas of Celano (the author of the *Dies Irae*) than he does with Zechariah.

Much of the science fiction literature simply assumes that there has been a nuclear war. Even the benign *Star Trek* series operated on such an assumption, and so do the future histories of Isaac Asimov, Poul Anderson (in his Nicholas van Rijn series), and Robert Heinlein. The world that has evolved is almost invariably at least as bad as the one which antedated the catastrophe and often times much worse—humankind sinking back into barbarism and savagery, made even worse by the presence of mutants produced by radioactive fallout

Thus, in *Lucifer's Hammer*, life goes on after the collision with the comet, but it is a life much like that of the Dark Ages with the ruthless warlords presiding over small territorial kingdoms locked in endless combat with their neighbors. Human nature, the writers say, following the popularizers of primate research, is basically evil, aggressive, destructive. All the apocalyptic events do is strip away the veneer of civilization and turn us back into savages.

In addition to the manmade holocausts, which usually end with the human race badly damaged but struggling on, and the extraterrestrially induced holocausts in which human nature is sometimes renewed but other times virtually eliminated (in one science fiction series, recently serialized in a magazine, genetic experiments produce god-like creatures who oppress and virtually destroy the descendants of the original human species), there are also the cataclysmic apocalypses that sound in their descriptions much like those in the scriptures but which result (like the comet collision in *Lucifer's Hammer*) from the blind working of astronomical fate—not infrequently ending completely the world and the human race (though somehow or other, accounts manage to get written after the apocalypse, often in ways never explained by the author).

For example, in Isaac Asimov's classic, "Nightfall," darkness descends: "This was the dark—the dark and the cold and the doom. The bright walls of the universe were shattered and their awful black fragments were falling down to crush and squeeze and obliterate him. . . On the horizon outside the window. . . a crimson glow began growing, strengthening in brightness that was not the glow of the sun. . . The long night had come again."

Thomas of Celano would really have liked that.

And in Arthur Clarke's "The Nine Billion Names of God," the Mark V computer, programmed by Tibetan monks, does indeed speak the nine billion names of God. The universe has had its purpose and "overhead, without any fuss, the stars were going out."

There is, however, one fascinating exception, a writer who continues to practice the apocalyptic tradition in a style that would please Zechariah and Deutero-Isaiah. His name is Raphael Aloysius Lafferty, and he was born in Neola, Iowa, in 1914, of Irish immigrant parents. A self-educated electrical engineer (for thirty-five years before he turned to writing full-time), Lafferty has a literary style that reminds one of Gilbert Keith Chesterton and a creative imagination filled with light, fire, and divine lunacy.

For Lafferty, apocalypses, even savage ones, are gracious and often comic.

In his novel *Past Master,* Thomas More is rescued from the headman's block by a people who are able to reach back into history and bring him into another era in which he is charged with saving a world that is coming apart at the seams. More does brilliantly and ends up on the headman's scaffold once again. After having been world president and king for nine days, he's doomed to die again. His allies, led by a marvelous young woman named Evita (and a boy named Adam, who dies repeatedly only to be born again), storm the scaffold but are driven back. "The boy Adam, in particular, died magnificently, as he always did." Evita destroys More's enemy, but More himself is executed—possibly—though a stranger does appear on the platform and speaks with him.

Thomas seemed both excited and pleased.

"Will it work, do you think?" he cried loudly, with almost delight. "How droll. Can a man have more heads than two? I'll do it, I'll go with you."

Then there is apocalypse.

"But one thing did really happen at that moment. At the moment that life flickered out of the beheaded corpse, the worlds came to an end.

"All life and heat and pulse went out of the world. It died in every bird and rock and plant and person of it, in every mountain and sea and cloud. It died in its gravity and light and heat, in its germ-life and in its life-code. Everything ceased. And all the stars went out.

"Was it for a moment? Or a billion years? Or forever? There is no difference in them, when the world is ended, when there is no time to measure time by.

But all of this is not yet quite the end; in fact it might not be the end at all for, as Lafferty concludes the book:

"Remember it? Then it happened?

"Be quiet. We wait.

"The spirit came down once on water and clay. Could it not come down on gell-cells and flux-fix? The sterile wood, whether of human or pro-grammed tree, shall it fruit after all? The Avid Nothingness, the diabolically empty Point-Big-0, is it cast away again? Is there then no room for life? Shall there be return to real life?

"Well, does it happen? Does the reaction become the birthing? What does it look like?

"Will we see it now, in fact and rump, the new-born world?

"Be quiet. We hope."

In the book *Apocalypses* (Oh, yes, Lafferty is well aware of what he's up to), there is a long novella called "The Three Armageddons of Enniscorthy Sweeny," in which a chronology is presented of the life and times of the picaresque genius Enniscorthy Sweeny, 1894 to 1984—including the election of Robert Taft as president of the United States in 1948 and Douglas MacArthur in 1952, John XXIII as Pope in 1958 and Richard Nixon as president in 1960. In 1984, Enniscorthy Sweeny himself dies (and the year is no accident) and his opera Armageddon Three is performed, apparently beginning the process that leads to the end of the world. The final entry in the chronology is 1984: "the situation worsens." After the chronology, the world may or may not end, but one is not quite clear because, as one preacher, warning of the end of the world, says in the tale, "When the world is finally destroyed will it act as though it is destroyed? Or will it be the most casual and nonbelieving cinder ever?"

It is quite clear that "just at the winddown of the years, the world and its people have gotten mighty mean. They were the meanest and the rottenest people that anyone ever saw." Enniscorthy Sweeny may not have been dead either; he may simply have been sitting in the tree like Mad Sweeny, the king in ancient Irish legend, and his wife Mary Margaret, who stood beneath the tree and crooned, "Aw, c'mon down, Sweeny." It would appear that some people set Sweeny's tree on fire to roast him to death and that began the final fire of the world.

"So Final Armageddon was burning and raging out of control, and the World was ending.

"That's funny. The people didn't act as if the world were ending. But they didn't act quite as if it were going to continue either.

"They behaved as though they didn't very much care whether it ended or not.

"Thus, the end of the world and the end of Enniscorthy Sweeny—maybe, and then, maybe not, because it would appear that Sweeny had been killed many times before and kept coming back."

But the wildest of Lafferty's apocalypses is in his brilliant story—perhaps his masterpiece—*And Walk Now Gently Through the Fire*, a tale about the Ichthyans, the "queer fish," a group of people who keep alive a strange version of Christianity after "The Great Copout":

> ... the Day of the Great Copout was worldwide. As though at a given signal (but there had been no signal) people in every city and town and village and countryside of earth dropped their tools and implements and swore that they would work no more. Officials and paper shufflers ceased to officiate and to shuffle paper. Retailers closed up and retailed no more. Distributors no longer distributed. Producers produced nothing. The clock of the people stopped although some had believed that the hour was still early.
>
> The Last Day had been, according to some.
>
> "The Last Day has not been," said a prophet. "They will know it when it has been."

The leading characters of *And Walk Now Gently Through the Fire* are the Thatcher family—Judy, the young mother, and her two early teen-ager children, Trumpet and Gregory. The head of the family, one John Thatcher, had been one of the Twelve, a leader of the Ichthyans, but he had been killed. However, he rose from the dead for a brief period of time to pass on his leadership function to his wife, who casually jots off Epistles, such as the Epistle to the Church of Omaha in Dispersal.

Judy was a Queer Fish. She was also, according to the story, "a young and handsome woman of rowdy intellect." Her son Gregory, who clearly has an important role to play, is tempted by a minor devil early in the novel: "His name was Azazel. He wasn't the great one of that name but one of his numerous nephews. There is an economy of name among the devils." Azazel asks Gregory to "command that these stones be made bread."

"Does it always have to start with those same words?" Gregory asks in response. He is then instructed to cast himself down from a height because, "if you are one of the elect you will not be dashed to pieces." Gregory dodges the temptation: "I'll not be dashed to pieces yet. It's high but not really steep, not a good selection." And finally Azazel offers him the "world and all that is in it." Greg Thatcher grins, "It really isn't much of a world you have to offer. . . really, where is the temptation?" However, Gregory does not give the devil the traditional dismissal. "I'll not say, 'get thee behind me, Satan,' for I wouldn't trust you behind me for one stride."

Trumpet and Judy, alas, are killed in a fierce battle, and Gregory and a certain Levi Cain band together with a group of other young people named Simon Cannon, Tom Culpa (his name meant Tom Twin), Joanna Cromova (daughter of Thunder), Andy Johnson, Mattie Miracle, and Peter Johnson—who seems to be their leader.

Then, when "events have gathered into constellations," the big fire begins, though it is an acre of fire, fire through which the young Ichthyans must walk.

One may be offended by Lafferty's playful manipulation of the Christian symbols in this episode, offended because one believes that the symbols are too sacred to be manipulated or, alternately, offended because one believes the symbols are too false to be discussed. Still, one has to say that the apocalypses of R. A. Lafferty are the closest things in science fiction to Zechariah, who started the whole thing, because Lafferty's apocalypses are apocalypses of rebirth, renewal, and beginnings again.

He may, in other words, be right or wrong about the nature of reality, but he certainly is right about the nature of apocalypse.

There is one difference between the prophet and the engineer. R. A. Lafferty imagines wild, renewing, destructive, manic, re-creating apocalypses just as Zechariah did, but R. A. Lafferty's apocalypses are also comic as well as Comic—a phenomenon that might well have offended Zechariah and certainly would have offended Thomas of Celano.

But then, neither of these two worthies was Irish.

(An earlier and different version of this chapter appeared in the Journal of American Culture.*)*

21

Ellis Peters: Another Umberto Eco?

On a fine, bright morning in early May in the first part of the twelfth century (probably 1137), a short, stocky man in his late fifties, barrel-chested and with the walk of a sailor, can be seen before Prime picking out cabbage seedlings in the monastery gardens of the Abbey of Shrewsbury of St. Peter and Paul. The man is Brother Cadfael (pronounced Cad-VALE), a Welsh monk who is the herbalist of the monastery, in charge of providing the monastery community with both seasoning and medicine—rue, sage, rosemary, gilbers, gromwell, ginger, mint, thyme, columbine, herb of grace, savoury, mustard, fennel, tansy, basil and dill, parsley, chervil, and marjoram. In the background are peonies and poppies which also provide useful material for Brother Cadfael's healing efforts. The poppies are especially important in the first Brother Cadfael story, *A Morbid Taste for Bones.*

Thus there enters on the mystery scene one of the most fascinating detectives to come down the pike in a long time. Cadfael the crusader, the lover, the hero who entered Jerusalem with Godfrey of Bouillon, the captain of a ship with which the crusader army fought off pirates, now settled to spend the final years of his life tending a monastery garden, healing the sick and the infirm, and solving twelfth-century mysteries.

In the nine mysteries published since 1977, author Ellis Peters has re-created the world of England in the first years of the High Middle Ages, a time of innocence and vitality in the reborn Benedictine monasteries. Just as Umberto Eco has re-created the world of a Benedictine monastery of mid-fourteenth-century Northern Italy, so Peters gives us the picture of an English monastery two centuries earlier. Edith Pargeter (Ellis Peters' real name) is not a genius at the new art and science of semiotics as is Umberto Eco. Her books are not filled with the elaborate word games, the complex philosophy, the intricate puzzles of *The Name of the Rose*. Unlike Umberto Eco, she does not believe that the purpose of the title of a story is to confuse the reader. It is highly unlikely that Brother Cadfael will ever rise to the top of the *New York Times* best-seller list. Yet, for this reader at any rate, she is a far better storyteller than Umberto Eco. Moreover, her "medieval novels of suspense," as the covers of the hardback books say, or "medieval who-dunnits" as the British paperback editions call them, provide an interesting counterpoint to *The Name of the Rose*. Umberto Eco undoubtedly describes truth in his books. Ellis Peters, for her part, has only verisimilitude; and as any storyteller knows, verisimilitude makes for a better story than truth and may, finally, at the level of myth and symbol, be even more True.

Peters' stories can be said to have everything—colorful monks; touching young love; marvelous atmosphere; a fascinating and complex detective; and, most importantly of all, ingenious puzzles. If you are one of those mystery fans who feels cheated when the mystery is too easy, Ellis Peters will not disappoint you. If you hold tenaciously to the position that all the atmosphere in the world does not compensate for a dull plot, Peters is just the new writer you're looking for. Only P. D. James, as far as this writer is concerned, compares with Ellis Peters as the mystery find of the last ten years.

And Brother Cadfael is at least as appealing, if not quite so pretty, as Cordelia Grey.

In *A Morbid Taste for Bones*, Brother Cadfael is sent by Abbot Heribert (a well-meaning and pleasant but ineffectual leader of the monastic community) to accompany Prior Robert on a pilgrimage to Wales to bring the bones of St. Winifred (a saint whose head was chopped off by a pagan Welsh prince and then miraculously placed back on her body so that she could live to become the abbess of a monastery) to Shrewsbury Abbey, where she may be venerated as the Holy Patroness. Brother Robert—sleek, glib, ambitious—has his heart set on becoming the new abbot. He also has a rather low opinion of the herbalist, a Welsh peasant with a dubious background; indeed, often in the story, the other monks wonder about Brother Cadfael. He certainly is devout and careful in his monastic practices (though not above sneaking out after Compline to be on his mystery-solving business); yet has he not seen too much life to be a good monk?

As we learn, Cadfael is even more a man of the world than his brother monks realize. There have been many women in his life: Rischildis, his childhood sweetheart; Bianca, a Venetian; Arianna, a Greek boat girl; Miriam, a Saracen widow from Antioch; and many others too.

> Having known them was part of a harmonious balance that made him content now with his harbored, contemplative life, and gave him patience and insight to bear with these cloistered simple souls who had put on the Benedictine habit as a life's profession, while for him it was a timely retirement. When you have done everything else, perfecting a conventual herb garden is a fine and satisfying thing to do. He could not conceive of coming to this stasis having done nothing else whatever.

The Welsh townsfolk in Gwytherine are understandably reluctant to give up the relics of their little saint. One of the local squires, the leader of the opposition, is mysteriously murdered. An exiled English nobleman, in love with the squire's radiant daughter, is blamed for the crime. Cadfael must solve the mystery, free the young lovers, rein in the ambitions of Prior

Robert, and bring St. Winifred—or something that would be presumed to be St. Winifred—back to Shrewsbury.

As is often the case in the stories, Cadfael takes into his confidence one of the young people, this time Sioned (Joan), the gorgeous young Welsh heiress. Cadfael and Sioned wrap up all the loose ends and solve the mystery at considerable risk, with almost as much skill as Peters displays in bringing the tale to its gently ironic and comic ending. Cadfael admits that if he were thirty years younger, he would give Engelard, Sioned's lover, stiff competition. As it is, he returns to the monastery enjoying the wondrous little secret that is at the core of *A Morbid Taste for Bones,* only to learn a few years later that Sioned and Engelard have given their first son a wonderful Welsh name—Cadfael.

> "Well, well!" said Brother Cadfael, "I'm certainly gratified. The best way to get the sweet out of children and escape the bitter is to have them by proxy, but I hope they'll never find anything but sweet in their youngster."

One cannot find in contemporary mystery fiction a more appealing or satisfying introductory volume to a mystery series than *A Morbid Taste for Bones.* The second mystery, *One Corpse Too Many,* begins on a specific date in the early summer of 1138. The remaining stories bring us into the middle of September in the year 1140.

In *One Corpse Too Many,* civil war is rending the Shropshire countryside. The Empress Maude and King Stephen are contending for the crown of England, and Stephen, perhaps too easygoing, has finally been moved to battle. Shrewsbury town is in the possession of those who are loyal to the Empress. Stephen attacks and captures it and appoints his Aide, Gilbert Prescote, as Sheriff of Shropshire. After the capture of the citadel of Shrewsbury, the remaining garrison is summarily executed. Aline, the daughter of Queen Maude's garrison chief, takes shelter in Shrewsbury Abbey, which steers a careful course of neutrality between the two warring factions. Brother Cadfael, from the second position of Welsh neutrality, takes the lovely and vulnerable young woman under his wing. Like Sioned, she almost at once becomes a protege of the good Brother. King Stephen's loyalists are searching for her because she may know where the stolen silver treasure of Shrewsbury has been hidden. Moreover, two men loyal to the king are in love with her, one of them a dubiously loyal young Norman to whom she is attracted despite his apparently dangerous plots.

While Brother Cadfael and some other monks are preparing the bodies of the executed garrison for burial, they discover one corpse too many. Who is the corpse? Why was he killed? What connection does he have with the lost treasure, and how will threats to the lovely Aline be turned away, especially the most serious of threats, which comes from slight, dark, seemingly sinister young Norman, Hugh Beringar? Will Brother Cadfael be able to keep his freedom of movement as Prior Robert gains more and more power in the monastery?

One Corpse Too Many adds but one dimension to the already fully developed "formula" (a non-pejorative use of the term) of its predecessor, and now events are set precisely and deeply in historical context.

Hugh Beringar turns out to be very different from what we expected, and as the story ends, he has been appointed Prescote's Under-Sheriff, a position in which he will become a more or less permanent Dr. Watson to Brother Cadfael. And the happy, if sometimes bemused, husband of the fair Aline.

In *Monk's Hood*, it is December of 1138. The battle line has left Shrewsbury far behind. A guest in the monastery, Gervais Bonel, is suddenly taken ill from symptoms that Cadfael knows all too well: he has been poisoned with oil of monkshood, useful for creaking bones but deadly dangerous to those who swallow it. Despite Cadfael's efforts, Bonel dies and his stepson Edwin is accused of the murder. Cadfael believes Edwin is innocent and is powerfully motivated to save him because Edwin's mother, Bonel's wife Rischildis, is Cadfael's sweetheart, whom he has not seen for forty years.

In the meantime, political intrigue threatens the Abbey of Shrewsbury. Poor old Heribert was not diligent enough in supporting the King. He is summoned to the Papal Legate, perhaps to be replaced. Prior Robert confidently expects that he will be the new abbot. The implications for Cadfael are ominous. With the help of Hugh Beringar, Cadfael solves the mystery, saves Edwin, and is able to be a friend if not a lover to Rischildis. A new abbot, Father Radulfus, comes to the monastery, and Prior Robert's machinations are thwarted. The book ends with Cadfael wondering about Rischildis:

> He wondered if he could legitimately plead that he was still confined within the enclave until Rischildis left and decided that would be cowardly only after he'd decided that in any case he had no intention of doing it. She was, after all, a very attractive woman even now and her gratitude would be a very pleasant indulgence; there was even a decided lure in the thought of a conversation that must inevitably begin to have "Do you remember. . . ?" as a constant refrain. Yes, he would go. It was not often he was able to enjoy an orgy of shared remembrances.
>
> In a week or two, after all, the entire household would be gone. . . all those safe miles away. He was not likely to see much of Rischildis after that. Brother Cadfael heaved a deep sigh that might have been regret, but might equally well have been relief. Ah, well! Perhaps it was all for the best!

In *St. Peter's Fair*, the fourth of the Brother Cadfael chronicles, it is the thirtieth day of July, 1139, the Feasts of St. Peter and Paul, the patronal festival of the monastery. Brother Radulfus is safely ensconced as the Abbot and is steering "the rudder of this cloistral vessel" with a strong, firm hand. Fortunately for him and for us, Radulfus shrewdly recognizes all of Cadfael's talent and supports vigorously Cadfael's poking around into mystery and crime, sometimes even assigning him the role of monastic detective. The good herbalist still must occasionally slip out of the monastery after Compline, but usually when he is engaged in his investigations he has the full support of Father Abbot.

The fair in the monastery foregate bustles with prosperity. Just under the surface, however, there is sinister intrigue. Soon the Empress Maude and her half-brother Robert of Gloucester will land in England to continue the civil war. Conspiracies are afoot to draw the powerful Earl Renulf of Chester into alliance with the Empress. The King's spies are everywhere in the foregate, sniffing for plot and conspiracy. That's good news, too. Aline Beringar is pregnant, and in a few months, she and Hugh will have a child.

A prosperous merchant is murdered; a local boy is blamed. The merchant's niece is trapped, apparently defenseless against the schemes of an evil man. Cadfael to the rescue in what may well be the most exciting of all the chronicles thus far, complete with a chase across the English and Welsh countryside which would be splendid in a film. Or in a television series.

In *The Leper of St. Giles*, the summer of 1139 has turned to autumn; and Brother Cadfael, his mind very much on his captain in the Holy Land, the great Paladin Guimar DeMassarde, finds himself caught up in a drama of intrigue and conspiracy and viciousness involving the leper colony and the church of St. Giles, which the monastery administers. The great crusader, in Cadfael's opinion the greatest of them all, is on his mind because his granddaughter, Iveta, was about to be forced into a marriage of convenience arranged by her ambitious and greedy guardian. Suddenly, there is one and then another murder. The young woman is free from torment, a ward of the Abbot, and will doubtless soon marry the man she really loves. But Cadfael is not altogether satisfied. The killer of the first victim is in his castle cell awaiting trial and certain condemnation, but who killed Iveta's guardian, and what is the role of the mysterious leper called Lazarus, who has appeared transiently at St. Giles?

Cadfael knows, finally, that Guimar DeMassarde did not die in the Holy Land and comes to understand why he wishes to continue to be thought dead.

My favorite of all the Cadfael chronicles is *The Virgin in the Ice*. It is now December of 1139. A young woman's body is found in the ice, a victim of murder and apparently the daughter of a great noble family in Worcester which has been caught up in the battle between the Empress and the King. In fact, the virgin in the ice is not the Lady Ermina, and her murder was not part of a political conspiracy; but the story is also about sons, about the first son of Hugh Beringar, who has become now almost an adopted son of Cadfael, and also about a young man named Olivier, a Saracen in origin it would seem, who aspires to be a knight and who is the true love of the Lady Ermina and, as we begin to suspect toward the end of the story, also the son of Cadfael and his Saracen lover, Miriam. Cadfael straightens out the problems of the young people and sends them happily on their way. Even though Hugh Beringar, as Deputy Sheriff, should keep them in his district, he cooperates with Cadfael's plan to free the young couple. Hugh boasts proudly of his son: "Wait until you see him! A son to be proud of!"

> Cadfael rode mute and content, still filled with wonder and astonishment, all elation and humility. Eleven more days to the Christmas feast, and no shadow hanging over it now, only a great light. Time of births, of triumphant beginnings, and the year now richly celebrated—the son of the young woman from Worcester, the son of Aline and Hugh, the son of Miriam, the son of man.
>
> A son to be proud of! Yes, amen!

The Sanctuary Sparrow takes place four weeks after Easter, in the spring of 1140. The war has now moved far to the south, and peace reigns again in Shropshire. It has been a hard winter but a gentle spring, and Brother Cadfael is caught up in a spring mystery, a tale of twisted love. A young man takes refuge in the monastery with a mob from Shrewsbury in hot pursuit. He is guilty, they say, of robbery and murder. He is scarcely more than a child, a traveling performer, Liliwan, a Saxon orphan with no family, no home, and no one to love or be loved by—no one except the serving girl, Rannilt. Of course, Cadfael saves Liliwan for Rannilt, but unfortunately he is not able to save an older and more haunted pair of lovers. The principal love affairs in the Cadfael stories are usually among the gentry, sometimes among the nobility. But Rannilt and Liliwan, two of Cadfael's most charming young lovers, represent the dregs of medieval English society. They cannot hope for or expect much in life, but they have one another and they have their love, which will serve them well. Love, however, does not save the other couple. Hugh Beringar reflects on this tale, the most somber of the Cadfael chronicles:

> "Old friend. . . I doubt if even you can get Susanna into the fold among the lambs. She chose her way, and it's taken her far out of reach of man's mercy, if she'd even live to face trial. And now I suppose," he said, seeing his friend's face still thoughtful and undismayed, "You will tell me roundly that God's reach is longer than man's."
>
> "It had better be," said Brother Cadfael very solemnly, "otherwise we are all lost."

In the eighth of the Cadfael chronicles, *The Devil's Novice*, the wheel of the year has turned again, and it is the autumn of 1140. Political intrigue once more involves the Abbey of Shrewsbury and its persistent herbalist. A messenger from Bishop Henry of Blois to the Earl of Chester is murdered near the Abbey, part of a convoluted plot in which Chester will betray King Stephen and make common cause with the Empress Maude. Somehow connected with these sinister connivers is a new novice in the Abbey, a squire's son named Meriet, who tries desperately to fit into the monastic community but seems too much the knight, too much the warrior, and even too much the lover to have a true monastic vocation. The struggle raging in his soul and his resulting nightmares upset the peace of the monastic community, and Meriet, simultaneously passive and violent, is dubbed the devil's novice.

Only Brother Cadfael is able to see the link between this young man, in whom he sees a reflection of himself at the same age, and the treason that is abroad in the land. The devil's novice does not belong in the monastery, but Cadfael knows in whose arms he does belong and finally comes to see how treason in the country can cause treason in the families. The devil's novice is freed from the monastic community and freed from the even worse burden of conflict with a harsh but well-meaning father. The love of Isouda and Meriet is one that revives Cadfael's faith in the goodness of human nature despite all the treachery and conspiracies and schemings and connivings and treason. The former devil's novice, once a proud, stubborn, arrogant young man, becomes gentle and considerate, even of his enemies.

> "Child," said Cadfael, shaking his head over such obstinate devotion, but very complacently, "you are either an idiot or a saint and I'm not in the mood at present to have much patience with either. . . There, be off with you! Take him away, girl, and let me put out the brazier and shut up my workshop or I shall be late for Compline!"

Cadfael can well afford to laugh on his way to Compline because he has once again routed his old enemy, Prior Robert and the Prior's stooge, Brother Jerome, and also, in the course of solving the crime and freeing the devil's novice, he has arranged that the other novice in his charge, Brother Mark, will study for the priesthood.

One's choice of which tale one likes best is purely a matter of personal taste. Each one of the chronicles is a first-rate mystery story. The collection of them is a fascinating reconstruction of the religion, the history, the social structure, the culture, the politics, and the lifestyle of England in the twelfth century. Having read all the chronicles, one feels that one has become part of a little section of England around Shrewsbury between 1137 and 1140 and that one knows the monks and the townsfolk and the squires and the nobility almost as though they were friends and neighbors. Ellis Peters is well along the way toward the creation of what might be a monumental series of stories—pure pleasure for mystery fans and rewarding reading for anyone.

Perhaps the greatest achievement of the Cadfael chronicles is Peters' ability to help us feel and accept the common humanity that links us to these inhabitants' world, so very different from our own. There is a terrible temptation in the study of the past to what one might call temporal ethnocentrism: to be

so appalled by the barbarism and the ignorance and the superstition of other ages as to have contempt for the people who lived
in those ages and almost exclude them from the same human
race of which we are a part. The writing on the Middle Ages of
the late Barbara Tuchman has always seemed to me to be
especially prone to that temptation. Even *The Name of the Rose*,
a classic of its own kind, leaves us feeling at the end that Adso
and William of Baskerville were very, very different from us
"moderns."

Brother Cadfael and his friends and proteges and allies,
and even the criminals he hunts, are very much part of the same
human race to which we belong. Different from us? Yes indeed—
different beliefs, behaviors, biases than we have, certainly, but
still men and women with the hates and the fears, the ambitions
and the sorrows, the joys and the pain that we know so well. This
may be the greatest achievement of all in the Brother Cadfael
chronicles.

The elitist critic will dismiss the *Cadfael Chronicles* as
nothing more than (superbly crafted) entertainment that has
nothing to do with the "real world."

Mircea Eliade, on the other hand, spoke to me once about
the "Soteriology of the Mystery Story." He meant that the detective in the mystery plays a savior role; he is the one who by
solving the puzzle "makes things right again"—restores the
proper balance of the cosmos and reasserts the triumph (always
tenuous) of cosmos over chaos. The world is always looking for
saviors, and the lure of the mystery, he said, is that it provides an
arena where the savior can route disorder and "re-create" cosmos.

I have no doubt that he is right. The appeal of the mystery
tells us a good deal about the nature of human nature; and the
"new" mysteries in which the detective is a "bum" tell us something about the elitist view that there are no saviors, that cynicism
is the only appropriate intellectual and emotional stance, and that
chaos is stronger than cosmos.

To dismiss the mystery as "unreal" is, as I've argued repeatedly in this book, to confuse genres and to insist that only Realism is appropriate literature. And to dismiss it as entertainment is to forget that all culture is designed to entertain. One could as well write off *Hamlet* because it is both entertaining and unreal.

The extent to which grace is present in the mystery depends on the skill of the storytelling and the suspense of the battle between cosmos and chaos. Just as there are villains in the world, so there are saviors, men and women who, if they don't make everything right again, at least devote themselves decisively to the cause of cosmos over chaos. They are not infrequently men and women who have many of the characteristics of Brother Cadfael—patience, wisdom, sensitivity, humor.

So grace would be present in the chronicles of Brother Cadfael even if he was a layman living in twentieth-century California. The portrait of medieval monastery life is an extra layer of grace, albeit a charming one.

It also suggests that the religious life, which has responded to so many human needs and aspirations for so many centuries, may yet survive even this era of turbulence and trauma.

22

Film as Sacrament

The film *Places in the Heart,* for which Sally Field won the 1985 Academy Award as the best actress of the year, ends with a Baptist communion service in a small town in Texas during the Great Depression. As the cup and wafers are passed through the congregation and the camera examines the faces of each of the communicants, we become aware that all of the characters in the story are present, the good and the bad, the venal and the heroic, the living and the dead, the killer and the victim.

As I watched this ending, I found myself thinking, They aren't really going to try this; if they do, they're not going to get away with it. But of course, they did try it and they did get away with it—a moving and vivid portrait of the religious doctrine that Catholics call "the communion of the saints." Whether that was the term the film-makers would have applied to the final scene of *Places in the Heart* I do not know; nonetheless the idea or, perhaps more fundamentally, the image that we are all brought together in one by Jesus and, indeed, by the reception of the Eucharist which "re-presents" Jesus is the same as the Catholic doctrine of the communion of saints.

After the lights went up, the film ended, and everyone else left the theater in Chicago's Water Tower Place, I sat for a few moments staring at the blank screen reviving an old conviction: the film is the sacramental art par excellence; either as a fine or lively art nothing is quite so vivid as film for revealing the presence of God. Film in the hands of a skilled sacrament-maker is uniquely able to make "epiphanies" happen.

Many years ago, when priests still wore Roman collars most of the time, I went on recommendation to see Eric Rohmer's *Ma Nuit Chez Maude* at the Three Penny Theater in Chicago's Lincoln Park district. It was (and still is) a fairly run-down place, filled with a lot of slightly scruffy young singles. (And in those days most slightly scruffy young singles were also radicals. Remember?) I wasn't altogether sure who Eric Rohmer was or what *My Night at Maude's* was about. Judging from the advertisements in the front of the theater, I thought it discreet to turn up my overcoat collar and push up my scarf. What was a priest doing in that theater, seeing that kind of film, anyway?

The film was about Pascal's gamble. Like all Eric Rohmer films, it was a mixture of strikingly vivid scenes and endless French conversation punctuated by the brilliant use of the new French-language liturgy and a homilist preaching in the context of that liturgy to make even more forceful some of Mr. Rohmer's theological, not to say catechetical, points.

The penultimate scene occurs during a snowstorm on a hill above the French city of Clermont. The heroine admits to the hero that she has been having a love affair with his friend and, therefore, as much as she would like to marry him, she feels unworthy of marriage. The hero is disturbed by the news of the love affair but even more disturbed at the prospect of losing this thoroughly admirable woman. He stumbles, trying to say the right thing, and mutters, "But of course, I will always respect your freedom."

It is not a very good answer under the circumstances, at least not in words, but his attitude conveys forgiveness, which in the context is relatively unimportant, and continued and undying love, which in the context is all that needs to be said. Then a quick cut to the final scene: several years later, a warm beach in Southern France in the summertime, the hero, the heroine, and their two children—a happy family and a happy marriage.

I walked out of the Three Penny theater with my coat collar turned down and my scarf open as if to say to the young people there, "Yeah, guys, that's what I stand for, that's what we're all about."

And a third scene. It's the end of the semester. I am going to a theater in Tucson to see a film called *All That Jazz*, which I have hitherto avoided because, while I like jazz, I don't like movies about jazz. However, it won a Cannes Festival prize, so I figure that I'd better see it. I encounter my colleague Michael Hout and various members of his family, and we enter the theater together.

Very quickly, I discover that *All That Jazz* is not about jazz at all but about a man's experience with death. Ten, perhaps fifteen minutes into the film, I realize that the cuts away from reality to the dreamlike conversation between Joe Gideon and Angelique in fact represent Joe Gideon's "particular judgment." Angelique (superbly played by Jessica Lange) is the angel of Yahweh—no, she's more than that, she is Yahweh.

If you play *All That Jazz* over on your video player often enough, you will realize that this is precisely what the film-maker intended. Several times during the course of the film, for example, images of Angelique are preceded and followed by references to God. In one particularly dramatic instance, Joe Gideon (Roy Scheider and, by implication, film-maker Bob Fosse since it is clearly an autobiographical film about Fosse's open-heart surgery) laments the failures of his life.

"Well, look at all you've accomplished, Joe," Angelique says with a smile, as she flips through his press notices.

"But that's nothing," Gideon replies. "For example, I've never made a rose."

"Oh," Angelique laughs charmingly, "only God can make a rose."

In the subsequent cut to Angelique she's holding a rose in her hand.

At the end of the film, when a final television spectacular

is held to celebrate the death and departure of Joe Gideon, one is given two options for the end of the story—something like a John Fowles novel. In the concluding scene, the lifeless body of Gideon is zipped up in a plastic shroud to be carried to the morgue. In the penultimate scene, he walks down a long corridor toward a lighted figure at the end (in a clear reference to the literature on revival of those who have apparently been dead). At the end of the long corridor, one sees waiting for him with outstretched arms Angelique, the fair bride dressed in a bridal gown, with smiles of tender affection on her face.

Which is it, Bob Fosse asks us, the hard slab of the morgue or the warm softness of the marriage bed?

My sociological theory of the religious imagination fits perfectly the paradigm of *All That Jazz*—religion as experience, image, and story. Bob Fosse had an experience when he temporarily died on the heart surgery operating table, an experience of death. But the death he encountered was not horrible or terrifying but gentle, warm, affectionate—like his wife, his mistress, and his teenage daughter. The experience of death remained in his memory, symbolized by the image of a beautiful woman, and he tells the story in *All That Jazz* to ask us the question, Is that what death is really like? And, perhaps, Is the beautiful lover he encountered in his moment of death what God finally and after all really is?

The film is a sacramental art form par excellence. Sacramental films are not for the Church a luxury or a utility but a fundamental and essential necessity. Unfortunately, I conclude that in the present state of ecclesiastical culture this linkage between "the movies" and the Church is likely to continue to be unperceived.

For the purposes of this chapter and with all due respect to Marshall McLuhan and others who make important distinctions on the subject, I will subsume under the rubric "film" both the motion picture and television, especially since, given the popularity of VCR's, most people now will see even feature films at home. The distinction between the two art forms is not nearly so important as it might have been and is not, I think, pertinent to this book.

Of the three epiphanies, the one in *Places in the Heart* is the most accessible, so blatantly accessible that the film-makers almost pound us over the head to make their point. It is the sheer, gentle beauty of the scene, however, which rescues them from the charge of preaching or moralizing. Eric Rohmer is much less accessible to most Americans, partly because films with subtitles are always difficult to follow; partly because Rohmer is working in a cultural context that is not our own; and partly because his epiphanies are usually very delicate and indirect—God drifts across the screen like a very gentle spring breeze. Yet it is not necessary that an epiphany be recognized and described as such for it to occur in a film. The sacramental impact need not be explicitly felt. The sudden, dramatic contrast between the snow falling on the hill over Clermont and the warm summer beach will linger in the viewer's imagination for a long time, perhaps insinuating itself into the collection of what Paul Ricoeur calls the "privileged" symbols in the person's imagination. It is worth noting, by the way, that both *My Night at Maude's* and *Places in the Heart* make use of liturgical services—the latter for the very epiphany itself, the former for explaining beforehand what the epiphany will mean.

The question of the accessibility of the sacramental dimension of *All That Jazz* is more complex. Surely none of the major movie reviewers showed any awareness of what Fosse was up to in the film. And even Jessica Lange herself in published interviews did not seem to comprehend that she was portraying God. I would have thought that a typical American audience would have grasped this theme rather easily. Many of the people with whom I've discussed the movie comprehended the sacramental dimension with little difficulty; others saw it as no more than an erotic movie musical. In my sociology of religion classes (to whom I show the film every year), there is instant sensitivity to the religious theme of the film—once someone has suggested to them beforehand that it is appropriate and legitimate to search for such significance. On the other hand, unlike *Places in the Heart* and *My Night at Maude's, All That Jazz* does not, for the most part, rely on traditional Jewish and Christian religious imagery. It is almost as though Bob Fosse had to make up his own imagery to recount his experience (relying, for example, on an article by Elizabeth Kubler-Ross as repeated by a standup comic to tie together the religious themes of the film).

As I have argued in previous chapters, Catholicism has always believed in the sacramentality of creation. It has always held fiercely that God discloses Himself/Herself to us through the experiences, objects, and people encountered in our lives—grace is everywhere, as Georges Bernanos observed. The world is deprived not depraved, but even in its deprived and imperfect state, it still discloses God. The artist in the Catholic tradition is therefore the one who sees "the splendor of the form in the proportion parts of the matter" more clearly, more acutely, more perceptively, perhaps more obsessively than others. S/he shares with us that special insight into the true, the good, and the beautiful as it is displayed in material creation(s/he does not have to know that s/he is doing that, much less have an elaborate theological explanation for it).

The artist uses the materials of his skill and the insight of her art to stir up in our imaginations memories of our own grace experiences. These memories will help us to understand more clearly the experience the artist is recording. In turn, they will also be enhanced by our encounter with the artist's experience and our enjoyment of the work of art. (As I have learned, to my dismay, on the subject of Catholic social ethics, one cannot presume that young people, either in the seminaries or in the Catholic colleges, are being taught the Catholic philosophy that we were taught thirty and forty years ago, not even those parts of the tradition which were brilliant, insightful, and worth preserving.)

The artist, then, is a celebrant of grace (though s/he may not realize that's what s/he's doing and may not call what s/he's celebrating "grace") who appeals to our imagination in order to recall and enhance our own grace experiences. The artist through her work discloses God in the universe even more sharply and decisively than God has chosen to display Himself/Herself in the works of Her/His creation.

Film is especially well disposed for the making of sacraments, for the creating of epiphanies, because of its inherent power to affect the imagination. It is obviously not the only art form nor necessarily the best art form. It is certainly not (as ought to be obvious) always or even often used for sacramental purposes. Nevertheless, the pure, raw power of the film to capture the person who watches it, both by its vividness and by the tremendous power of the camera to concentrate and change perspectives, is a sacramental potential that is hard for other art forms to match.

The major advantages the film-maker has over the playwright are that he can change perspectives quickly in the same scene, forcing his audience to concentrate on that aspect of the scene on which he wants them to concentrate, and then shift with dramatic abruptness from scene to scene, filling the audience's imagination with images at rapid-fire speed. Thus the disclosure of God's love at the end of *Places in the Heart* is accomplished basically by the camera's moving from face to face in the congregation, which is made up of both living and the dead. In *Ma Nuit Chez Maude*, the vividness of the sacrament is achieved principally in the quick cut from the hill above Clermont to the Mediterranean beach. Fosse uses both techniques with surrealistic abandon and enormous effectiveness. The viewer's imagination is overwhelmed with so many dazzling images that s/he leaves the theater almost drunk with imagery. It is only on reflection and perhaps only after several viewings that one realizes all that Bob Fosse's camera has done to us.

As someone who is engaged in both, it seems to me that

epiphanies through film and screenplay are more vivid and normally more powerful than epiphany stories told through the written word. Nonetheless, the novel, I think, is capable of more complex and intricate and sophisticated epiphanies than the film. Thus, for example, the dramatic explosion of Claire O'Brien's character in the conclusion of Maeve Binchey's *Echoes* would be hard to achieve on the screen and, indeed, will not be quite so dramatic in a screen version of *Echoes*. Nonetheless, there does not have to be a choice between film and novel. Both are art forms with their own media, their own rules, their own power. The point here, however, is that the camera can create a sacrament far more quickly and vividly than can the written word.

Most films, it might be argued, are trash; whatever sacramental power the film might have is not normally used. One is prepared to concede the point, but that is not the issue in this article. Rather, the question is whether the Catholic Church, which of all the great religious traditions of the world most strongly supports the sacramentality of being, ought not to strive to cultivate, develop, promote, and facilitate the sacramental potential of the film.

There is, first of all, a good deal more sacramentality in films today than the average Catholic is likely to perceive consciously, in great part because s/he has not been sensitized to do so by teaching and preaching. Thus when I considered the five films I saw immediately after *Places in the Heart*—*Purple Rose of Cairo, A Day in the Country, Ladyhawke, Breakfast Club,* and *The Gods Must Be Crazy*—I saw homily material in each one of them, hints that are obvious and even easy to comprehend of the Being who lurks in beings. If the rich sacramental power of films that are currently being made is not being disclosed reflectively and explicitly to the Sunday congregations, the reason is that those who preach to those congregations have not themselves been sensitized to the enormous sacramental power of film.

Is there, I wonder, a homiletics course anywhere in the

United States which teaches the art of using a film in the Sunday homily?

Indeed, given the terrible condition of preaching, is there a homiletics course anywhere in the country?

The Church's inability to deal with the film as an art form can be explained by the fact that, in substantial part, the motion picture industry in Los Angeles was shaped by Eastern European Jewish immigrants who were mostly agnostic and very ill at ease with religion in any manifestation. At the same time, the Catholic Church in the United States was caught up in the midst of its urban immigrant experience and deeply committed to protecting a presumed fragile faith of the immigrants and their children. Under such circumstances, The Legion of Decency and the Hayes Office were perhaps inevitable phenomena, if not ones of which American Catholicism can be very proud.

Essentially, our concern with the film industry was that the immigrants and their children not be permitted to see too much female flesh on the screen. Having engaged, quite successfully as it turned out, in this defensive maneuver, and a narrowly defined defensive maneuver at that, and having protected the Catholic Church from explicit attacks (no matter how historically valid), we left the film to itself as essentially a worthless exercise in wasting time. That many or even most films were such can hardly be denied. Nonetheless, it was a strange posture for the Church that presided over the emergence of modern drama in the late medieval mystery and morality plays.

The Legion of Decency mentality is still very much with us, as was proved by the Church's bizarre response to the television miniseries *The Thornbirds*. Without anyone in charge apparently viewing the series, the decision was made to attempt to boycott it because it was a film, presented during Holy Week, about a sinful priest. The boycott was not particularly successful, though some advertisers did indeed drop out of sponsorship of *The Thornbirds* for fear of antagonizing Catholics. *The*

Thornbirds ratings were extremely high, in part because of the bishops' clumsy effort to bring pressure to bear against it.

It seemed to occur to no one that the novel was a story of sin and redemption, especially appropriate for Holy Week viewing, and that a much more intelligent response to it—since most Catholics would see it anyway—would have been an educational effort to draw out for viewers the sin/redemption themes.

Many Catholic lay people who I know caught the themes immediately. Perhaps it is expecting too much of the hierarchy that they be as sensitive to sacramentality in films as the laity. Nonetheless, one of the great adult religious educational opportunities in recent history went down the drain because of the hierarchy's knee-jerk reaction to *The Thornbirds*.

Grace, then, abounds in film, more so perhaps than in any other form of popular culture. Some/many/most (choose your own word) films are trivial and unimportant, but (a) in a number of films, the presence of grace is easy to spot and (b) of all the lively arts, film is that which ought to be most appealing to the Catholic heritage and even to the Catholic Church.

That we ignore it when we are not condemning it is sad proof of how much we are cut off from our own traditions.

23

Woody Allen: Romantic, Moralist, and Theologian

At the beginning of *Annie Hall,* Woody Allen appears on the screen. Life, he tells us, reminds him of the joke about the two Jewish women at a terrible Catskill resort.

"The food is no good," says one.

"And the portions are too small," says the other.

So with life, Woody tells us, there's not much in it and its all too short.

All Allen male characters from Fielding Melish in *Sleeper* through Zelig up to Mickey in *Hannah and Her Sisters* find themselves in the middle years of life devoid of direction and faith and hungry for a woman and for purpose. All of them are not unlike the self-description of Woody in the *Rolling Stone* interview: "I occasionally envy the person who is religious naturally, without being brainwashed into it or suckered into it by all the organized hustles. Just never occurs to such a person for a second that the world isn't about something."

And *RS* asks him, "Are you agnostic?"

"Agnostic—I mean, I know as little about it as anyone, you know?"

In one way or another, the Allen men pursue both the woman and purpose and, in one way or another, find the woman (or a woman) and a hint of purpose.

Agnostic Woody Allen may be, but then, as Morris Janowitz once said to me, an agnostic is someone who is afraid that there might be a God after all.

(You did note, by the way, that Woody did not give *RS* a straight answer to their question?)

Allen is also an incorrigible romantic, determined, except in *Love and Death,* to squeeze a happy ending out of his story and equally determined that his audiences get the point of the happy ending.

Thus in *Annie Hall,* the hero loses Annie at the end but observes, just in case there is any doubt left in the audience's mind, that the search for happiness in human relationships is what life is all about and that therefore we keep on trying.

It's an Ingmar Bergman point and Allen admires Bergman enormously: if there isn't any God or any purpose, and there may or may not be either, at least we have each other and we have love.

At the end of *Sleeper,* Melish, having won the girl (Diane Keaton as in so many other films), notes that there are only two certainties in life—death and sex and death doesn't leave you nauseous.

In *Stardust Memories,* his 1980 film about a film-maker making a film (and hence in substance and style both a tribute to and a parody of Fellini's *8 1/2*), the God question becomes more explicit. Woody wanders Fellini's beach and encounters an extraterrestrial in the form of a ball of light equipped with a computer voice (and, by the being's own admission, a 1600 IQ).

Why is there human suffering?
"That question is unanswerable."
Is there a God?
"That is not the right question."
Why should I make films when there is so much wrong with the world?

"We like your films, especially the early, funny ones. Anyway life is not so bad, like when you're with Isobel."

There then follows an exchange between the ET and the director about which of the two women in his life he should marry. The ET enthusiastically endorses Isobel.

What's the matter, are you my rabbi or something?
Then: Should I give up making films and become a missionary?
"You're not the missionary type. You help others by telling funnier stories."
[Exit ET.]

"To you I'm an Atheist," the Allen character says in *Stardust*. "To God I'm the loyal opposition." And in *Love and Death*, he observes, "If it turns out there is a God I don't think He's evil. The worst you can say about Him is that basically He's an underachiever."

A few scenes after his conversation with the Alien, the film-maker savors the loveliness of Isobel (Charlotte Rampling). She is embarrassed and flattered as he stares at her, making her all the more attractive. Life is not all bad as long as there are people like her in it. Perhaps she is a hint of an explanation.

Mickey in *Hannah* says the same thing with much more positive emphasis and perhaps tells us where Allen is in his own quest (as he watches a Marx Brothers movie after a suicide attempt):

I just, I just needed a moment to gather my thoughts, and be logical, and put the world back into rational perspective . . . and I went upstairs to the balcony, and I sat down, and you, now the movie was a film that I'd seen many times in my life since I was a kid and I always loved it. And, you know, I'm watching these people up on the screen, and I started getting hooked on the film, you know?
And I started to feel, How can you even think of killing yourself? I mean, isn't it so stupid? I mean, look at all the people up there on the screen. You know, they're real funny, and what if the worst is true?
What if there's no God, and you only go around once and that's it? Well, you know, don't you want to be part of the experience? You know, what the hell, it's not all a drag. And I'm thinking to myself, geez, I should stop ruining my life . . . searching for answers I'm never going to get, and just enjoy it while it lasts. And . . . you know . . . after all, who knows? I mean, you know,

maybe there is something. Nobody really knows, I know "maybe" is a very slim reed to hang your whole life on, but that's the best we have. And . . . then I started to sit back, and I actually began to enjoy myself . . .

It is an argument that goes much further than Bergman ever does and which would not be unfamiliar either to Blaise Pascal or that philosopher and mystic's modern disciple, the Catholic film-maker Eric Rohmer.

Pascal's "wager"' is that there is nothing lost by betting on God because if it's the right bet then you're on the winning side and if it's the wrong bet you don't lose anything and life is happier anyway for seeming to have a purpose.

The similarity between Mickey's expression of the "wager" and the same theme in *My Night at Maude's* led some people to say that Woody's theory had become Catholic in *Hannah* in a much more profound way than Mickey's temporary conversion earlier in the film, which stirred up so much laughter.

Perhaps. Though at the end of the film, the fact that the "wager" is supported by the joys of family life (a "hint" that the wager might be a good bet? If there are such joys, maybe, maybe there is also Joy?) is so like the conclusion of several of Bergman's recent films that it might be more appropriate to say that Allen has changed from being a Jewish agnostic to being a Lutheran agnostic!

In Thierry de Navacelle's book *Woody Allen on Location*, the author reports a rumor that Woody is about to become Catholic, a rumor that is not subsequently confirmed.

That is a matter for his personal life which, as I will note subsequently, must be sharply distinguished from the religious issues that obsess his films.

In passing, however, I must note as a priest that (a) I think it would be wonderful if he became a Catholic; (b) he would not stop being Jewish—to become Catholic does not mean to give up anything of your past, but only to add something to it; and (c) Pascal's gamble is all any of us have when push comes to shove, and it's as good a reason as any for slipping in the back door of the household of faith.

I tremble at the thought of how the New York Archdiocese would react to any attempt by Woody to actually enter the front door of the Church. I suspect that, led by the wondrous Father Smith from Dunwoodie, the Archdiocese would turn him down. Better, should it be an issue, that he cross the East River to his native Brooklyn and ask for Bishop Sullivan who was never, thank God, a rear admiral!

(I also note that, as my friend Jessica Rosner has observed, a study linking the work of Allen and Rohmer would be fascinating—the links with Bergman are obvious but perhaps superficial; the links with Rohmer are, I think, much deeper. The big difference is that, having wagered with Pascal for a long time and being steeped in a Catholic tradition all his life, the Frenchman plays out the gamble against the setting of the sacramentality of the ordinary, with a good deal more—what should we say?—savoir-faire than the American.)

I don't think there is that much change in the religious themes of the later Allen films (though I am one of those who think they are getting better. Like most people, I don't share Allen's dissatisfaction with *Hannah*, which is, I think, his masterpiece even if it is not as imaginative as *Purple Rose* or *Radio Days*). I see the wager in some form, often attenuated, in almost all his pictures, with the exception of the very funny (maybe the most funny) *Love and Death*. I see it especially in the happy endings that he imposes, usually with the moral made quite explicit, on most of his work.

The hero, even poor Zelig, gets the girl or at least a girl or at least the promise of a girl; and Allen says implicitly or explicitly, "Already all right, you've got her. Isn't that enough for now? Maybe she's a hint of something else. So you want more than hints? What can I tell you? Isn't she a good enough hint?"

This position, I argue, is Pascal's wager, romance with a vengeance, and sufficiently sacramental to be Catholic if you (or he) wants it to be.

All right already.

Manhattan is my least favorite of Allen's films (although the New York photography is sensational). It was the first of his films I had seen, and I thought it anti-Semitic and too much a New York Jewish joke. I laughed at the jokes because an appreciation of New York Jewish humor is required for survival in the sociological profession. I laughed, but I was the only one in the theater in Tucson who did laugh, because, I suppose, I was the only U. A. faculty member in the house.

Why should nonacademic goyem in Tucson, I asked myself, be forced to watch all this self-hatred from New York Jews?

Since then, I have learned that when Jews make such jokes about themselves, it is not anti-Semitic. I also realized that the picture intends to be critical about the mess New Yorkers make of their romantic lives.

I still don't like it.

On the other hand—and to the essential point of this essay—once one realizes that Allen is a moralistic romantic, one understands the romance of rebirth and renewal in the hero's return to his teen-age sweetheart. Mariel Hemingway is as powerful a symbol of fresh life and new beginnings as you are going to find in any contemporary film, a sacrament of rebirth for a tired middle-aged man of which there are few equals. On the level of realistic expectations, the relationship is nutty. On the level of romantic symbolism, it is brilliant. She is the happy ending, which Allen puts on his films and hopes for in life, raised to the tenth power.

The difference between Mariel as symbol and Mickey's theological argument at the end of *Hannah* is merely one of image opposed to explicit propositional reflection.

I therefore argue that Allen is a theological film-maker as well as a moralistic romantic, that his theology has always been that of Pascal, that the woman in the happy ending is a reinforcement of the bet—a sacrament for its validity if you will—and that whether he ever becomes a formal member of the household of the faith is less important (as far as his work is concerned) than the clear sacramentality of his vision.

A Catholic without knowing it? That says too much. Rather, I would suggest that having a little bit of faith in the possibility that happy endings (however tentative) in this life hint at a Happy Ending is like being a little bit pregnant. Once you begin to think about sacraments (without using the word), you are hooked.

Or to put it in yet another fashion, if you push romanticism far enough, you are skirting dangerously close to the thin ice on which you see the sign "Catholicism—St. Thomas Aquinas, Prop."

Or more recently, "David Tracy, Prop."

I am not so inclined to say that Allen is now skating near that thin ice as to say that he's always been close to it, but before he didn't see the sign.

Allen is the best of contemporary American film-makers. If he continues in his present trajectory, he could easily become the best ever. He is a comic, of course, and always has been. Indeed his greatest appeal has always been comedy, but he is also a Comic. His comedies are romances, but they are also Romances. He has not recently become a theologian. He has always been preoccupied by God. He is, as the *Rolling Stone* interview demonstrates, a God haunted person, even if he is very dubious about Her existence. The only change I see from *Sleeper* or *Bananas* to *Hannah* and *Radio Days* is that the God question has become more explicit and the tentative answer, if not more confident, at least a little more detailed.

(In some films, *September* and *Interiors*, the God question is muted—or transformed into the question of how humans can relate to one another. These are the least popular and the least successful—and certainly the least comic of the Allen films.)

Perhaps, also, there is a greater tendency in some of the later films—the Mia Farrow pictures—to see the ideal woman, the girl who one gets at the end of the story, the sacrament, as a wife. Her promise of joy is not merely physical sex (which in *Sleeper* is described as producing nausea afterwards) but in family relationships. The girl who is God becomes domesticated. The God who may still be absent may also lurk at the hearth.

It is inappropriate to link the recurrent religious quest in the Allen films with his own personal life. He leaves little doubt in his pictures that he is as God-haunted a pilgrim as are his characters. But he properly insists in the *Rolling Stone* interview that the films are only very loosely autobiographical. He is not Fielding Melish or Mickey. Diane Keaton is not Annie Hall. Mia Farrow is not Hannah. To suggest that they are is both offensive and ignorant. No storyteller (except the bright young folk from creative writing classes who produce narcissistic tripe for the literary magazines) is so foolish as to be literally autobiographic. Even the two great "autobiographic" novelists of the century— Proust and Joyce—changed the facts of their lives to fit the story they wanted to tell. "Marcel" is not Proust. Stephen is not Joyce. In both cases, you may learn a lot about their experiences from the novels and a lot about their hopes and their agonies. But you are not reading a memoir; the protagonist is necessarily different from the author if one is telling a story and not recording history.

Searching for the real-life counterparts of characters in a story is usually a waste of time and also offensive. While the characters may resemble real people, they are—even in Saul Bellow's stories—creatures of the author and not of God. They are what the author needs for his tale and not the people who exist in the world beyond that tale.

Thus it may be a good line to say that, on the basis of the news stories about him, Woody Allen started out in a Jewish family and has ended up in an Irish-Catholic family; but such a conclusion cannot legitimately be drawn from his work and is irrelevant to his work—at least until he himself tells us the link between his own experience of the important women in his life and the women in his films.

Is *Hannah* a love poem to Mia? Perhaps it is; if it is, it's a powerful tribute to her. At the present, however, that is a matter between them and does not impinge and should not impinge on our evaluation of his theology.

Is Mia the sacrament? Well, maybe, and heaven knows one could do worse, but the issue does not compute until Woody Allen is ready to tell us about his personal religious quest in some other format than his films.

Despite his fondness for New York in jokes, Allen is a great comedian, a successor to Chaplin, perhaps even more comic than Chaplin. My favorite "in" joke (I mean, I do visit New York, and rejoice that all I need to do is visit it) is in *Sleeper* where the Rip Van Winkle character asks how the atomic war started. He is told that a man named Albert Shanker obtained control of the bomb. Having jousted with the perpetually outraged president of the teachers union, I literally rolled off my chair and, God forgive me for it, rejoiced in seeing my adversary put down.

Still, it is a joke that wouldn't fly in Tucson or almost anyplace else.

But if the man wants to tell New York jokes at this stage of the game, let him tell them. Indeed, let him tell any jokes he wants to tell because it is humor that has provided the opening for him to become the most explicitly theological film-maker in America today.

Who else makes films that honestly and unambiguously ask about the existence of God and the purpose of life and suggest tentative answers that, as I contend in this chapter, are acceptably Catholic?

That the Catholic Church is utterly unaware of his theological concerns and of the presence of grace lurking in his films (presentably revealed by such worthies as Mariel Hemingway and Mia Farrow) proves nothing at all. As I have argued repeatedly in this book, the fact that bishops and theologians are insensitive to the rumors of angels, the presence of grace, in popular culture only proves that they are insensitive to grace and not particularly concerned about it.

If Allen's theological concerns become yet more explicit (though how can you be more explicit than Mickey's outburst in *Hannah*?), will it affect his humor? I am sure the critics will say so because it is the kind of thing that critics feel constrained to say. It seems to me, however, that there is another development taking place in his most recent work which suggests a different kind of humor—the compassionate and nostalgic (though I don't like that word) wit of *Purple Rose* and *Radio Days*.

I give away a few years to Woody, but I find myself trying also to re-create the world of the early thirties and forties with both amusement and fondness. So I understand his sentiments about old films and radio programs and decoder pins. I realize that they are funny and still innocent and that if one looks back on that era with sympathy and sensitivity, one may learn much about the nature of human nature which we have forgotten in our more affluent and more manic present.

Thus I wonder if he is trying to interpret or reinterpret the world of forty years ago for us in an elegiac and bittersweet wit that is warmer and less brittle than the wit of his earlier films. If that's what he's up to, it is a very brave and very interesting development. Whether he finds in the memories of those times yet another sacrament, hint of an explanation, rumor of angels remains to be seen.

His turn to the elegiac may be utterly unrelated to his theological concerns, a purely artistic and creative development. Or it may be a creative innovation that has been made possible by a decision to ride with Pascal's gamble for the moment. Or . . .

But then for that we'll have to wait and see.

Moralist, theologian, romantic—not exactly the Woody Allen of the ordinary feature story or clerical denunciation; but on the face of the data, I don't see how any of these titles can be denied him.

Catholic? In one sense, I contend, most certainly.

In the other sense? Well, that's up to Herself and to him, isn't it?

But surely a searcher for the Holy Grail. As I said at the beginning of this study, the font of Romance in the Western World is the legend of the Grail, the story that the Grail is the girl is God.

And in the Irish version of the story, the searcher gets the first two and by getting them earns a promise that the third will be his, too.

It is a version that I think Woody Allen would rather like.

24

The Soteriology of Clint Eastwood

The Western hero has always been a savior. Sheriff, marshal, cavalry officer, wandering gunfighter, honest cowpoke — Buck Jones, Tom Mix, Jimmy Stewart — the hero rides into town or on to the ranch to save the townsfolk or the people on the ranch from the powers of evil. Sometimes he collects the girl and settles down to become part of the new world that is a-borning (usually represented by a church and a school). Other times like Shane or the Lone Ranger he rides off into the sunset.

As John Cawelti has observed, the western is a mixture of convention and invention, of that which will offend us if they leave it out and that which holds our attention because it is variation on the essential theme.

While occasional anti-heroes are tolerated (the Maverick brothers for example) an original and successful western is one in which the hero is modeled after the convention but is still different enough from it to make us sit up and take notice.

For a quarter century the Clint Eastwood persona has dominated the western film, a hero and an anti-hero, a product of the rigid convention of the western genre and yet someone still absolutely unique. From the first of the "spaghetti westerns" directed by Sergio Leone (*A Fistful of Dollars*) to the most recent directed by Eastwood himself (*Pale Rider*), from the "man with no name" to the preacher with no name, the Eastwood character has fascinated millions of moviegoers, in great part one suspects because while he is always the same, he is also always changing.

It's about the change from the "man with no name" to the preacher with no name that this chapter is concerned. The transformation, I argue, is in substantial part the result of an insight by Eastwood himself that the character he and Leone created was a proto-Christ figure and that the more Christ-like he became, the more fascinating he would be. In *Pale Rider* he appears, coming down a mountain be it noted, in response to a young woman's explicit prayer to God for a savior. At the end, Shane-like, he rides up the mountain as the girl cries after him. But unlike Shane who simply goes over the mountain, the *Pale Rider* (who stands not for death as the book of Revelation suggests but for life) ascends (or perhaps only seems to ascend) into heaven.

Eastwood knows what he's doing. He senses, I think, that the "man with no name" had these soteriological characteristics within himself from the beginning and that if one purifies the dross from the earlier versions, one arrives at the essential paladin, the stripped-down western hero, the man who dies and rises again to save others.

I am not suggesting any explicit theological merit for Eastwood's films as I do for the films of Woody Allen. Rather I am noting that they reveal, ever more starkly, our hunger for a saving paladin and the impact on the shape of the savior figure in our culture of Jesus of Nazareth. Their effectiveness is in great part based on the increasingly self-conscious use of powerful Christ imagery which stirs deep if not always conscious resonsances in those who watch the films.

We all need or want (at least in our tradition) a savior.

Eastwood portrays for us a kind of savior which we find immensely satisfying.

While theologians may grow ever more obscure in trying to account for the puzzles of Christology (who was Jesus) and Soteriology (how did he save us) and while the Vatican makes life miserable for theologians not content with repeating the obscurities of the Councils of Chalcedon and Ephesus, popular culture knows who Jesus is and how he saves and reflects back to us the structures of the Jesus image as he lurks, resilient and powerful, in our imaginations.

I'm not suggesting that Jesus is exactly like the preacher in *Pale Rider* (nor do I think Eastwood is either). Rather I am contending that the preacher with no name is a portrait of someone who is much like Jesus and who hence vividly reveals our own Jesus images to ourselves — far more effectively than do the frivolous (because unintelligible) disputes of theologians and the Vatican.

The preacher kills, he makes love, he carries guns — behavior in which Jesus did not engage. He is more like the "winnowing fan," the "purifying fire" of which John the Baptist spoke — an avenging angel — than the Jesus of the New Testament. Yet, for all of that, he is a vivid reflection of the Jesus image in our culture, and as such far more meaningful for our imaginative life than most Sunday sermons which purport to be about Jesus but which in fact pervert the meaning of the Incarnation.

The preacher in *Pale Rider* is human — in fact a powerfully attractive human, especially to women but to men too.

The temptation for the Catholic preacher to make Jesus seem superhuman usually ends up by presenting him as someone who is less than human, unattractive to both men and women. Especially perhaps to women.

Even at his worst the man with no name was never inhuman. Moreover the transformation in him since 1964 pushes him to the edge between human and divine where any more development might well deprive him of his humanity and take from him his role as a popular culture symbol of the Incarnation.

To begin with, the Eastwood paladin represents the distilled essence of the western hero; courteous, laconic, soft-spoken, fearless, and unbelievably quick on the draw. Indeed, the character stops only a half step away from caricature. Only the resolute restraint of the actor prevents the persona from becoming comic. An extra twitch of the eye, for example, when he says, "Long walk!" to Michael Moriarity at the end of "*Pale Rider*" would have destroyed the illusion completely.

All western heroes are quick on the gun, but no one is quicker than the man with no name. In fact, his quickness is so wildly improbable that it hints, even in *Fistful of Dollars*, at superhuman qualities. We know as we watch him that there is going to be a shoot-out. We know that the "bad guys" (as clearly identifiable as if they wore the black hats of yesteryear) are going to get their just desserts, we know that no one could possibly draw and shoot with such deadly accuracy.

Yet we suspend our credibility and wait on the edge of our seats for the gunfight to begin. Justice and goodness will triumph as surely as it did in the days of Tom Mix, even if as in *The Outlaw Josey Wales* at least one and possibly two characters fall a fraction of a second before the shooting begins.

Moreover, to a greater extent than any of the other western heroes, the man with no name is a man of mystery. The loneliness and isolation of the paladin (nowhere to lay his head, in scriptural terms) is pushed almost to caricature. He rides in on his mule or his white horse, hat tilted forward on his head, cheroot in his mouth, back erect, face expressionless, a man with no past and no future and a dangerous, indeed lethal present.

The townsfolk eye him nervously, sensing how lethal he is, but unsure who he is.

We watch him eagerly because we know who he is and that the forces of evil had better beware. Their most dangerous opponent in the whole history of western films is on the scene.

They may hurt him before the story is over. But he will destroy them. Our savior is at hand.

All of this is convention, but the skill of Leone and later Eastwood himself is to be found precisely in the fact that they push convention up to its absolute limits without destroying our willingness to suspend credibility. The invention, even during the years of the spaghetti westerns, was to combine mystery with deadliness in such a way as to make us want to believe in the man with no name. Surrounding him with mists, making him seem to the other characters (and eventually even to us) to come back from the dead, having him appear suddenly and without warning at the end of the street — these ingenious directorial tricks made him seem even at the beginning of the series as someone intruding not only from a mysterious place in this world but perhaps as a being from another world. What began as style through the years turned into substance.

It is a tribute to Eastwood's skill as an actor and a director that he has not become so much a prisoner of the man with no name (and various equivalents who might have names such as the heroes in *Two Mules for Sister Sara* and *Hang 'Em High*) that he can play no other role — as the late Basil Rathbone was captured by Sherlock Homes and Raymond Massey by Abraham Lincoln. Dirty Harry is perhaps a modern, urban version of the man with no name, but not nearly so much the paladin, to say nothing of the Christ figure that the gun fighter has become.

In the early films, the man with no name is not possessed by his savior role. Thus in *Fistful of Dollars* he appears merely as someone riding through a Mexican town who cynically exploits warfare between two families to make money for himself.

Then the savior role is forced on him (as it often is on apparently cynical western heroes) by the need to save a beautiful woman (Marianne Koch) and her child from oppression. Next he must pay for his goodness by terrible suffering (a theme which runs through all the films). Then he becomes an instrument of terrible vengeance against those who had tortured him, murdered their enemies, and threatened the few of decent people left in the town.

After the final fight, he is saved from an ultimate ambush by an old man whom he had befriended and protected — another recurrent theme. (Repeated in *High Plains Drifter* when the dwarf finishes off the last would-be killer and in *Pale Rider* when Michael Moriarity disposes of the chief enemy).

Then Shane-like, he rides out again, with a semi-comic (but unsmiling or almost unsmiling) last line.

By *High Plains Drifter* the man with no name has become a predestined savior and avenger. He rides into the town of Lago (alongside a chill lake which may be an allusion to Dante's hell — especially since he changes the name of the town to Hell before the story ends), apparently a gunfighter looking only for a shave and a bath. But it soon develops that he must avenge the murder of Jim Duncan. the late town marshal, who had been bull-whipped to death with the connivance of many in the town and the silence of the rest.

It is deliberately left unclear who the man with no name is. Might he be Duncan come back from the grave? He seems to materialize out of the mists at the beginning of the film and disappear into them at the end. Yet no one in the town recognizes him as Duncan. Or might he be an angel of vengeance? Or God himself coming to impose justice? Or simply what he pretends to be — a gunfighter caught up in the vibrations of the Lago which demand that wrong be righted?

But if the last is the case, why does he say to the dwarf at the end when the later says he never did catch his name, "You know what it is."

In *High Plains Drifter* the mystery is deepened, the savior role made more intricate and complex (the town is saved after being punished) and explicit if grim religious issues are raised. But the man with no name has also become gratuitously violent and hence perhaps less attractive than in previous films. We liked him more as the cynic turned savior by chance than as the grimly determined avenger. Moreover, unlike the Outlaw Josey Wales who was also heavily into vengeance, the man with no name shows no sign of gentleness at the end. He is a bit too much the grim reaper, too much the angel of death to be as attractive as he used to be.

When he appears again, fourteen years later, (on what seems to be the same white horse, by the way) he is a changed man — still indeed the man with no name, but now without a gun or a cigar and now with a roman colar tucked away in his pack. Moreover, he is always gentle to everyone, an occasional trait of the man with no name now become the hallmark of the preacher with no name. Now he is indeed the knight without fear and without reproach, not so much an avenging angel as a protecting angel for Megan (the fifteen year old who summoned him by her prayer) and her mother Sara and Sara's suitor as played marvelously by Michael Moriarity.

Nor does the preacher want to get into gunfights. His guns are left at the hotel. If he must eventually do battle with "Stockburn" (The Devil? The one who would burn the stock?) the reason is that this fight has occurred before (Stockburn may have killed him) and perhaps will occur again. The gunfight becomes a war in heaven.

You can, by the way, usually tell the bad guys in Eastwood films because they wear light colored cattle dusters, while Eastwood's duster is always darker, a nice twist on the white hats and black hats of the past.

Finally, he treats women, most notably Sara and Megan, with enormous respect, something that was only an occasional trait of the man with no name. No longer do we see the obligatory scene in which the hero drags a not altogether unwilling woman off to bed — in earlier films almost as de rigeur as dynamite, fire and a Gatling gun. On the contrary, he merely says softly, a request and invitation in response to her offering, "Sara, close the door."

Eastwood has kept the invulnerability and the skill of the

man with no name and added the goodness of Shane. But Alan Ladd as Shane was as incredible as he was admirable. The preacher with no name still forces credibility on us because of the electricity we feel in his character and because we therefore want him to be real — even if his quasi supernatural origins and nature ought to make him even more improbable than Shane.

I am not sure what is more interesting, the transformation of the Eastwood western persona or the fact that even its earliest, spaghetti manifestations, the raw material for such transformation was already present.

By *Pale Rider* he is surely a messiah. But even in *Fistfull of Dollars* the messiah role was already present, waiting to be developed.

It is most unlikely that either Leone or Eastwood thought in messiah terms in the early nineteen sixties. Rather the "convention" of the genre forced such raw material into the character they were inventing. Only with the passage of time, did Eastwood come to understand where the dynamic might lead. If his Ascension into heaven at the end of *Pale Rider* is so much more powerful than the earlier Ascension of Shane, the reason (in addition to the fact that Shane had created the paradigm) is that there is much more complexity and mystery and ambiguity built into the character of the preacher and much more self-conscious use of the messianic symbolism.

An admirable man, so good and so strong as to be almost more than human to begin with, suffers and dies to save others, then comes back from the dead to save them again and finally, after routing their enemies, leaves them behind with a promise of continued protection.

In a culture where Jesus had not appeared such symbolism would not have been possible.

In a culture which remembers Jesus but tends to forget how mysterious and ambiguous and disconcertingly attractive he was, such symbolism may well be necessary.

Pale Rider is not great art perhaps, but it is a great western precisely because the latent messianic symbolism of the western has rarely been used with such skill and imagination — or by an actor who is able to convey so well the mysterious and attractive ambiguity which must have marked Jesus when he walked among us.

Pale Rider is also a judgment on such works as *Jesus Christ Superstar* and *Godspell* which try to cope with the mystery of Incarnation by reducing Jesus to the merely human. *Pale Rider* does not eliminate mystery. It does not tell us finally who and what the preacher is precisely and exactly. Like Jesus, the preacher doesn't say. And like us, Sara and Megan and the rest of the folk in the mining camp are not sure either; they don't know quite what terms to use to describe their experience.

They also understand, as many theologians and curial officials do not and cannot, that words are inadequate tools to describe an encounter with the overwhelmingly sacred. Words — like theologies — may be necessary, but in the end they hide almost as much as they disclose.

A Jesus who does not disconcert is ultimately not the real Jesus. For two thousand years we have tried to rework Him so that he fits into our categories, our plans, our need for power and control. We connive to identify Him with our cause and turn Him against our enemies and their causes. He slips away from us, as elusive as He was in His own time. Just when we think we have Him, at the very moment we think we have eliminated all uncertainty about Him, we discover that whoever we have signed up for our side, it isn't Jesus any more.

Is Clint Eastwood aware of all these implications of the preacher with no name?

I don't know and, in truth, I don't care. He does understand that Jesus is mysterious, attractive, haunting, enigmatic, irresistible — more than many theologians and bureaucrats and parish clergy seem to understand. For the moment that is enough.

He also seems to understand how much we miss Him.

Does not Megan, at the end of the film, crying out with

much more passion than the little boy in Shane (perhaps with the passion of Mary the sister of Lazarus) speak for us all when she shouts, "We love you, preacher! We all love you! I love you, preacher! I love you!"

That, one must say, is what it's all about.

25

The Comics: Philosophy Arcade for Commuters

The ballerina stands on a rock in a pond and announces, "I am woman, fear me."

The penguin, wearing his usual bow tie, responds, hand on chest, "Fear you?"

"I have struggled hundreds of years and men still believe me to be powerless." She begins her dance and the penguin joins her.

"Yet after only a couple of weekends in Moscow"—the pas de deux is now taking place on a flat surface in another world—"I managed to humiliate the entire American Marine Corps."

The penguin and the woman are now in a spotlight on a stage. "With fifteen minutes in a hotel room, I've toppled an American religious empire and its king."

The ballet continues against a pink background. "And with twenty-four hours in a D.C. townhouse I've singlehandedly helped determine who would or wouldn't lead the entire free world in 1988."

Now they are back on the rock in the pond, though the rock seems much higher.

The ballerina takes her bow. "Men! If you can't join 'em, beat 'em."

"Yeek," says the exhausted penguin.

It is Sunday June 14, 1987. The Embassy, PTL, and Gary Hart Scandals are in the immediate past. We are in "Bloom County," and the penguin is the inimitable Opus. In fact, we are on the Sunday comic page. In six panels, Berke Breathed (I doubt the name is real) has summarized the sex scandals, interpreted them, dismissed the absurd ideology of unisex, and emphasized once again the enormous power of women to disconcert, dismay, and unnerve men. Moreover, the ingenious critique has been accomplished in the summer of 1987 (*Witches of Eastwick, More Die of Heartbreak*) without a trace of the hatred of women which usually accompanies the acknowledgement of their power to overwhelm.

We are in a full-color arcade of philosophy and social criticism.

We turn the page, and beneath Gary Trudeau's attack on Ronald Reagan, we find Cathy prying a huge stack of mail out of the box on the wall of her impersonal apartment building—engagement announcements. In the winter, she says, she gets only bills. In the summer—engagements, weddings, births. And a post card from the "Cote d'azur where I'm showing off my new size 4 body in a bikini on board a yacht owned by this really cute French guy named Philippe."

In the final panel, we see Cathy on the floor, muttering to herself, "Winter mail goes for the wallet. Summer mail goes for the heart."

Cathy wants someone she can plan with, a long-range, long-term, lifetime relationship, but she is shocked when her boyfriend Irving proposes a vacation together: "Are you crazy? I'm not ready for that big of a commitment!"

She does not represent a rejection of the "woman of the

eighties" choice of career and independence. Rather, she stands for the ambiguities and uncertainties of such a choice—as well as the humor involved in the self-deceptions and rationalizations of her world.

We move up the page to "For Better or Worse." The husband is in the bathtub, escaping, as he says, from all his worldly cares. His wife opens the door, a smile on her face, a hint perhaps of romance. "Can I come in?"

She continues, "What's that—a new bar of soap. You always start a new bar of soap before the old one is gone."

"So what?" he demands.

"So what? I'm left with a row of soggy little lumps in the soap dish, that's what!"

The argument is interrupted by an argument outside the door between their two kids.

"Mom, Michael says I'm only six—but I'm six an' a half. Tell him I'm six an' a half."

And what does the mother say? "Honestly, you two! If you're going to argue about something, make it something worthwhile!"

Another parent in trouble is Ted in "Sally Forth."

His daughter and her friend Molly are setting up a lemonade stand. The cute little blond tyke wonders if she can ask her father for some business advice.

Of course she can. "I can probably give you a simplified version of some of the basic business principles that might be helpful in running a lemonade stand . . ." Next panel: "I'll try not to get too technical on you. What's your question?"

Clutching her pitcher of lemonade, the kid asks, "Should we set it up as a partnership or as a subchapter S corporation for tax purposes?"

Final panel: Sally enters the kitchen carrying a box. Ted is slumped at the table.

Sally: "What's with the frown, Ted?"

Ted: "Kids are too darn sophisticated these days."

Next we turn to "The Far Side." A somewhat battered pooch slumps in the chair of a room full of very elite poodles. "So Raymond," says mama poodle to the junkyard dog, "Linda tells us that you work in the security division of an automobile wrecking site."

In this wild and weird arcade we have entered on the peace of a humid summer Sunday, we can find an incredible variety of beings, stories, and messages: there are dogs (Fred Basset and Marmaduke); cats (Garfield and on some Sundays Bill the Cat from "Bloom County"); tigers (Hobbs of "Calvin and Hobbs"); parrots ("Kudzu"); beagles (sometimes thinking they are World War I fighter aces); Vikings (Hagar the Horrible and Broom Hilda); and such old friends (usually in very modern dress) as Moon Mullens, Dick Tracy, Mary Worth, Winnie Winkle, and Blondie.

Something for everyone.

Also, unless one is completely biased, some of the best wit, social commentary, and moral philosophy to be found anywhere in contemporary America.

And the arcade is open every day of the week.

"Whom do you write for?" I ask old pro Jim Lawrence who is trying to persuade me that Blackie Ryan belongs in the comics.

"Commuters," he replies. "They're the ones who read the comics every day."

A philosophy arcade for commuters.

One of the characters in "Bloom County," almost as appealing as Opus, is Michael J. Binkley, a young man whose bedroom is equipped with a closet in which all his anxieties are kept, a closet which he describes the day I write this chapter as a "bastion of metaphors and metaphysics, of my furies and fears, both subtle and sublime."

"And," he adds, as eels crawl out of the closet and tangle in his hair, "sometimes not so sublime!"

In one strip, Binkley is awakened from his sleep and, below his Wayne Newton poster, cowers under his sheet and stares at the closet door from which a voice bellows, "On your feet brave knave, adventure awaits."

In the next panel, a knight in armor appears on a mount that seems to be a two-legged dragon with a tail and a unicorn. The dragon sniffs curiously at Michael. "Time is short and the world is vast," says the knight. "Hurry we have much to do and see . . . Fantastic horizons! Enchanted kingdoms! Magical lands beyond imagination with chocolate dragon and white satin maidens who look like Madonna with her hair combed! So hop up, lad," he extends his hand, looking a bit like Sean Connery. "There's a whole life of meaningful personal discovery ahead of us!"

"I'm afraid I can't. I have a science report on snails due in class tomorrow."

"Suit yourself! Away!" The knight and his mount bound back into the closet.

Under his covers again, Binkley reflects, "Someday when I've got kids, a dog, a mortgage, liver pate rotting in the 'fridge and a chrysler mini-van in the garage, I'll say to myself, 'Binkley, you poor miserable bored yuppy . . . you never went for the gusto.'"

As I tell the Sunday congregation, the knight is Jesus and you're Binkley.

Speaking of Yuppies, another night Binkley awakens with a monster on his bed. "Guess what we have waiting in your anxiety closet tonight? Fifteen and one-half million young urban professionals!"

"No, not Yuppies, anything but yuppies!"

"We also have a truckload of youngish upwardly mobile mothers!"

"Yummies? Those are worse!"

"And maybe a few sniveling lawyers, indecently machiavellian!"

"Slimes!" Binkley cowers in a corner.

"And gay urban professionals!"

"Guppies! Run! It's the attack of the over-used media acronyms!"

In yet another strip, a "liberal"—balding, sad-eyed, droop-shouldered—sits with Opus in a bar.

"The whole thing started when I bumped into Jackie at the carrot juice counter during a 'save the whales' benefit picnic. She said I ought to write that book we'd discussed back at Berkeley in '68.

"So I said, 'what the heck,' and borrowed an old Smith-Corona from Abbie at the world hunger council, scraped a few bucks together and published that little baby myself.

"I titled it 'The American Rich: Forgotten Financial Fascists.' It went through 22 printings. I netted over a quarter million."

"Slurp," says Opus, draining his glass.

"Today my accountant ran up and gave me a hug and said, 'Congratulations, Larry . . . you saved $91,000 last year with Reagan's tax cut.'"

An agonized pause for a whole panel.

Then a scream: "WHAT'S A LIBERAL TO DO?!"

"Hit me again," Opus says to the bartender, "and put it on that guy's tab."

These three strips from what may be the best of the contemporary comics illustrate the genius of the comic strip philosophers at their most skillful—a sensitivity to the absurdities and contradictions of our lives; a quick grasp of the ironic; and deft, rapid depictions of the absurd and the ironic made all the more effective because of the presence of other species (like penguins) who seem to have acquired our traits. (Two buffaloes stand casually at an office water cooler in "The Far Side," looking like young executives trying to seem important, with the caption, "water buffalo.")

With the exception of "Doonesbury," the best of the comics do not permit themselves to be ideological. Both the left and the right are legitimate prey for their criticism—as the bards and the poets of Ireland made fun of anyone and everyone. The comics are, for that very reason, more lively, more pointed, and more effective than any of the social commentary to be found on the op-ed pages. With most columnists, you can predict after the first sentence, indeed often after the headline, what the rest of the column will say. But the ironists of the comic pages must catch your attention in their first panel and hold it for the few seconds it takes you to consume the strip. They have no time for pomposity and predictability. They must strike and strike quickly and then, like Binkley's dragon, bound out of the arcade until tomorrow.

At their best then, the ironic philosophers of the comic page are both deft craftspersons and highly sophisticated artists. Their genre imposes on them rigid constraints of time, space, and convention. To be able to say a lot and say it in a way that gains attention and obtains laughter requires enormous skill. The moral criticism involved, for example, in the brief interlude of the husband and wife fighting over bath soap appeals to both the common experience of human intimacy and the ethical and religious ideals that we all know should preside over such intimacy but which frequently do not—more because of inattention than because of malice. The cartoonist has perhaps four panels—six on weekends—and no more than five or six bits of dialogue to say these things vividly and concretely. Yet he can often drive home his moral or philosophical point with more power than a year of Sunday sermons.

The homilist who does not find material for a homily in almost any day's comic page has lost all sense of creative imagination.

An amoeba in "The Far Side" is splitting off from another. "No, Elizabeth," screams presumably the parent, "Don't go!"

Sound familiar?

Moreover, the story strips ("Rex Morgan," "Brenda Star," etc.) are often drawn with considerable sophistication, borrowing many techniques from films and cramming an enormous amount of subtle communication into a single frame. While the story strips seem to be in eclipse at the present, some of them are quite capable of creating enough suspense to make you wonder what will happen the next day, no small feat given the constraints of time and space.

At their best, the ironists of the funny papers compare well with the cartoons in the *New Yorker*. I realize that it is heresy to say so, but "Cathy," "Bloom County," and "The Far Side" are as good as if not better than the revered *New Yorker* drawings—and are read by many millions more people.

At this point in the present chapter, the readers may have divided into two groups—those who think I'm out of my mind and those who not only agree completely but wonder why I bother to argue the point. The latter read the "funnies", the former do not.

The latter position was summed up for me by a priest who heard that I had been working on a possible story strip called "Blackie Ryan's World" (in which with my characteristic weakness, I fear, of biting off more than I can chew, I tried to combine a story with a joke a day). "I'm not surprised," he sneered. "Your stuff is comic strip material anyway."

I thanked him for the compliment and said that some of the most polished work in America was to be found on the comic page.

To repeat a theme that runs through every chapter of this essay, a genre must be judged not by the worst of the work done within it but by the best. Some of the "funnies" are terrible. But since there is intense competition for space on the comic page, the level of skill displayed is remarkably high. One who dismisses comics as worthless trash either has not looked at them or is so blinded by his own ideology and snobbery that he does not understand either the irony that pervades the page or the skill necessary to drive home an ironic point under the severe constraints imposed on the cartoonist.

One looks not to the op-ed page nor to the canned

comedy of TV for the Mark Twains and the Will Rogers of contemporary America but to the comics.

Yet they are still derided, mostly by those who don't read them, "Doonesbury" and "Peanuts" perhaps excepted. Most editors realize how important they are to the economic survival of their paper. If such lofty journals as the *Washington Post* or the *Boston Globe* should attempt to abandon their comic pages (and thus really imitate the *New York Times*—whose ancient decision about comics was not based on principle but on the practical necessities of the time), they might just have to go out of business.

It is humiliating to journalists whose self-image was molded by *All the President's Men* to realize that many more Americans read the comics than read the editorials and op-ed page and the latest reports of a Washington scandal. While the comics have helped make and sustain American journalism, they arc trcatcd with a strange mixture of economic fear (you have to have the damn things) and contempt (for the blockheads who read them). Hence the size of comics and the space available to them and the money paid for them is under constant pressure.

Perhaps some editors read the comics and understand how good they are, but being self-respecting members of the intellectual elite, they would not dare admit it to anyone else. It is too bad, because if there is one thing that American journalism needs in this day of inflated self-image and collapsing public image, it is the ability to laugh at itself.

The appeal of the contemporary comic is that its irony leaps to our own sense of irony (often vestigial) and helps us, however briefly, to laugh at ourselves as we see our own faults and foibles in the humans and the animals and the "creatures " depicted on the page.

The "Far Side" again: A couple sitting in a parlor. A duck is ambling down the corridor. The wife says to the husband, "Here he comes, Earl . . . Remember, be gentle but firm . . . We are absolutely, positively, NOT driving him south this winter."

The philosophy of the comic arcade is practical, not

theoretical (despite Hobbs, the imaginary tiger of the little boy Calvin), moral not metaphysical, ironic not didactic. It is the social criticism of the bard, not of the Ph.D. with tenure. But most professional philosophers have turned to logic of one sort or another; and most social critics merely repeat ideologies that are innocent of the capacity to laugh at or criticize the self.

Socrates would not be a distinguished professor or an op-Ed page columnist or a writer for *The Nation,* much less for the mom-and-pop journal *Commonweal.* He would be a cartoonist on the funny pages. That's where the action is if you're looking for social criticism to which people listen.

Spiritual growth requires perspective on the self, a capacity for detached irony about one's own foolishness and pretensions, rigidities and weaknesses, pomposity and self-righteousness, self-deceptions and defense mechanisms.

You're not going to find any devastating critiques of these propensities of human nature in theology books or in spirituality tracts these days. For the most part, they currently pursue, with undeviating humorlessness, political ideologies in which self-doubt is not permitted because it interferes with interminable denunciations of the current target groups (white male heterosexuals being the favorite these days). If you are doing black theology or feminist theology or gay theology or third world theology, you would commit a grave sin should you engage in irony or laughter at yourself. You are part of a sacred cause, a spokesperson for the oppressed (who, by the way, never did elect you to that role). Irony and laughter are singularly inappropriate for such a person.

Yet irony is, finally, an essential ingredient of any valid theology. For irony sees the folly of human pretensions; it is the counterweight to all idolatries. The fundamental dictum of irony is quite simple: "A human is not God."

The immediate corollary of that dictum is "And when we act like we're God, we're usually pretty funny."

And a practical policy, a moral conclusion from these two

dicta is "The best way to resist the temptations to think that you're God and to act like you're God is to acquire the ability to laugh at yourself."

Since theologians speak about God (or at least are alleged to), they are readily tempted to speak as though they have been endowed with divine wisdom. Since churchmen speak for God (or allege that they do), they are similarly tempted to solemnity that, one suspects, would embarrass God.

Both groups desperately need a sense of irony so that they can laugh at themselves and see themselves in proper perspective. There are few better sources of irony in the world than the comic pages.

Irony, however, is required for more than the humility that ought to be a virtue zealously pursued by those who engage in theological reflection. It is an absolute prerequisite for theology. Without irony one forgets the essential nature of human nature as creature, indeed funny creature. Pomposity, self-importance, and self-righteousness make theological reflection impossible because they turn the theologian into the object of the reflection; and the theologian is by definition not God.

An irony that I suspect is not lost on God.

I am reasonably certain that She is a comedienne. Otherwise she would not have made us so funny.

Like Cathy at her mailbox or Binkley faced with his anxiety closet. Or Snoopy taking on the Red Baron. Again.

Humans are God's comic page.

26

Catholicism and Popular Culture

Let us recall a scene from William Kennedy's film based on his novel *Ironweed*. Helen is about to die from stomach cancer. She enters a Catholic church; kneels in front of the statue of St. Joseph; and in a tone of voice one would use in talking to a close friend, pleads her case. It is a self-serving plea, but Helen admits as much and seems to imply that the Saint is on her side and expects something more than an objective presentation. At the end, she finds a ten-dollar bill on the vigil light stand. She is able to die in a clean room, clad in her favorite kimono after a shower, surrounded by the few precious things she still possesses, and listening to Beethoven's version of the "Ode to Joy."

I would suggest that there are two modes of reaction to that scene.

In one mode, we can consider the following points as we watch the scene:

1) The scene, like much of the rest of the movie, is filmed in the soft color that is supposed to indicate nostalgia, as if light was different in 1938 than it is today.

2) Ms. Streep's celebrity image makes it difficult for us to take her seriously as a hooker and a drunk.

3) The interlude is an exercise in sentimentality and superstition, cute perhaps but not realistic.

4) It is also a manifestation of the author's Irish-Catholic obsession with salvation for his characters. The money from St. Joseph is an artificial *Deus ex Machina* intervention.

5) It is certainly not in the book. Kennedy is playing to the galleries so that his grim story will not be completely rejected by the movie-going public.

Having analyzed the scene and torn it apart, one can later leave the theater with considerable self-satisfaction. One has destroyed William Kennedy, Pulitzer Prize notwithstanding. One is part of the ranks of serious critics who refuse to be taken in by trash. One is upholding standards. One is a tough-minded, sophisticated literary thinker.

It's worth five dollars (seven in New York, I am told) to walk away from a movie house with such feelings of satisfaction.

Isn't it?

Let's consider the second mode.

One sits in the theater utterly dazzled by the wit and the brilliance of the scene and revels in the acting, the dialogue, the atmosphere, the twist in the story line.

Then later, perhaps for days, one turns the scene over in one's mind and imagination, thinking, reflecting, speculating.

One has not, in this case, destroyed William Kennedy. One has rather become a coconspirator with him.

Following the work of Walter Ong and a suggestion of Ingrid Shafer, I would suggest that we call the first sensibility *agon* and the second *empathos*. In the first, we are the adversary of the author (film-maker, etc.). In the second, we are the creator's somewhat reserved but open-minded and open-spirited ally. In the first, we seek to find fault; in the second, we seek first to enjoy, then later to reflect and understand.

I think it reasonably obvious that most of us approach works of culture from the empathetic sensibility. We are predisposed to enjoy a work instead of enjoying its destruction. We are entertained by the work itself not by an *agon*, a struggle with the author. We are inclined, by nature or nurture, to be magnanimous instead of mean spirited.

As more and more young people graduate from college, however, and join the ranks of what I would call the "half educated," the sensibility for which we stand may diminish in society. By "half educated," I mean the kind of person who has had a couple of courses in literary criticism or even an introductory course and is convinced thereby that sophistication and intelligence require that one approach a work of culture as an adversary, as an agonist with an axe in hand.

It is a free country, and if one pays for a movie ticket or buys a book, one has every right to find whatever amusement one wants. My point, however, is that for most of human history the notion that entertainment is not the first purpose of encountering a work of art would have been unthinkable. It is an indication of the mixture of puritanism and academicism which dominates high culture today that the suggestion that we seek entertainment from culture sounds dangerous if not heretical. Culture means work, struggle, criticism, *agon*.

I do not think it at all accidental that the agonistic approach to culture became part of our life at about the time universities began to give tenure.

To make my point more strongly, in most eras of human history, if someone asserted that the first question about a story is not whether it is a good story, one which holds your attention and entertains you, then that person would be thought mad.

With reason.

Enjoyment and intellectual work are not the same thing. Nor is it true, despite the Puritan ethic, that one earns the right to the former by engaging in the latter.

The argument against enjoyment is that it constrains us to abandon our critical faculties, to substitute imagination for intellect, and to be come a consumer of trash, a favorite word of the agonists.

In fact, this argument is not true. Someone who is well educated and not merely half educated can revel in a film or a book or a musical composition and still have his critical apparatus in full operation in, to use a computer metaphor, background mode. Such a person is resonating to the work with the totality of her/himself and not just with an aggressive (and macho) intellect. By being open and generous to author and work, such a consumer frees the resources of the whole personality to resonate with the work. The agonistic resonates with narrow, adversarial intellect.

I propose a test: read a dozen book reviews from your local paper or the *New York Times*. Then grade the reviews on a score from zero to nine according to whether you think the author of the review had made up her/his mind whether s/he was going to like or dislike the book beforehand. Giving the reviewer the benefit of the doubt. I would wager, nonetheless, that only a few reviews will rank above five and that the average will be much below it.

The agonist knows what s/he is going to dislike before participating in it. Indeed the purpose of the agonist is not to participate but to judge or, better, to confirm a judgment.

The Meryl Streep scene I described at the beginning is a perfect example of how necessary empathos is in consuming a work of art. Granted that all the agonistic observations cited above may be true, they nonetheless miss the point of the scene completely. Even as critical intellect, the agonistic approach fails.

The scene is about grace, the most powerful, if comic (and most powerful precisely because comic) revelation of grace in a grace-drenched work. In case you're in doubt, Kennedy says of the same monologue in the book (with St. Joseph absent), "a will to grace if you would like to call it that."

Walter Ong suggests that *agon* is a male approach and that the world is developing in a direction where *agon* is less needed and empathos more needed—that womanly styles and sensibilities are now more important for the species. Be that as it may, the direction of evolution in the consumption of culture is, I think, in the opposite direction. Young people are being trained by our universities to think that if you don't approach culture with the style and perspective of an academic critic, you are uneducated and capable only of enjoying trash.

I do not fault the academic critics or the book review editors and writers. Men and women are entitled to earn their living or to make a few extra bucks or to win tenure. I would note in passing that the best critics are those who are able to enjoy first (I cite my friends Robert C. Marsh and Roger Ebert by way of example) and then judge. I condemn, rather, the mentality that says the sensibility of the academic critic is the only way or the best way or the educated way to approach culture.

I denounce, therefore, the heretical notion that you cannot trust the human imagination, the human capacity to enjoy and to be entertained. I suggest that the agonistic approach to culture in which young people are indoctrinated is not without taint of snobbery: those who approach culture with adversarial intellect, it is suggested, are more intelligent and better educated than those who simply enjoy culture and are entertained by it.

Note the unshakeable first premise of the position: it is either adversarial intellect or surrender to trash. That reflective intellect can operate in "background mode" while enjoyment is taking place is a possibility that the agonist cannot abide, cannot, in fact, even discuss.

The agonist is almost necessarily mean-spirited. If you are always on the attack (upholding standards in the pose of the professional critic or the book review editor), there are few works that can possibly please. You settle only for the perfect, and since nothing is perfect, you're never satisfied. You may never be entertained, but you have a hell of a lot of fun attacking.

About nothing is the agonist more mean-spirited than genre differences. Thus, a columnist of the *Chicago Tribune*, one of the most mean-spirited of reviewers, after praising the work of Elmore "Dutch" Leonard, observed that Leonard is the best in his genre but that it is an inferior genre.

Why, one wonders, does that need to be said? Is it really necessary to compare *Finnegans Wake* with *Glitz?* Why is the columnist not ready to permit Mr. Leonard his own genre? Why is he not content with judging the author's work by the canon of rules appropriate for that genre?

Undoubtedly, Mozart is superior to Linda Ronstadt, but so what?

Could not one respond that *"Canciones de Mio Padre"* is superior to much of the noise that passes for modern music and that Mr. Leonard is a better writer than some of those precious authors who clutter the so-called literary magazines?

To the agonistic sensibility, there is only one genre that is "serious" and that is the "serious" genre or "literary" or academic or whatever one wishes to call it.

Now I am prepared to admit that the best work in the literary genre (let's say a story by Flannery O'Connor or Louise Erdrich) is superior to the best in other genres (at least ordinarily), but so what? Making comparisons across genre lines (the implicit assumption of much book reviewing) is like comparing apples and oranges. Moreover, such comparisons ignore the painfully obvious fact that in the "literary" genre as in every other genre, there is much writing (film-making, music, etc.) that is graceless and inept and dull.

The agonist rejects genre differences and is profoundly suspicious of enjoyment and of the possibility that the intellect can continue to function when entertainment, pure and simple, is taking place. Moreover, he also is profoundly suspicious of any work that people, ordinary people, enjoy. As a rule of thumb in the agonistic world, if a work is popular, it is no good, indeed trash.

Rock and Roll, for example, is surely trash—and possibly blasphemous and pornographic trash. Not only do people like it, but teen-age people, God save us all, like it. To be concerned, as I am, about the religious themes in some rock music is to endorse pornography.

I happen to like Ronstadt, but being Catholic and having a catholic sensibility as well as a Catholic sensibility, I think I can enjoy both. I can find grace in both. And perhaps Grace. (In Ironweed, glory be to God, I find grace and Grace in superabundance.)

Another example, one I think is an excellent litmus paper, is the work of the rock singer Madonna. Is one willing to be open and generous and listen to the cry for renewal in her "Like a Virgin," the cry of every human heart to be treated like someone new and surprising and wonderful? Or is one so put off by the paraphernalia and accoutrements that one does not hear the grace? If you are not a teen-age girl, it is easy, I think, to be agonistic with Madonna—but at the cost of missing the grace.

For the true agonist, "best seller" and "trash" are synonyms; grace is excluded. So, too, is Grace.

My point here is not that if it's popular it has to be good. It is merely that if it is popular it may possibly be good; and if it is unpopular it may very well be good but it might also be terrible.

I think these are modest points, but your true agonist cannot admit them.

Especially when the agonist is a Catholic cleric or hierarch arguing against the importance of culture and especially popular culture to the Church.

While I was working on this book, I happened to read a collection of essays on "evangelization." The level of intellectual honesty in the book was demonstrated by the fact that not once did any of the authors note that the Church's official teaching on birth control was a major barrier to "evangelizing the unchurched."

One of the essays was devoted to an analysis of American culture, an analysis that was long on moral fervor and short on nuance and evidence. Apparently, the priest who wrote it felt that you win people to the Church by denouncing them. A

Benedictine (and hence a man who ought to know better), he contended that the media has (sic) turned us from a nation of book readers to a nation of TV watchers and that such rock music celebrities as Bruce Springsteen shape American culture.

"Media" of course is a plural word (perhaps the priest is too young to know any Latin), and in fact, book reading is at an all-time high in America. Moreover, the image of Springsteen as a malign influence on American culture could only be held by a man who had never listened to the "Boss's" music or read his lyrics.

However, this doubtless sincere priest represents a typical attitude among American Catholic clergy. They parrot without reflection or evidence the cliches of the critical agonistic conventional wisdom ("vast wasteland"), immune both to the meaning of their own heritage and the possibility that grace might lurk in popular culture.

To such people, the argument in this book will seem quite mad.

Nonetheless I make the argument:

1) Popular culture gives us strong hints of the nature of human nature.

2) Catholicism, a religion of sacramentality, must be sensitive to the possibility that grace may be found in the "stories" that ordinary people enjoy.

3) In fact, while much of popular culture is worthless (as is much of "serious" culture, too), some of it does indeed contain signals of the transcendent, the presence of grace, rumors of angels.

4) Hence, popular culture has theological, homiletic, and catechetical implications. We must listen to the rumors of angels.

There are two reasons why we are disposed not to listen:

A) We (church leaders and clergy) do not value culture.

B) Like the Benedictine priest cited above, we have nothing but contempt for culture that appeals to the ordinary folk in our congregations. We have joined the ranks of the elitists and betrayed our own.

One can hear four different attitudes among Catholics about culture:

1) Art (herein defined in the broad sense as any work of culture) is, if not evil in itself, at least very dangerous because it can actuate such terrible human vices as sensuality and pride. The most religion can concede to art is grudging toleration.

2) Art is a luxury that a religion with the time and the money can pursue, but when a church is under pressure and does not have the financial resources to deal with basic human problems, it can scarcely be expected to be interested in or to encourage the various arts.

3) Art is useful. It can be used to teach religion and to defend it, to make religious points, influence religious thinking, and resist the evil and pagan influences that permeate a society and indeed permeate the art in society.

4) The arts are essential because the arts make sacraments. The arts reveal to us the presence of God lurking in His/Her creation. The Church sponsors, encourages, promotes art, not because art is useful (though it may be) but because it cannot do without the artistic sacrament-maker.

While all four attitudes have existed in the history of Christianity and in the history of Catholic Christianity, in its finest moments, Catholicism, perhaps more than any other of the world's great religious traditions, enthusiastically embraced the fourth position. To the builders of the great thirteenth-century cathedrals, the light streaming through the stained glass revealed God as light of the world. That was enough and that was everything. But in worldwide Catholicism of the late Counter Reformation and the American immigrant Church since the early nineteenth century, that position has no longer been dominant. Even today, in fact, it is not unreasonable to assume that it would be very much a minority opinion within the American Church. The first position is still stubbornly lurking in the minds of the clergy from their seminary training (novels, I was told in the seminary, were a waste of time), and the principal emphasis is on the second and third position. The first three positions are all agonistic, either implicitly or explicitly.

Father Edward McKenna and I are presently engaged in trying to develop an opera out of my story *The Magic Cup*, a harmless enough activity and for me one that doesn't consume much time; but a priest said to me, "How can you justify spending time writing an opera when there are poor and hungry people in the world? Isn't it a waste of time, and worse, couldn't you be spending that time doing real priestly work?"

I could have pointed out to this priest that he spends a lot of time at night watching television. I could have pointed out that in his suburban parish the only contribution he makes to the cause of the poor and hungry is an occasional sermon that demonstrates very little understanding of anything that his parishioners can do, let us say, about the famine in Ethiopia or the poverty in the inner city of Chicago. The "preferential option for the poor" has replaced "protection of the faith of immigrants" as a catch phrase in American Catholicism. It is only necessary that one repeat it, not do anything about it. Thus, the bishops may announce in their pastoral letter that they are endorsing the "preferential option for the poor" without any need to keep open the inner-city parochial schools that are the major help the American Church offers the poor. The chairman of the committee that issued the pastoral can close down one such school rather dramatically, at the very time that he is denouncing middle-class Catholics for their lack of enthusiasm for the "preferential option for the poor."

It is merely required that you talk about poverty and not that you understand it or do anything about it yourself. In a Church where everything is to be evaluated against the "preferential option," nothing else matters; opera-writing and film-making are devoid of value. The shallow pragmatism of the immigrant church is reborn under a new title, as anti-intellectual, anti-artistic, anti-human as ever.

If I were to talk to this priest about sacraments, he might well react the way the sometime-dean of Holy Cross did in an embarrassing review in the *New York Times Book Review*. The only meaning he could imagine for sacraments was a definition of the seven official Sacraments of the Church. He presumably is the greenwood.

So when I write of epiphanies in films or rock music, the typical product of American clerical education will wonder what a film or a rock piece has to do with the sixth of January. When I say that the creator of a film or a rock singer is a "sacrament maker," the same typical product of clerical education will wonder what the relationship is between a movie and Baptism, Penance, Eucharist, Confirmation, Anointing, Orders, and Matrimony. How can a film director or a screenplay writer or a singer make a sacrament when there are only seven and Jesus has already made them?

When I was in the seminary, there was at least a chance that one would read Maritain or some similar author on art and religion. At the present time, such reading is extremely unlikely. And the younger clergy, if one's impressions are to be trusted, are even more illiterate than we were at their age—which is pretty Illiterate indeed! Only they are illiterate in a population now one-and-a-half times more likely to go to college than its white Protestant counterpart. Under the circumstances, one can expect nothing professional in the way of film writing, film-making, film sponsoring or film criticism from the institutional church. (There is perhaps an occasional happy exception in film-making, as, for example, *The Fourth Wise Man*.) Film and television may be useful, but they cost too much.

Someone who talks "sacrament" and "epiphany" to such a mentality isn't even heard. One points out that Catholics by the scores and by the hundreds are moving into the lively arts as writers; directors; producers; and in the new generation of brilliant young actors and actresses and singers and stars. One is then told that their parish will administer the sacraments to them or maybe we ought to have an occasional communion breakfast for them or maybe we should challenge them about the superficiality of their lives and about their obligation to exercise "the preferential option for the poor."

We don't make films, we don't criticize films, we don't encourage film-makers, and we don't embrace film-making as an absolutely decisive and essential sacramental activity. Who, for example, besides a crazy man like the present writer, would suggest that one of the qualifications for the new Archbishop of Los Angeles should be some sensitivity to the importance and to the possibility of film-making as sacrament in the modern world?

There has been no more pathetic manifestation of the stubborn, amateurish pragmatism with which American Catholic ecclesiastics approach the arts (it is important not that a church be beautiful but that it be cheap and efficient) than the disastrous Holy Week "mission" attempted in the Archdiocese of Chicago in 1984. The idea was a brilliant one: the popular new cardinal would preach on television the first four nights in Holy Week. The television camera was viewed as a pulpit, the television audience as a congregation, and the Archbishop as a mission preacher.

Professionals TV directors and producers, if given a chance, would have warned vigorously against such a view, but they were not given a chance. It was said (by me, alas) to someone in power: "Hey, Joe will be competing with Dan Rather, Tom Brokaw, Joan Collins, Maude Adams, Victoria Principal, and the Great Communicator. We can't do that to him. Even Sheen could not get away with four half-hours four nights in a row, and even the Great Communicator wouldn't try it."

The Cardinal tried it just the same. For, despite repeated pleas to the priests who somehow managed to wrestle control of the project so that they would write the script and plan the programs (their qualifications for such roles were invisible), professional film-makers were never given a chance to turn the Holy Week project into something appropriate for prime-time television. The result was a stiff, awkward, disastrous travesty, aired not only in Chicago but, through WGN, in every city and country where there was cable television.

"Is he that much of a creep?" a teen-ager asked me in Tucson with a disdainful twist of her lip.

"No," I responded, "he may be many things, but I wouldn't call him a creep."

There are ways television could have been adapted to the Lord Cardinal's personality. Professional television people would have been able to make recommendations about such tactics. Perhaps the most appropriate strategy would have been a twenty-five-minute story by the best Catholic film-makers in the country (and paid for without clerical discount; we're patrons of the arts—remember?—not bargain hunters) and a brief personal conversation between the Cardinal and someone else about the meaning of the story. To do that would mean that the two priests who possessed personal power in the production of the program would have had to yield to lay people. When it comes to power, the clergy are notoriously unyielding.

The whole mess was symbolized by the response of one of them to a question my sister asked: "Why didn't you have the Cardinal wear contact lenses so we could see his eyes?"

"That would be vanity!"

An issue of professional competence, in other words, is blurred and covered over by converting it to a question of personal piety. It is apparently not vain for the Great Communicator to wear contact lenses when he talks to the people of the United States, but it would be vain for the Cardinal Archbishop of Chicago to wear such lenses instead of hiding his (very attractive to women, I'm told) brown eyes behind cola bottles. Television—"film in your home"—for the purposes of this book was not important enough an art to study and master. It was merely a tool to be used for preaching a mission. Anybody who wore a Roman collar could use that tool. A marvelous opportunity for religious film-making was wasted because it could not be comprehended and because, if comprehended, it would then be seen as too expensive. Instead of doing it right, you put the Cardinal on in an awkward, embarrassing context for four nights in a row and, moreover, you pretend the whole affair was a huge success.

In a church where that ethos prevails, the sacramental potentiality of art cannot be understood or, if understood, applied to the life of the church. Maurice de Sully, the Bishop of Paris who presided over the beginning of Notre Dame de Paris, would be utterly astonished by such a mentality.

I see very little change over the last thirty years. There was more comprehension among the clergy and the religious about what I am arguing in this book when I was in the seminary than there is now. In a recent interview, Cardinal John O'Connor of New York, a contemporary of mine, more or less (rather less than more), said that the novels of Francois Mauriac were important to him in the seminary and still are, an opinion that caused me to notably enhance my respect for the Cardinal—anybody who likes Mauriac can't be all bad. However, there is no novelist today who has influence on Catholic seminarians and probably no other writer either, including Mauriac, who is as good as he was forty and more years ago.

There was a literate subculture in the seminary in O'Connor's days and in mine a decade or so thereafter. That the beauty of the form shining forth in the proportioned parts of the matter reveals God was given credence by some seminarians in those days but is likely to be understood by very few seminarians or young priests today. The pragmatism of the immigrant Church—despite everyone's expectations—has not died among its clergy. It has been replaced by a new pragmatism, concerned not so much with protecting the faith of the immigrants to the exclusion of all else as with achieving, normally through very simplistic methods, justice for the Third World, the poor, the oppressed, the homosexuals, women, etc., etc.

It is not my intention to deny the importance of the cause of justice. Quite the contrary, it is extremely important. However, it is no more served adequately or effectively by shallow, simple-minded anti-intellectualism and anti-humanism than the cause of protecting the faith of the immigrants was served by the shallow-minded pragmatism of the Legion of Decency a half century ago. The more things change in clerical culture, in other words, the more they remain the same.

Thus, hope for a rapprochement between the Church and the lively arts, like so many other hopes for the future of the American Church, must rest with the lay people, especially the ever-increasing number of Catholic laity engaged in the fine and lively arts. Even they will need at least a few priests to understand what they are doing and the importance of their work. Some-where, even these lay people must find a priest who is not a shallow, simplistic, anti-intellectual pragmatist.

Good luck to them on their search.

If all art is dismissed with such shallow pragmatism, a fortiori the popular art represented by L'Amour, King, Fosse, Springsteen, Lafferty, Peters, Cosby, Eddings, McCaffrey, Ron-stadt, Madonna, and similar craftspersons of popular culture is simply too unimportant to merit any attention at all. Moreover, the critical, conventional wisdom of the elitists who dismiss Comedy and Romance (as their predecessors have down through the ages, each generation in turn refusing to learn from the errors of their predecessors) is available to justify this stance of teachers and leaders and thinkers, such as these may be.

The suggestion that Comedy and Romance may be the Catholic story form par excellence will seem to such deadly serious, pseudo-pragmatic folk the worst kind of nonsense.

There does not exist, in other words, among the leaders and teachers and thinkers of American Catholicism today, a rhetoric of discourse which would enable them to consider the possibility that grace is present, indeed abundant, in the lively arts.

In the Catholic Church in the United States today, there is no awareness that the good, the true, and the beautiful reflect God in the world and no sensitivity to new art forms that are spectacularly capable of manifesting the presence of God in the world.

Such a church scarcely is worthy of the name Catholic.

Yet the process of creation in the fine and lively arts continues; in the men and women who do this work is to be found the hope of a future resurgence of the traditional Catholic sensibility.

Listen to one of them who, while "lapsed," considers herself "forever bound more thoroughly by irritation and the need to understand than if I went to Mass three times a day and took it all for granted."

"As a Catholic child one is taught to believe in symbols, to understand . . . that the world is form containing spirit, that the word can be made flesh, that one should celebrate the union of body and soul in the Eucharist. Metaphor becomes second nature, the first lesson, and we must struggle in order to be touched with grace."

Art—fine and lively—is ultimately Eucharistic and hence touched with grace.

The kind of grace that make our ears pick up and our heartbeat increase when we hear, "Once upon a time, long, long ago there was a woman who was about to die. She had lived a very painful life in which she did many wicked things and many wicked things were done to her; and just before she died she went into church and knelt down in front of a statue of St. Joseph and . . ."

Index